"Whether you are a learned tarot practitioner or newbie reader, Ms. Greer's work will surely shed new light on intricate, and often unseen, details of the cards. Her influence in the field cannot be overstated. So, I'm delighted she is focusing here on some of the most misunderstood cards in the deck, the court cards. By seeing sides of ourselves and the energy of others around us reflected in the 'people' cards, we gain a deeper level of understanding of our readings. Her techniques for exploring the multidimensional layers of the cards while utilizing them to plumb the depths of one's own psyche are clear to grasp and accessible to all. I will forever be indebted to Mary K. Greer for sharing her wealth of tarot knowledge. Her books prepared me for a satisfying lifetime relationship with tarot. I consider her a mentor I've never met but for whom I am certainly grateful." —Rachel True, creator of *True Heart Intuitive Tarot*

"I'd like to say that this is Mary K. Greer's most important work, but everything she brings to the field of tarot is noteworthy. She is a dedicated scholar, and her innovative way of studying these seventy-eight cards has changed the game time and time again. For anyone on the path to self-discovery, this book belongs on your shelf. I have no doubt that it won't be long before my new edition becomes as well-worn as the previous ones." —from the foreword by Theresa Reed, the Tarot Lady, author of *Tarot: No Questions Asked*

"This book has lived at the top of the stack in my tarot library since the 1980s. Both workbook and guidebook, it is an essential, user-friendly read for those looking to pinpoint and synchronize their life with the cards." —Carrie Paris, creator of *The Relative Tarot*

"Mary Greer is a tarot scholar and a gifted reader of the cards. In *Archetypal Tarot* she takes numerology a step further by reducing your birth date and given name not only to a number but also to a series or constellation of tarot cards that speak of your destiny or life direction. While acknowledging the irrational nature of this endeavor, she is wise enough to recognize that this irrationality is actually its strength. The system and the tarot constellations that it forms allow us to step past our separateness and to see ourselves as a part of the universal whole, with a life path determined by the Soul of the World and not just our egos." —Robert M. Place, author of *The Tarot: History, Symbolism, and Divination* and creator of *The Alchemical Tarot*

ARCHETYPAL TAROT

What Your Birth Card Reveals

About Your Personality, Path, and Potential

MARY K. GREER

foreword by THERESA REED, the Tarot Lady

WEISER
BOOKS

In memory of my parents

Rita Alice West Greer and John Cox Greer
who encouraged me to follow
my own destiny.

First published in 2021 by Weiser Books, an imprint of
Red Wheel/Weiser, LLC
665 Third Street, Suite 400
San Francisco, CA 94107
www.redwheelweiser.com

Previously published in 2011 as *Who Are You in the Tarot?* by Weiser Books, ISBN: 978-1-57863-493-4.
The 2021 edition includes a new foreword and a new preface.

Parts of this book were originally published in *Tarot Constellations* by Mary K. Greer
(North Hollywood, California: Newcastle Publishing Co., 1987).

ISBN: 978-1-57863-748-5
Library of Congress Cataloging-in-Publication Data is available upon request.

Cover and text design by Kathryn Sky-Peck
Cover Illustration: Roue de Fortune, from *Tarot Egyptien, Methode d' Etteilla*,
1870, Editions Dusserre, Paris/Private Collection.
Typeset in Adobe Jenson Pro

Printed in the United States of America
IBI
10 9 8 7 6 5 4 3 2 1

Acknowledgments

I particularly want to thank Angeles Arrien from whom I first learned about Lifetime and Year Cards. My gratitude next goes out to the thousands of clients, students, and friends who allowed me to explore these personal cards with them and who offered so many insights into how the cards function in their lives. My fellow tarot readers over the years have been a great inspiration and are equally too numerous to mention—thank you, all. In addition to the many people mentioned in my earlier book on this subject, *Tarot Constellations*, I'd like to add Wald and Ruth Ann Amberstone, who have freely shared their own concept of Birth Cards with me. When I was writing the earlier version of this book, my young daughter, Casimira, regularly reminded me that there is life beyond tarot. My grandson, Eli, now does the same. I would also like to thank Red Wheel/Weiser and especially Amber Guetebier, who asked me to update and expand this classic for a new generation, and editor Mikayla Butchart, who saved the day by carefully checking all the famous birthdays. Any remaining errors are solely my own.

Contents

Foreword

I have many tarot books on my shelves. Some are in pristine condition, a sign that it may have been read once . . . or quite possibly never finished. But there are also a few that seem to be in a somewhat shabby condition with bent corners, tattered covers, broken spines, notes in the margins, and warped pages. These are the books that have been my most trusted companions on my tarot journey.

Mary K. Greer's *Who Are You in the Tarot?* is one of those battered books, a replacement no less for the original *Tarot Constellations*, which ended up falling apart from so much wear and tear. It is a book I turned to again and again in an attempt to understand myself and the people around me.

"Who am I, and what is my purpose?" That's a question I've been trying to answer since I was a tiny, inquisitive tot. My parents never seemed to provide a satisfactory response to my query. Neither did my priest or teachers, although they tried. It's a big question and one that doesn't have a simple answer.

I'm not the first person who pondered their place in the Universe, and I certainly won't be the last. The search for self is never-ending, and many people have attempted it since the beginning of time.

Because my quest to understand myself wasn't answered on the home front, off I went in search elsewhere. My journey led me to the metaphysical section of a bookstore, where I purchased a tarot deck on a whim. When I got home, I opened the box, removed the plastic wrapping around the deck, and spread the cards out on the bed. The images captured my imagination immediately.

What were these symbols, and could they tell me the future or, better yet, unlock my secret reason for being here? As I pored over those cards, I began to see stories unfolding, of the past, present, and future. Different characters emerged, representing the people around me—and suddenly, I saw myself in those images, and parts of me that no one else seemed to understand. "Aha, I'm a Queen of Swords! That explains my sharp tongue and thirst for knowledge. No wonder I don't fit into this family!"

I identified so hard with this Court card that I couldn't see myself any other way. So, for a while, I felt like the mystery of me was solved. But as I said before, this question doesn't have a simplistic answer.

While my own interpretations satisfied me, there were moments where I wondered if there was more to this thing called life ... and these seventy-eight cards. Was my destiny a one-dimensional card trick? Or was I more than that logical, cool-headed Queen? I certainly didn't always feel like the rational one. In fact, I tended to operate more with a keen street sense, an animal instinct that often defied logic. Everything was a sign. What's that all about?

When I stumbled upon Mary's *Tarot Constellations*, I found myself going down a whole new tarot rabbit hole, one that I never knew existed. Using my birth date, numerology, and the Major Arcana, I was able to peel away different layers to get to the core of that question, "Who am I, and what is my purpose?"

Through Mary's methods, I learned the Judgement card was my Birth Card—and the High Priestess my Soul Card. Although I still feel the Queen of Swords describes my feisty, independent nature, these two cards indicated that my purpose was to assist other people in their transformation— and that intuition would be the guiding force in my life. This explained why I often made decisions that seemed utterly illogical (so NOT the Queen of Swords!). I tend to follow my gut and have always been deeply in tune with what I call my "signs from the Universe." The cards also explain my career, which I like to say, "happened by accident." (It might have been in the cards all along!)

Diving in further, I discovered that Justice was my Hidden Factor, and my greatest lessons centered on taking responsibility for my actions while developing mercy for other folks. As I began putting these pieces together like a personal mandala, I became curious about my loved ones. Digging into their archetypes allowed me to understand them better, which made communication easier.

For example, knowing my daughter has the Chariot as her Birth Card explains why we seem to be at odds from time to time. In the past, she viewed me as "judgmental," while I thought she was domineering. Learning how to compromise (and keep my opinions to myself) paved the way for a healthier dynamic.

One of my favorite parts of this book is the section on the Year Cards. You can find out the card that governs your year by adding your birth month and day with the current year. I use this method to determine yearly themes to focus on. Right now, I'm starting a Death Year. Mary says that it's "time to shed old skin for new growth." I'm in the midst of significant changes, so it not only makes sense but helps me to remember that no matter what is moving out of my life, it's for the best because my Temperance Year is not too far off in the future.

As you can see, this book is a valuable resource for self-knowledge and plotting out the best course of action—one that is aligned with the pulse of the Universe. The title of this new edition, *Archetypal Tarot: What Your Birth Card Reveals About Your Personality, Your Path, and Your Potential*, is a perfect description of what you'll find within these pages. The wisdom contained within is timeless.

I'd like to say that this is Mary K. Greer's most important work, but everything she brings to the field of tarot is noteworthy. She is a dedicated scholar, and her innovative way of studying these seventy-eight cards has changed the game time and time again. For anyone on the path to self-discovery, this book belongs on your shelf. I have no doubt that it won't be long before my copy is as well-worn as the previous ones.

—Theresa Reed, author of
Tarot: No Questions Asked: Mastering the Art of Intuitive Reading

Preface to the New Edition

I first learned about Birth Cards from Angeles Arrien in a tarot class in San Francisco in 1977. We both taught tarot in colleges only a few blocks from each other. I took her private class, centered around the Crowley-Harris Thoth deck, with a small group that eventually birthed several prominent tarot teachers and authors. The entire twelve-week class focused on the meaning of the Major Arcana as Birth Cards, cards whose numbers were a result of adding the month, day, and year in which you were born and on Year Cards for the current year. Of course, everyone also calculated the cards for the important people in their lives. As a result, each lesson became personally relevant. The cards themselves gradually assumed the role of teachers and guides through life.

As a result of that initial class I began calculating and interpreting birth and year cards at the beginning of every reading I did for others. I also researched the personal cards of famous people and of everyone I knew (having gathered the data for astrological purposes). In the forty-plus years I've been using this technique, it has become my favorite way to introduce the Major Arcana to students so they are invested right away in a personal relationship with the cards. There is no better way to develop an immediate visceral understanding of the Major Arcana's place in tarot.

For this new edition of my book (previously published as *Who Are You In the Tarot*) I queried more than 150 tarot practitioners about how they use Birth and Year Cards. Certain themes were related to me over and over again.

While some people don't use Birth Cards at all or find the concept illogical, others say they are the best way to introduce someone to tarot by giving them a sense of ownership—"this is *my* birth card." Several people talked about how these personal cards work like a compass to help them navigate their life journey, stay on their path, and remain aligned with a sense of purpose. Others emphasized insight and understanding of on-going themes, lessons, goals, and plans, helping a person find a sense of order and meaning in both inner and outer experiences. The cards also offer direction for self-improvement and "how best to show up in the world." A few people spoke of the empowerment that comes when they embrace their own rhythm and honor their unique strengths and weaknesses.

When it comes to Year Cards, one person explained that the Year Card "shows the way the wind is flowing so the client can set their sail accordingly," while another appreciated that by observing multiple years he could discern cycles of similarities when cards repeated.

For professional tarot readers this "portrait in cards" is a great way to open a session by providing insight into a client's personality and by keying in to their mode of receptivity, and thus establishing an instant connection. As an overview, these cards can zero in on reoccurring issues, often surprising a client by answering questions before they are even asked.

Quite a few of us have found that printing a "Tarot Profile" with Birth and Year Card descriptions, along with pictures of the cards, makes a lovely birthday gift or a present for the parents of newborns.

Through the years I've learned to view my own Hermit/Moon combination with ever increasing appreciation as my guides to both self-acceptance and potential growth.

In working with Year Cards I've found that while I can speculate as to the significance of cards particular to the current or forth-coming year, the deepest insights come years later when I reflect on what the major learning was for me in that year. For instance, a Death year rarely heralds the physical death of someone close to a person. Rather, if I ask a client for a year that includes the most impactful death of a close one, the card of that year makes clear what significance that death had for the person in terms of a life lesson or understanding. Just as people can often remember exactly where they were when they heard John Lennon was killed or that a plane crashed into New York's Twin Towers, so, too, many people will remember the year of the coronavirus pandemic. What did that world change mean to you? Like an unforgettable dream image, the meaning can continue to unfold itself through the years.

This brings us to the fact that I am writing this new preface in the midst of COVID-19 and the California wildfires of 2020. I've asked tarot readers what their Year Card means as a major lesson or experience for them this year. The year card calculations result in cards from the **Lovers** to the **Tower** in a bell-curve range of possibilities. With more than 450 responses from online tarot enthusiasts I found the following year card trends.

6-**Lovers** was about choices and being more nakedly honest in relationships in an attempt to harmonize with the self-love and self-care that the pandemic required.

7-**Chariot** felt like exerting willpower to try and manage or control juxtaposing needs and wants while hurdling forward into an uncertain future.

One person who had 8-**Strength** noted that in prior Strength years she "muscled through" difficulties but, being physically vulnerable, she is now drawing on spiritual energy as a more effective resilience technique.

Those with the 9-**Hermit** connected it with isolation and introspection but also the unforeseen completion of many projects and hopes.

A 10-**Wheel of Fortune** year brought attention to life's ups and downs. It also required initiating changes that focused attention outward and onto new opportunities.

Those with 11-**Justice** focused more on the social issues, protests, and maintaining equilibrium and balance while seeking the truth.

The 12-**Hanged Man** increased sensitivity to sacrifices and restrictions. Life felt suspended with forced delays and inaction; yet surrendering to it allowed for seeing things from a different perspective.

13-**Death** necessitated change, endings, closures: a forced letting go and discarding of attachments and old ways of doing things.

14-**Temperance** called for healing, compassion for others, and, for some, attention to drinking patterns, and the regulation of their physical and mental patterns.

The 15-**Devil** seemed to be about temptations, power struggles, and issues of tenaciousness—keeping or breaking bonds—as well as deep shadow work and struggles with responsibility versus shame. Some people found comfort by laughing at the hubris that one can control anything.

With 16-**Tower** it seemed like things were crashing down and some were wondering where to leap to free themselves from destruction. Others found themselves liberated from ordinary social and work constraints.

I recommend that you add the month and date of your birth to the year 2020 to determine what major impact, challenges, or life lessons you experienced then and what new insights are available now.

Introduction

This book teaches two major concepts. One focuses on your nature, and the other on the nature of tarot.

1. You are composed of many facets, or different aspects, of Self. Each of these has its own set of skills and abilities that you can more easily access once you recognize them. Getting to know the cards that best represent *you* teaches you about these selves and gives you more options for effective and meaningful action in the world. It also increases your compassion and understanding about the differences in how other people function.

2. Tarot can be organized into a variety of patterns to enhance study and understanding. The tarot constellations, in particular, reflect correspondences among the cards that numerologically reduce to the root numbers one to nine. These result is nine core principles that give you a powerful way to work with the lessons and opportunities of life depicted by the tarot.

The Original Edition

In 1981, after fourteen years of studying tarot and seven years of teaching it, I began writing books on tarot that emphasized personal growth and insight using self-teaching techniques. At the time I was on the faculty and administration of New College of California in San Francisco, a liberal arts college where I taught for eleven years and was director of Independent Studies. I was also doing graduate work in methods of experiential and right brain–oriented education. The motto of the college was "Learn how to learn," and its core methodology was Socratic, which meant that much of a teacher's task was asking questions and teaching students how to ask questions. These approaches became central to my work as a tarot reader, teacher, and author.

Who Are You in the Tarot is an extensive revision of my second book, *Tarot Constellations* (1987). I began that work with an impassioned plea:

> You are your own teacher. All rules given here are made to be broken. Question everything I say and accept nothing until it brings you results you can perceive. As you go through this book, clarify for yourself your intentions in working with the tarot: What do you want to learn from it?

I still advocate breaking rules (when common sense supports that) in order to learn what rules are worth keeping. This work presents a variety of what appear to be nonrational techniques of determining cards that could have special significance for you. In the process of discerning a personal meaning in these cards, you can quickly establish a relationship with the tarot that is unique to you. These personal cards become friends and guides that help you connect with the rest of the deck and find meaning in your experiences. As you go on to explore the personal cards of your friends, family, and clients, you will begin to appreciate the different approaches people take to life, resulting in compassion and understanding where before there may have been puzzlement or frustration.

Correspondences to specific cards, whether via your birthday, name, or personal characteristics, are esoterically and imaginally significant. *Esoteric* means "within" and refers to things that are obscure, enigmatic, or mysterious and, thus, things that are incomprehensible to the rational, scientific mind. By *imaginally*, I mean internal, emotion-laden symbols and images that motivate your actions and give meaning to life. This book offers a symbolic or mythic rather than scientific approach to the world and to your psyche. These correspondences help you explore the things that inspire, motivate, and challenge you, but the techniques have to work for *you* if they are to be truly useful. So try them out, add to the meanings given here, use what works, and let go of what doesn't.

Tarot and Your Destiny

This book is based, in large part, on the idea that you were born during a phase of the solar year, marked by a calendrical date. Its energy harmonizes with something that your spirit, soul, or a higher consciousness chose to develop in this particular lifetime. This energy is described by your birth date, based on a calendar that embodies our Western culture and its historical timelines. You were also named in such a way that you were further linked to your family, culture, and heritage. To make the most of this material, I suggest you assume the magical mind-set: that a "Greater You" or Higher Self chose those factors that would help you succeed at your soul purpose. Your destiny is to actualize these potentials to the best of your ability—whether you have an understanding of Lifetime Cards or not. Although this premise is debatable, you will probably find that acting "as if" it were true brings tremendous benefits in terms of a sense of meaningful direction and a compassionate understanding of yourself and others.

The tarot cards, numerologically considered, provide a visual tool for ascertaining both the potentials and pitfalls you have set for yourself through your birth date and name. They provide a method of looking at and even communicating with that energy, so that you can know when and how you are actually living it in the world.

The tarot cards associated with your birth date and name form your individual mandala: your pattern of personal destiny. Although your destiny is also mapped in your astrological natal chart, or can be calculated by traditional forms of numerology, none of these other perspectives allows you to work with the power of the picture, each one of which expresses a thousand words and tells a thousand times a thousand stories. Only tarot introduces you to personal power figures with whom you can dialogue and ask for guidance in achieving your highest destiny.

The tarot deck has seventy-eight cards, normally divided into three groups:

+ 22 Major Arcana, or Trump or Key Cards

+ 40 Number or Pip Cards

+ 16 Court or People Cards

The Number Cards and the Court Cards when combined are called the Minor Arcana; they are both divided into four suits representing the four elements:

Wands = Fire   Cups = Water
Swords = Air   Pentacles = Earth

This book also emphasizes a division of the tarot into nine "tarot constellations" and their accompanying principles (see chapter 1).

The 8-11 Controversy and Astrological Correspondences

With much of this book based on the numbers of the cards, I've had to face a dilemma concerning what to do about Strength and Justice. Traditionally, in continental European decks, epitomized by the classic Marseilles-style tarot dating from the 17th century, Justice is number 8 and Strength is number 11. There are, however, several variations in the number sequences found among the earliest tarot decks, including one early woodcut deck in which both Strength and Justice are numbered 8.[1]

In 1910, occult scholar Arthur Edward Waite made tarot history by publishing a new deck with designs by Pamela Colman Smith, a member of his mystical order, in which these two cards are counterchanged. In the Waite-Smith deck, Strength is number 8, and Justice number 11. This was to accord with a secret at the heart of the Hermetic Order of the Golden Dawn, where the cards were given Hebrew letter, astrological, and number correspondences (known as alpha-astro-numeric correspondences), such that Strength was aligned with Leo, and Justice with Libra.

Both numbering systems are common today, which requires each new tarot author, deck designer, and practitioner to make his or her own 8-11 choice. It becomes even more essential when working with numerological systems. My observation is that whichever numbering system you learn well first becomes mentally imprinted and difficult to dislodge. And, as Gareth Knight suggests in his book *The Treasure House of Images*, perhaps all orders limit the tarot's possibilities.

In appendix A, I discuss in detail the historical, functional, and personal aspects of this "8-11 controversy," and why both systems are valid. Meanwhile, this book uses the Waite-Smith, or Golden Dawn, numbering system in which *Strength is number 8 and Justice is number 11*, with occasional suggestions for working with the continental European–style decks. Feel free to adapt and make adjustments where appropriate.

Likewise, all astrological correspondences for the cards are based on the traditions of the Hermetic Order of the Golden Dawn and, therefore, decks influenced by Crowley/Harris, Waite/Smith, and Paul Foster Case.

How to Use This Book

Photocopy any charts that you'll want to use repeatedly. Write in this book. I also suggest keeping a tarot notebook or journal. You can use a blank book, a three-ring binder, a set of computer or physical file folders, or a combination of these. A flexible format allows you to add to and expand your notes as your knowledge and interests grow, while a lovely journal can offer a sense of pleasure and appreciation. Or use a physical journal for dialogues and a computer journal for things you'll want to cut and paste. What works for one person will not necessarily work for another. Consider including any of the following:

- card interpretations and associations
- your own symbol dictionary
- tarot-related images, sketches, music, and quotes
- explorations and comparisons of different decks
- card spreads and layouts
- readings done for yourself and/or others
- dialogues, processes, meditations, and card mandalas
- Lifetime Cards of family and friends
- your Year Card graph and observations about it

The internet and cloud computing offer many options for creating personal journals. It's easy to include pictures, video, and audio, plus links to helpful resources. For instance, blogs can be set to public, private, or members only and can connect to social networks—just as you desire. You can access your online journal anywhere and share only what you want. However, be aware that anything made public on the internet is subject to copyright issues either through your use of another's works or by others infringing on your rights.

Although this book is designed for you to use alone, you may progress faster through interactions with other people. Find a tarot partner or form a tarot study group. You'll also find discussions and study groups on internet tarot forums covering many of the processes talked about here. There's no reason to feel alone in your tarot journey or to think that I or any other author is your only source of information.

Chapter 2 contains several processes that you can use to explore the personal significance of your Lifetime and Year Cards or, in fact, any tarot card.

If you wish, jump ahead to Chapter 3 to calculate your Lifetime Cards. While the order of chapters provides you with tools, methods and concepts, the book, as a whole, should be seen as a flexible resource. Read sections in the order that most interests you.

Researching Your Lifetime Card

As with any psychological typing system, you need to ask, what is this telling me about myself and how can I use this information? When I first wrote *Tarot Constellations* and through all the years since, I've informally investigated the relationship between people and their Birth Cards. I encourage you to do the same, and, for this reason, I've included a list of famous people that fall under the different constellations for you to explore.

What I discovered is that Lifetime Cards have nothing to do with a person's public persona, career, ability to succeed, or with their being an innovator in their field—the very reasons why they are famous. So you'll have to look under the surface of their celebrated facades. True, a few trends seem to emerge that I've woven into the card descriptions. But, the majority of Lifetime Card descriptions came from what I've learned from friends, family, students, clients, and other tarot professionals with whom I've explored this topic.

Their constellations seemed to describe the kind of life lessons with which they are continually confronted and the kinds of subtle inner urges that motivate their choices and actions.

Lifetime Cards seem to describe the kind of life lessons with which individuals are continually confronted and the kinds of subtle inner urges that motivate their choices and actions.

So, if one's soul purpose is not a job, field of endeavor, outer talent, or list of accomplishments, what is it? Instead, it appears to be an inner compulsion, yearning, or questioning and the need to follow wherever this takes you and learn everything you can from it along the way. It is an underlying force or urge that gives meaning to events and personal interactions such that they are experienced as deeply meaningful and fulfilling.

Most of the younger famous people I have listed are pop celebrities and Internet entrepreneurs, because these are the names with which most of us are familiar. What we know of them is all-too-often fictionalized, sensationalized, and carefully manipulated by the media machines behind them. Their public personas may have little to do with who they really are. I include them simply to spur your own search.

To get anything from the lists of famous people, you need to research and find their most heartfelt statements—autobiographical quotations that reveal what really touches them, what they truly believe in, what they struggle with, and what they stand for. It is not what you see on the surface but what lies hidden underneath. Look for themes that motivate and drive a person throughout his or her life. What songs most express what a songwriter truly feels, despite the ups and downs of the moment? What is an innovative architect or filmmaker always struggling to achieve? What conditions present their biggest challenges? What do they believe in? What both sustains a person and impels him or her to action? And, as you discover these core themes, ask how you experience similar issues in yourself.

You will find, though, that the best source for understanding the Lifetime Cards are by examining how they function for you and for people you know.

CHAPTER 1

Constellations, Principles, Archetypes, and Beliefs

You are embarking on an adventure with this book as your guide. This is a magical journey, illuminated by what I call the tarot constellations. The universe that we gaze at in the night sky above us was first mapped into meaningful groups by the ancient Chaldeans, "the sky gazers," six centuries before Christ. In the West, we identified these groups as constellations; named them for mythical beings, animals, and objects; and told stories about them that served as guides to the meaning and purpose of life. Similarly, the tarot deck is another map of consciousness evolved by our predecessors and transmitted to us, in which we now chart the journey of our Self. A semi-mythical philosopher by the name of Hermes Trismegistus described the relationship between the inner and outer universe like this:

> That which is above is like that which is below and that which is below
> is like that which is above, to achieve the wonders of the one thing.

Called the Hermetic axiom, this phrase is central to all alchemical and metaphysical philosophy and the key to an understanding of the use of symbols such as the tarot.

Consider, however, that the astronomical and astrological constellations are not actually connected star systems; they are imagined collections of points of light, some originating relatively near us and some far more distant, that appear related only from our personal viewing platform, which we call Earth. Because of our own inner need for personal meaning, humans throughout history have projected our own consciousness upon the night sky in the form of complex patterns and pictures. Nevertheless, the meaning we find in them is completely valid: When we gaze at the stars, we see ourselves clearly. As author Joseph Chilton Pearce has aptly said, "Man's mind mirrors a universe that mirrors man's mind."[2]

Tarot Constellations
and the Nine Basic Principles

According to the *American Heritage Dictionary*, constellations are "groupings of objects, properties, or individuals," especially ones that are "structurally or systematically related." Most events and concerns current at any particular time in your life are "constellated," or clustered, around specific core issues. To the extent that constellated issues within you influence your actions, they also define your character.

The cards in a reading reflect your current constellated issues—both inner and outer. These constellations are made up of cards that resonate to the same theme, of major and minor intensity, and each card within a constellation gives a different perspective on the theme. The more situations in your life that fit the description, the more you are involved in a core issue or dilemma that will continue to project itself and its meaning onto outer events until it has been dealt with. The positions in a tarot spread break the constellation down into several constituting properties. Much like a constellation in the sky, which is a grouping of stars defining the lines of a figure and representing a story, a tarot spread pictures you and tells a story about you. Thus, spreads are also constellations picturing the events that have come together to form your current story.

More important for our purposes, there are a set of nine tarot constellations consisting of the Major Arcana cards plus the Minor Arcana cards of the same root numbers 1 to 9. (The Court or People Cards will be dealt with separately.) These nine sets of cards constellate or cluster around nine basic principles. The division of the Major Arcana into nine similar groups, called "The Qabalah of Nine Chambers" (see appendix B), appears in the writings of MacGregor Mathers and Aleister Crowley, members of the Hermetic Order of the Golden Dawn, from which emerged two of the most influential decks used today: the Waite-Smith and Thoth Tarot decks.

The Constellations Discovered

I was first introduced to the concept of "tarot constellations" in 1978 by Angeles Arrien, who taught tarot using the Crowley-Harris Thoth deck. She explained how she was playing with the cards one evening and had laid out both the Major and Minor Arcana in groupings based on the numbers:

All the 1s together and all the 2s, etc. She then included all the cards that added up to each of the nine single-digit (root) numbers. For instance, since $17 = 1 + 7 = 8$, the 17th card, the Star, was placed with the 8s, and so on.

She was arranging the groups into patterns when the phone rang. It was Joseph Campbell, author of works on mythology and symbolism, with whom she was leading a workshop at the Esalen Institute. He was excited by a realization he had recently had of how constellations are not just in the sky and stars, but such pattern groupings occur everywhere in our lives. Angie says she stood there as Campbell spoke and looked at the cards she had just grouped together all over the floor and saw that they were "tarot constellations." To the extent that constellated patterns within yourself determine your character, they become patterns of personal destiny—major forces that motivate and direct your life.

Chart 1: The Nine Principles of the Constellations

1. The Principle of Will and Focused Consciousness
2. The Principle of Balanced Judgment through Intuitive Awareness
3. The Principle of Love and Creative Imagination
4. The Principle of Life Force and Realization of Power
5. The Principle of Teaching and Learning
6. The Principle of Relatedness and Choice
7. The Principle of Mastery through Change
8. The Principle of Courage and Self-Esteem
9. The Principle of Introspection and Personal Integrity

Using the Lifetime Cards in a Reading

Imagine that you have come for a tarot consultation. I may begin (even before knowing your question) with the tarot constellation determined by your birth date—your Personality, Soul, Hidden Factor Cards, followed by your Year Card. These are all explained in this book.

From the information contained in your Personality and Soul cards, I gain some idea how to communicate with you in a reading. This understanding may modify how I interpret a card or the extent to which I emphasize its importance. These personal cards also suggest how you can best hear what the tarot has to say.

During the process of describing your basic characteristics and life issues, my intuition tunes into your potentials and possibilities. You'll most likely find that this basic information resonates with you and affirms that there are reasons for acting the way you do. If you have the Chariot as both your Personality and Soul Card, for instance, it is natural for you to protect your inner feelings. You are not just hiding behind a mask of bravado, or a role in your life, but also that is the sanctuary within which you develop your abilities. Nevertheless, that sanctuary must eventually be torn down when you have learned what you need from it. As a Chariot, if your life is currently in upheaval, we will look to see if you are breaking through an old and restricting identity that is now holding you back.

Thus, even before an actual reading has commenced, you have some insight as to not only "what" but also "why" something is occurring in your life. This is especially pertinent if you are asking the question, Why is this *always* happening to me? Repetitive occurrences can often be traced to the lessons inherent in your Personality, Soul, and Hidden Factor Cards—those cards that answer the question, What have I come here to learn? The Minor Arcana number cards of the same constellation show the kinds of life situations in which you are most likely to experience these lessons. Often, after only a few minutes of my describing the characteristics of your particular constellation pattern, you will begin to see for yourself, in the images on the cards, their relevance to your life.

Next, I calculate your Year Cards for the last several years and for the next three to five years. From the description I give of these cards, you begin to see a developmental pattern forming—for instance, how the choice of one year is acted on in the next, or how you move from an inner or more reflective state to a social or more aggressive energy. You can see how this allows you to experience complementary lessons in succeeding years. For instance, in a Chariot Year, you attempt to maintain control over opposing instincts and drives, but in the Strength Year that follows, you learn to come to terms with your instincts so that you can act in harmony with that power from within. Such an opportunity will not last forever—you have only a limited time to directly face your inner "beast" and discover what you truly "lust" after. Then you will move on to your next lesson, carrying with you what you learned this time around. Thus you begin to see each year as an exciting opportunity for growth. The lessons of the current year usually directly affect the situation for which you've come to the consultation.

This process can take from a quarter to a third of the time I allot to a consultation. By the time I ask for your specific question or issue, you already may have had your most pressing questions answered. Your immediate concerns are now placed into a larger perspective, so you see them as part of an entire life pattern. This is a major purpose of the tarot constellations.

Archetypes and the Tarot

The tarot cards hold great personal significance because they symbolize your inherent and eternal human characteristics, which psychologist Carl Jung labeled "archetypes." These archetypes, visualized and projected upon two-dimensional painted cards, speak at the deepest levels of secrets veiled behind your everyday personality.

The events in your life develop around myriad patterns or themes, in a way similar to the themes of ancient myths. Once you begin to perceive such patterns, you realize that your life is not meaningless but has great mythic and spiritual significance. M. Esther Harding, a Jungian psychoanalyst, says:

> The fact that the path unfolds in this way, step by step, leading the individual on, often by quite unexpected turns, towards the goal of wholeness, must mean that there are in the psyche patterns or rules of development analogous to the patterns operative in the physiological realm—such as that, for instance, which leads to the growth and development of the embryo. Surely we should not be surprised to find in the psychic life such a priori patterns . . .[3]

Harding goes on to say that men and women, by finding such wholeness within, and in freeing themselves from the conflicts and division in their own lives, will "be doing something constructive towards the solution of the very problems that are devastating mankind."[4] A world free of conflict and division can only exist if it is inhabited by people who have first freed themselves from conflict and division.

In the concepts of Jungian psychology, the term constellated refers to a particular archetype made up of interlocking factors, possessed of great power, and activated by an excess of energy. This constellated archetype can dominate your psyche unless you understand its energy and integrate it into your personality. Otherwise its qualities will be projected onto other people whom you deem more powerful and capable. You will then feel either inadequate and inferior or egotistical and bombastic in that area. Yet the values inherent in that archetype are accessible to you, and you will gradually assimilate them.

Although at any point in your life an archetype may constellate in your psyche, at birth you are born into a particular constellation. This is actively demonstrated through your astrological chart calculated for the exact minute of your birth. Yet another level of this "birthmark" is the archetype whose energy is constellated on the date of your birth, symbolized by the tarot card corresponding to the numerological sum of your birth date. When you are named, another energy is constellated, which it is your task to assimilate. These apparently "chance" occurrences become more understandable if you accept that your Greater Self chose your birth circumstances so that you could develop particular characteristics, face specific kinds of challenges, and focus on fulfilling a self-determined goal. Your name given at birth, with its cultural, familial, and generational significances, indicates the social constellations with which your soul desired to work. If you change your name, you choose to express new archetypes that reflect new energy constellations. Often when you release an archetype into consciousness, it cannot fit back into its old container, so a new one—a new constellated formation, a new name—must be made for it. Each year of your life is also defined by a particular confluence of energy, represented by an archetype whose passing influence gives you the opportunity to understand and integrate its values and lessons into your Self. If that energy already exists in your name or in the date of your birth, it becomes activated and more accessible than usual. You must deal with it directly and constructively, or its powerful effects can be destructive rather than beneficial.

You could say that the cards determined by your birth name and birth date represent the major tensions with which you will struggle all your life. Cards that express you only at certain times or under particular circumstances may show secondary issues. Jungian analyst Marie-Louise von Franz calls these constellated archetypes "a mass of dynamic energy" and "a factor of psychological probability." According to von Franz, the constellating of an archetype actually creates an inner pattern or structure in the psyche. Oracular techniques, she says, are attempts to get at these basic structures so that the psychological probabilities can be read. To quote her: "Divination oracles are an attempt to contact the dynamic load of an archetypal constellation and to give a reading pattern of what it is."[5]

The central archetypal constellations in a person's life—with which they must cope through an entire lifetime—are the forms of one's chosen purpose and are expressed in the birth date and name given at birth. This personal data deeply represents what one is destined to *realize*, meaning both "to make real" and "to comprehend the meaning of."

Another way of looking at the Self choosing its own destiny is the image of the child or fool in the act of playing a game of chance, that is, gambling. When dice (one of the oldest forms of gambling) are rolled, the "luck of the throw" determines the move. Fate supposedly rules that moment. But, according to Jung's theory of synchronicity, everything that happens at any given moment in time is meaningfully related. Fate then becomes a synchronistic phenomenon.[6] Thus, synchronistic events—which seem to be unique, sporadic, and unpredictable—happen within a larger firmament that we are rarely, if ever, able to see. Coincident events mirror the constellation, with each event illuminating a small portion of the greater field—i.e., the archetype that is seeking expression. I see this in the image of the Fool in the tarot, who throws fate—and himself—to the wind. He simply steps into and goes with an existing current, although he cannot see it. He trusts his destiny, and eventually he may come to recognize its modes and perimeters.

But, you may ask, how can a number tell me what my central archetypal constellation is? Scientifically speaking, we live in a time-space continuum based on mathematical "relativity." We measure both time and space in numbers. Again, according to von Franz:

> Number gives information about the time-bound ensemble of events. In each moment there is another ensemble, and number gives information as to the qualitative structure of the time-bound clusters of events.... I think we have to see that number is an archetypal representation or idea which contains a quantitative and a qualitative aspect.[7]

Von Franz references Richard Wilhelm, a translator of the I Ching, who explains that the Chinese felt the future could be predicted by knowing how a tree contracted into a seed. Thus, "if we know the kernel point of a situation [such as one's life], we can predict its consequences." I interpret "consequences" here to indicate what one's life stands for. Von Franz continues: "Now what that means in psychological language is that if we know the deepest underlying archetypal constellation of our present situation, then we can, to a certain extent, know how things will go."[8]

In this book, I attempt to give you some of the tools for discovering your "kernel" constellation.

The Nature of Beliefs

The tarot cards act as mirrors enabling you to look at your experiences with some objectivity. The tarot images mirror our beliefs about life and literally depict the hereditary and societal belief structures that we have been born into, specifically in our Western culture. They show great affinity with Hermetic philosophy, Qabalah, astrology, numerology, Jungian psychology, mythic and symbolic psychologies, alchemy, and other esoteric metaphysical systems.

Each of these describes a particular framework of reality, much as scientific systems describe the kind of structure that exists within atoms and molecules. One of the most basic frameworks can be imagined as similar to the dance of Shakti and Shiva (deities of the Hindu pantheon), in which their tracings would resemble a web out of which our universe is constructed. And as Shakti and Shiva express the basic duality of female and male, their framework would be described in a sort of binary-code arrangement: on/off, order/chaos, conscious/unconscious, black/white, energy/matter, masculine/feminine, good/bad, the blinking in and out of manifestation.

Each individual contributes to the mass beliefs that together form our society. As long as we act in accord with a belief, whether we think it's a good one or not, we perpetuate it. Most of the time we are not aware that our actions are based on beliefs. We just "do what comes naturally." Why question our every move? we ask ourselves. Just be "natural." But is it natural to blindly follow a set of beliefs and ideas inculcated in us, first by our parents and teachers, then later by employers, politicians, and television? That is what most people do. They call it natural, but it has nothing to do with Nature. It is habitual and reactive rather than active; it leads to a sense of powerlessness when caught in the crossfire of conflicting beliefs from each of one's many teachers.

Beliefs are helpful as well as harmful, and most of our beliefs are only helpful in the appropriate context. The problem is that they tend to become generalized as rules of conduct, and the reasons for them are forgotten. For instance, some people are taught never to put a hat on a bed or chair. They nag everyone around them, and nasty disagreements can be started from finding a hat on the bed. Few people question where this idea came from. ("It's just good manners.") Actually, this idea has a practical source. Many communities even today have problems with head lice. They can spread very quickly from a hat to a bed, then to someone else. If you don't live in a lousy environment, you need not be concerned about a hat on the bed. It is a rule of conduct cut off from its origin. Bad effects may follow, but they are imposed or created out of the fear, not directly as a natural consequence. Other beliefs are more insidious: "If you go out in the rain you will catch a cold." But this idea is not found in some cultures, where getting caught in the rain is not seen as having any relationship to catching a cold.

When people believe and expect that psychic things happen in their lives, they look for and notice them. If you find benefit in developing your psychic sense, why not believe in it? If you don't want war but believe it to be inevitable, you will act with an expectation of hostility and violence. One of the first things for you to do is to become aware of your emotions and beliefs!

One of the basic tenets of all metaphysical systems of thought is that we create our own reality in accord with our beliefs. These beliefs form the actual structure of that reality and hold it together. But in some sense, these beliefs are arbitrary. This is why, for instance, you can believe in precognitive dreams and experience them often, while another person who does not believe will find "proof" in each case that it was prior knowledge or coincidence. A skeptic will not experience anything counter to his beliefs until a related belief changes, allowing him to perceive another reality, that is, crack open his universe.

Perhaps you have recently read a book that you read years ago, but now you discover that it says something entirely different. How could you have misread it in the first place? Because you didn't notice things that didn't fit into your belief system. Beliefs direct your perceptions, as well as your emotional responses. I try to use the terms *I think* . . . or *I believe* . . . very consciously in this book to point out a personal belief of mine that you may or may not hold. But even if I don't use these words, you should know that they are implied at all times. If you do not hold a similar belief, you may not find significance in what I say, or you may ascribe a completely different meaning to it. At the least, question the ideas I express, while remaining aware that there is an infinite variety of beliefs. Nevertheless, I urge you to maintain a "willing suspension of disbelief" to the extent that you approach the ideas and exercises in this book with an attitude of fun and nonchalance. You must be willing to come play with me, to try out the suggestions here to see if they can teach you something new; then, by all means, develop your own rules for the game.

CHAPTER 2

Techniques for Working with Your Personal Cards

This chapter contains several ways to gain personal insights into what your Lifetime and Year Cards (including the Minor Arcana Lessons and Opportunities Cards) and the Court Card Significators mean to you. I ask you to begin by first exploring a card with which you most closely identify (before you learn what cards are determined for you in the following chapters), or you can skip ahead to the next chapter and calculate your Birth Cards and come back to this chapter when you are ready to work more deeply on your cards.

Much of this book necessarily consists of my telling you about the traits and characteristics of the cards and constellations. While this may be helpful, it is also limiting and may keep you from accessing your own inner wisdom. Just as no book that tells you the meaning of dream symbols will ever adequately or accurately explain your own dreams, so too, my interpretations do not fulfill the task of exploring your own range of possibilities. I encourage you, however, to explore other books and to continually add to your repertoire of meanings so as to deepen your appreciation for the cards.

Your First Exercise

Right now, look through your tarot deck, face up, and find a card in the Major Arcana that you think best depicts how you like to think of yourself. To do this, take the twenty-two Major Arcana from your deck and go through them looking at the pictures. Eliminate all the cards that are not the most complete expression of this Self (even though they might depict some piece of the whole). Keep eliminating cards until you get down to three to five cards. Spread these in front of you and choose the card that best depicts who you feel you are.

The card you first selected will always have a special place in your heart. It may depict an ideal Self or a part of you that you feel very comfortable with, like a favorite, well-worn shirt, or it could be a part of you that is hidden from others or a self-image with which you struggle to actualize or try to reject.

Use the instructions that follow to dialogue with your card.

Dialoguing with the Cards

You will be dialoguing with a figure on your card. This is an ideal, first assignment for your tarot notebook.

1. Find your card in the list of Card Questions that follows these instructions. Read through the questions and pick one as your starting point or make up your own question to ask your card. Write it down.

2. Select a figure or object on the card that seems most receptive to a conversation (objects can talk in this magical realm). Give him, her, or it a name (like Lion or Moon or Priestess) and address your question to that figure.

3. Allow yourself to *write the first response that comes to mind.* Be spontaneous, without censoring or hesitating. If you feel silly or stuck, then go along with it and make up the silliest thing the figure would say. This helps to break the ice and get the conversation moving. Play the Fool. Continue asking the same or related questions and making up responses in an impromptu manner.

4. Ignore handwriting, spelling, grammar, or anything else that might get in the way of the back-and-forth conversation. Continue for at least twelve to *fifteen minutes.* Once you are used to the process, you can write as long as you like, although a timed writing can help you keep focused.

5. You might find that your handwriting changes the longer you write, becoming looser and more childlike. This indicates you are bypassing the normal restrictions set on your thinking mind and freeing up your "inner knowing" to be directly expressed.

6. You will probably come to what I call *thresholds*. A threshold is a point at which you feel you have written enough and it is not really necessary to go on; you may suddenly feel weary or distracted or simply complete. You have reached a barrier beyond which your thoughts do not usually go. If you truly want to know yourself, *now* is the time to act on your intention. Simply acknowledge to yourself, "I am at a threshold." Then make the intention to go on, saying to yourself, "I choose to go on to what is on the other side." You'll find that what seemed like a brick wall now has an open gate through which you can easily pass. Go through only one or two thresholds the first few times you do this. When you gain confidence, you can move through more thresholds.

As you continue your dialogue, you might want to ask:

+   What is the significance of _____ symbol in the card?

+   How can I use this symbol in my life right now?

+   Why am I so attracted (or repelled) by you?

+   How can I best face the problem or challenge shown here?

+   How can I triumph through the qualities depicted?

+   Why did I choose to dialogue with you (addressing the particular figure or object with whom you are dialoguing) and what do you have to teach me?

Don't be surprised if the figure begins asking you questions! Your responses to these questions are especially significant. Any resistance to the questions implies that you are at a threshold.

Card Questions

You can always ask the general, all-purpose question, What do I need to learn from you? However, since each card has its own particular characteristics and issues, you may want to address these directly. If you'd like a kick start, select one or more of the sample questions that follow for the card with which you've chosen to work.

The 22 Cards of the Major Arcana

The Magician (1): What is my own personal magic? How do I focus and direct it? Who is my magical Self? How can I use the four suits or elements in my life? How can I communicate in four ways?

The High Priestess (2): My inner wisdom: How do I become aware of your knowledge? What questions must I ask in order to know myself? How do I go within? What are my dreams or intuition trying to tell me? How can I achieve your calmness and serenity?

The Empress (3): To what am I giving birth? How do I grow in beauty? What is rich and lush in my life? How does my physical environment nurture me, and what am I nurturing? What wants to creatively express itself through me?

The Emperor (4): Where does my power lie? How can I establish my own authority? What must I rule within myself? In what direction have I chosen to focus my energies? What rules or boundaries do I need to consider or construct?

The Hierophant (5): What do I need to learn from my problems? How do I learn? What religious, moral, or social factors do I need to consider? On what values do I base my decisions? What do I have to teach? What beliefs must I question?

The Lovers (6): What do I need to share openly about myself? What choice(s) do I have to make? How can I accept others for whom and what they are? What do I want and need from relationships? What opposites can I embrace?

The Chariot (7): What energies must I harness in order to move toward my goal? Where am I going? How can I control my instincts and keep myself centered? What would make me feel victorious? What mastery is necessary for this?

Strength (8): Beast: Who are you? Where does my strength lie? Where can I use my strengths? How can I balance power with love and lovingly express my power? How do I work with my desires (or with my rages)?

The Hermit (9): What am I searching for? Where should I look? What do I need to know about the path I am on? What do I need to complete? What wisdom have I learned that I can share with others?

Wheel of Fortune (10): What is changing and how can I best handle those changes? What does Fortune want from me? What is my destiny? What does the season or cycle call for? How do I reach the center and leave the ups and downs on the perimeter?

Justice (11): What needs to be negotiated, reconciled, or adjusted? Where is fairness or justice needed? On what basis can I judge or evaluate something? How can I be true to myself? Which of my needs can be balanced with the needs of another?

The Hanged Man (12): What are my current hang-ups? Where do I feel stuck, or what's suspended? What happens if I view things from a different perspective? To what do I need to surrender? What requires humility? How do I feel misunderstood or unappreciated?

Death (13): What needs to die? What must I sever in order to grow anew? How can I release any unnecessary patterns? What will letting go relieve me of? What needs transformation? What bare bones basics or essential supports do I need to get back to?

Temperance (14): What is my art? What things must I adjust or combine? What trial and error experiments can I try? How can I revive my interests and renew my spirit? What energies and resources are available for healing? What needs compassion or forgiveness?

The Devil (15): On what ambitions do I focus my energies? What do I hate or fear? Where do I feel bad or guilty? To what do my feelings bind me? How do I free myself from these bonds? What knowledge will free my thinking? How can mirth and humor help?

The Tower (16): Where has pride made me vulnerable? How can I express my angers and aggressions? What could be ruined? What personal barriers have I built up? What must I do to break through rigidity and constrictions? What needs liberating?

The Star (17): How am I a star? What talents and abilities do I esteem in myself? For what am I hoping? What could make my dreams come true? Where am I most free? What needs conservation or renewal? How can I work with the stars or the greater flow and patterns?

The Moon (18): What is troubling me or making me feel uneasy? To what secrets or undercurrents do I need to be sensitive? How can I draw on hidden resources? Where has my own evolution brought me? What must I digest from my past in order to move on?

The Sun (19): What makes me feel optimistic and happy? Where do I experience joy and love? What do I reveal when I open myself fully? How am I successful? What lights up my world? Where do I need to be careful of burnout?

Judgment (20): What does my purpose ask of me? How will I recognize my calling? What can I do to be part of a new aeon and recognize my kinship with others? What needs to be recovered or resurrected in my life? What requires a judgment call from me?

The World (21): What potentials within me seek manifestation? Where do I want to travel? How can I express freedom within structure and dance on my limitations? What would fulfill my highest goals? How am I already whole and complete?

The Fool (22): Where am I going? How am I being foolish? What wisdom is there in my folly? How can I trust? What would it look like to live more spontaneously and joyfully? What do I learn by being naïve, innocent, and irresponsible?

In the rest of this book, you will discover cards that are particular to you based on several factors. In my opinion, the dialogue process is the best way to get to know these cards and what they signify for you—to establish a personal relationship with them. Come back to this process often.

The Triumph Exercise

The following exercise shows you how to discover meanings for yourself while in the midst of a reading. It works even if you have never seen a tarot deck before. I use this procedure in my own professional consultations at those times when I look at a card in a spread and realize my mind has gone blank. Sure, I've felt panic wash over me when I think, "I can't remember a thing about this card! What will I say?" And, yes, it happens to everyone. I then take myself firmly in hand and go through the steps I've outlined below. Usually I choose to lead my client through them, since I've found that the reason I blanked is that my client often holds the essential piece of the puzzle that opens up the entire reading and empowers the client. I've learned to trust this.

While I call this ""The Triumph Exercise"—because it uses only the Major Arcana—the principles apply to all seventy-eight cards. When they were first created, the Major Arcana were called the trump suit (*il trionfos*) because, in games, they triumphed over the suit cards. The term also may come from their being pictorial representations of the carts in triumphal processions commonly found in Renaissance Italy. Each cart contained persons and symbols portraying an allegorical story of the triumph of a virtue or universal principle (such as Love, Justice, Time, Death, etc.)[9] Applying this today, the Major Arcana, as "Trump Cards," represent the ways we can "triumph" in a situation.[10] A contemporary definition of *trump* given by the *American Heritage Dictionary* is "a key resource to be used at the opportune moment." As the Major Arcana are also referred to as "Keys," these terms indicate that the information you receive can be used to open to opportunities and prevail successfully in any given situation.

Use any of your Lifetime or Year Cards with this exercise to discover more about them. If you want to try it immediately, then separate the twenty-two major cards from the rest of the deck, mix them thoroughly face down, spread them in a fan, and while asking, What can help me triumph in my life right now? select one at random.

The card I have selected is: _____. Write it down here in this book or in a journal right now. (Always read with a tarot deck and pen or pencil in hand.)

Describe the card. Be liberal with adjectives and descriptive phrases. What is going on? Write quickly. Don't think about what you are going to

say before writing. Surprise yourself. (For example: *A magician is*
in a garden full of flowers in full bloom. He is standing before a table on
which are spread symbols of all the elements: his tools, perhaps. He has
a rod in his raised right hand. He is pointing his left hand toward the
earth. Only one leg of the table is visible.) You will probably describe
this card differently each time you see it, noticing things that you
were unaware of previously, while ignoring others.

If you haven't done so already, describe how the figures feel in the
situation you've described. What is their attitude or mood? What
does the situation feel like? (*For example: He is concentrating as if manifesting*
something or channeling some power with complete confidence. It seems as if he
wants to demonstrate how to do something.)

Make at least one fictitious fantasy statement about the card, beginning
with the phrase *What if* . . . Do it off the top of your head right now, without
thinking about it, and in a spirit of fun. (For example: *What if the Magician*
were a storyteller, improvising a tale for his supper, in which he must use each
item on the table.)

Next, repeat the basic elements of what you wrote in the statements above,
but now use the first-person, present-tense *I am* . . . form. You become the
figure in the card and assume the characteristics you described. Also, take
the words *what if* off your fantasy and transform it into part
of the same declarative sentence. (For example: *I am a magi-*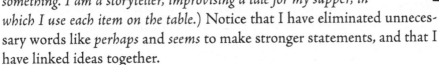
cian in a garden of flowers in full bloom. I am standing before a
table on which are spread symbols of all the elements: my tools. I
have a rod in my raised right hand and am pointing my left hand
toward the earth, channeling power with complete confidence and
concentration. I am totally focused on demonstrating how to do
something. I am a storyteller, improvising a tale for my supper, in
which I use each item on the table.) Notice that I have eliminated unnecessary words like *perhaps* and *seems* to make stronger statements, and that I
have linked ideas together.

Now transform your own statements into the first-person present tense: Immediately you will see that some statements are very appropriate to your life right now. Underline these.

Turn each of your phrases into a question. Depending on the phrases you used, ask yourself, for instance, *What am I concentrating on in my life now?* From the above example, you might ask, *What elements or tools am I using?* and, *What is the story I am improvising and how can it feed (or reward) me?* You can even go back to the images on the card and ask, *How could I use each item on the table in my improvisation?*

Examine all the images you used as symbols of events, beliefs, and choices in your life; that is, of the reality you are creating. As another example, a description for the Empress might be *A woman, big with child, sits*

in a very rich field, which becomes *I am a woman big with child sitting in a very rich field.* Then ask yourself, *What kind of child or creation am I pregnant with?* and, *What sort of riches surround me?* And another example: A description of the Justice card, such as, *She appears to be in a courtroom or in some rigid setting; she is trying to be stern and just and looks as if she will take nothing less than her due* would become *I am in a rigid place of judgment; I am stern and just, and I will take nothing less than what is due to me.* Then create questions from these phrases: *What is rigid about my setting or in my environment? What is being judged? Where in my life am I trying to be stern and just? What do I feel is due to me?*

Now list several questions of your own, based on your description of your card.

Answer your questions as honestly as you can, focusing on your current life situation.

Since each card is a way you can "triumph," you must now consider the card you drew as an opportunity for growth, or a challenge to meet, while also portraying the qualities required to do so.

How can you triumph? What are the highest qualities you see in the card? What characteristics does it suggest that you value or that you would like to develop? Write down at least five qualities you see. Do this quickly, without thinking about it first.

In this exercise, it is important to avoid negative statements; instead, transform them into their opposite, beneficial qualities. For example, if you wrote that you can triumph through being "not afraid," what positive qualities are implied? Courage? Loving your fear? Determination? Compassion?

Transform any negative statement from your list above into its triumphal qualities.

Now put these qualities into a statement in the first person, present tense, using one of your words as the active verb, so that you are affirming that you have those qualities in yourself.

To further amplify the meaning that this one card can hold for you and to confirm its relevance, return to this page tomorrow and write in the space below a quick review of what happened in the twenty-four hours since beginning this exercise. Note especially how thoughts, assumptions, and events might relate to your card, or how you used its qualities in your activities.

Card _____   Date (1st review)_____

Observations or synchronicities: Date (2nd review)_____

Review the same card in seven to ten days to see if you can add further perspective. Use a pen of another color the second time, so you can differentiate your comments.

This is a basic interpretation technique that can actually be used in any reading and with any card that has a pictorial scene on it. After doing it several times, it will begin to feel natural and proceed easily as an automatic process seen holistically in your mind's eye. Done in depth, it can provide you with as much information as you receive from an average multicard reading and will be more relevant to the issue than any meanings you will find in a book. You will gradually define the cards according to your personalized criteria and in terms of actual situations, truly making the cards your own. This is the essence of personalizing the cards and of discovering tarot for yourself. Here is a summary of the technique:

Chart 2: How to Read a Tarot Card

1. Simply describe the card! Be liberal with adjectives and descriptive phrases. What is going on? How do the figures feel in the situation you've described? What is the atmosphere?

2. Being careful to use the exact phrases from the previous step, repeat what you've just said, but in the first person, present tense, "I am . . ." (or, if reading for another: "You may be . . .")

3. Turn the statements into open-ended s and answer them. For example: "How am I/you being devilish?"

4. Examine the images as symbols of events, beliefs, and choices in your life. In what ways are they beneficial or limiting?

5. How can you triumph? What qualities does the card have that you value or that you would like to develop?

Spreads for Getting to Know Your Cards

Pages 32 and 33 show two examples of how to use spreads to learn more about the wisdom your personal cards have for you. Cards drawn randomly can open up whole new perspectives and suggest directions you hadn't considered before. Remember, the responses are from the point of view of the card with whom you've chosen to communicate—whether it be one of your Lifetime or Year Cards or a Court Card Significator or any other card in the deck.

If the questions in these positions don't suffice for what you need right now, then change them. You can photocopy the spreads for your own use.

Finally, take one of your Lifetime Cards through the twenty-one steps in my book *Mary K. Greer's 21 Ways to Read a Tarot Card*. It is guaranteed to reveal dimensions to the card and things about yourself that you never knew before.

"Getting to Know You" Spread

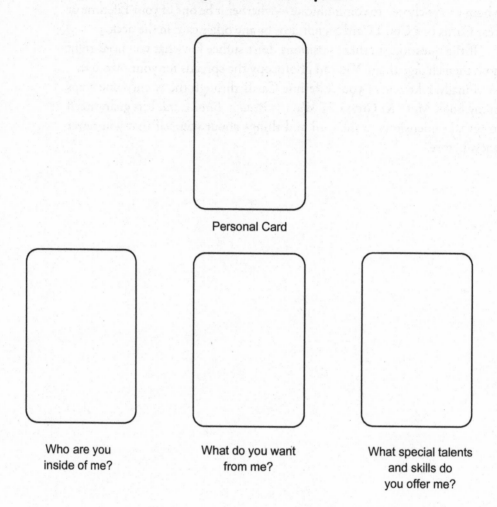

Personal Card

Who are you
inside of me?

What do you want
from me?

What special talents
and skills do
you offer me?

Archetypal Tarot

An Advice Spread

What do I need to pay attention
to in the outer world?

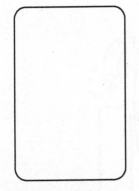

What do I need to pay
attention to in my inner world

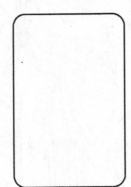

Personal Card

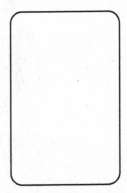

What needs to be broken
through, changed, or
illuminated in my life?

What can I do to listen to you
more clearly?

THE FATES

CHAPTER 3

Your Birth Cards

Lifetime Cards

As I've mentioned, one of the most helpful concepts I've found in working with the tarot is what the inspirational speaker and teacher Angeles Arrien named the "Lifetime Cards." I have used this concept extensively as a major part of my tarot work and, with Angie's permission, I introduced it in my book *Tarot for Your Self*. All together, the Lifetime Cards refer to a set of cards that are determined by (1) the date of your birth (called Birth Cards); and (2) the name given to you at birth (called Name Cards), as these apply to you throughout your entire lifetime. (For clarification of the card names used in this book, refer to appendix C: Summary of Card Names.)

Fate and Destiny

The cards determined by your birth date (and by your birth name) are based on the Gregorian, or New Style, calendar, which was not adopted in England and the United States (then the American colonies) until 1752. There are literally hundreds of different calendars in use in the world today, such as the Chinese, Hindu, Hebrew, Roman Catholic ecclesiastical, and Muslim calendars. These not only have different month names but also different beginnings for the new year, and they compensate for the solar year's "extra" one-quarter day per year in a wide variety of ways, usually by the device of a leap year. The oldest continuous calendar seems to be the lunar calendar of the Chinese—in use since 2397 BCE! Our own version was originally taken from an Egyptian calendar modified by the Romans and "rectified" by Pope Gregory XIII in 1582.

So, you might ask how such an arbitrary system could have any validity for us. Have you ever tried thinking in another time system? There are many languages that do not have words for *past, present,* or *future;* they think, for instance, in terms of what "has manifested" and what "is being manifested."

Yet that definition is not quite right either, because we have no words for what they experience.

We are tied to our own perception of time, inculcated from childhood. Ask any five-year-old when their birthday is, and they will probably know the date and some idea of how long until their birthday. Our definitions of time literally structure how we perceive it, and we are not really free to rid ourselves of this learned understanding. By being Americans or Westerners, we are "fated" to relate to time in the way we do, and to "know" that February follows January. It is part of our cultural conditioning, and just as our chromosomes give us a certain "fate" in our genetic conditioning—Caucasian, Negroid, Asiatic; straight red hair and green eyes, or kinky black hair and brown eyes, etc.—so we are fated to experience time through our cultural heritage and the calendar and clocks to which it adheres. This is nothing we have individually "caused," nor are we in any practical way "responsible" *for* it. We are responsible for what we are going to do *with* it.

Many spiritual teachers point out that before birth your soul chooses the kind of life you need to experience in order to complete your physical-plane education, and that sometimes your soul will choose a short life of pain and suffering in order to develop much more quickly or to help with the growth and learning of the whole planet. Who are we to say? I like to believe that at some level my Greater Self sees a larger plan, but in the meantime I can only work with what I've got. To this way of thinking, the life you are "fated" with can be described psychically by your name and birth date, just as it can be mapped physically by your chromosomes. Your birth name and birth date are lifetime keys to your inner psychic Self *as you perceive yourself through your culture, language, and ethnic heritage.*

By understanding the significance of your Lifetime Cards, including your various Birth Cards and Name Cards, you can take responsibility for what you choose to make of your destiny: This is free will.

Methods of Adding Your Birth Date

There are many different ways to add the numbers in your birth date. All of them result in the same single-digit or root number! All of them are valid in their own way. However, since we are looking for twenty-two possible results for a Personality Card, then a method of adding dates that maximizes these results will serve us best. That is why I recommend the addition method below. The most important thing is that you always use the same method and that you get to know that method's patterns and intricacies for yourself.

Your Personality and Soul Cards

In any tarot reading, I always first determine a querent's Personality Card and Soul Card, based on their birth date. With only this information, we are able to see what a person most needs to learn in his or her life, and what lessons will bring this person to an understanding of this urge.

Using your birth date, let's numerologically calculate your Personality, Soul, and Hidden Factor Cards.

First, to find your Personality-Soul combination (destiny pattern), add together your month, day, and year of birth.

For example (using Mexican artist Frida Kahlo's birth date, July 6, 1907):

Month (July, the seventh month of the year) =	7
Day =	6
Year =	+ 1907
	1920

Add the digits in the resulting number: 1 + 9 + 2 + 0 = 12.

If You Get a Sum Between 1 and 22:

The resulting number is your Personality Number, which in this example is 12 and corresponds to the 12th card of the Major Arcana (the Hanged Man). *Your Personality Card indicates personality characteristics that you develop easily and lessons that you learn early in your life as they seem to resonate with your essential nature.*

Add together the digits of that sum, (in this example, 12: 1 + 2 = 3), to find your Soul Number. Artist Frida Kahlo's Soul Number (3) corresponds to the 3rd Major Arcana card, the Empress (3). *Your Soul Card shows your soul purpose: those qualities in yourself that you must express and use in order to feel fulfilled in whatever you do.*

THE HANGED MAN.   THE EMPRESS.

If You Get a Single Digit or a Sum Greater Than 22:

In a few cases, the first sum is a single digit ($2 + 0 + 1 + 4 = 7$). Or, more often, the number will add up to more than 22. Since there are only twenty-two cards in the Major Arcana, reduce the number to 22 or less (this will result in a single digit).

For example (using rock singer Mick Jagger's birthday, July 26, 1943):

Month (July, the seventh month of the year) =	7
Day =	26
Year =	+ 1943
	1976

Add the digits in the resulting number: $1 + 9 + 7 + 6 = 23$
Because this sum is greater than 22, add the digits again: $2 + 3 = 5$

THE HIEROPHANT

In this case, the 5th card, the Hierophant (5), is *both* Personality and Soul Card. Anyone whose sum is a single digit (1 through 9) has the same number for both cards and is specifically working on their soul purpose in this lifetime. It makes the person more focused and directed, although they can lack flexibility until life's lessons force them to be more pliant and adaptable.

If You Get 19:

There is one case in which more than two cards can appear. If your first number is 19, you will have three cards.

For example (using Martin Luther King, Jr.'s birthday, January 15, 1929):

Month (January, the first month of the year) =	1
Day =	15
Year =	+ 1929
	1945

Add the digits in the resulting number: $1 + 9 + 4 + 5 = 19$
Add the resulting digits: $1 + 9 = 10$
Add the resulting digits: $1 + 0 = 1$

It is only when your birth date totals 19, like that of Martin Luther King Jr. above, that you will have such a triple sequence. For your use here, you can consider the Sun (19) as your Personality Card, the Magician (1) as your Soul Card, and the Wheel of Fortune (10) as your Teacher Card

THE SUN.   THE MAGICIAN.   WHEEL of FORTUNE.

(more about the Teacher Card later). People with this sequence must learn to communicate their individual creative expression. Their personal identity and sense of Self will be inextricably combined with their life and soul purpose. Their ability to relate to others will depend on a harmony of vision and sense of shared purpose.

If You Get 22:

If your birth date adds up to 22, you combine great impulsiveness and great mastery, a fine line to balance. The number 22 represents 0 (The Fool), since there are twenty-two cards in the Major Arcana, and in numerology, 22 is a Master Number signifying great wisdom or great folly. It reduces to 4 (The Emperor). While you might consider 4 (The Emperor) to be your Soul Card and 22/0 (The Fool) to be your Personality Card (especially when figuring your Numerological Lessons and Opportunities Cards), I find that in practice they work as a unit. Don't expect Emperor-Fools, like Woody Allen, to sit still for anyone's system.

THE FOOL.   THE EMPEROR.

For example (using Woody Allen's birth date, December 1, 1935):

Month (December, the twelfth month of the year) =	12
Day =	1
Year =	+ 1935
	1948

Add the digits of the resulting number: 1 + 9 + 4 + 8 = 22 (The Fool)
Add the digits again: 2 + 2 = 4 (The Emperor)

Chart 3: Your Personality and Soul Card Chart

Determine your own Personality and Soul Cards as follows:

Add: The month you were born: _____

           The day you were born: _____

           The year you were born: _____

           Equals: _____

Add each digit: _____ + _____ + _____ + _____ = _____

If you have a double-digit answer, add again: _____ + _____   = _____

My Personality Number is _____ (the higher of the two numbers if 22 or less).

The Major Arcana card corresponding to this number is   _____

                                                   PERSONALITY CARD

My Soul Number is _____ (the single-digit number in your final reduction).

The Major Arcana card corresponding to this number is   _____

                                             SOUL CARD

(Note: If you are a 19-10-1, the Wheel is your Teacher Card.)

The Hidden Factor or Teacher Card

In addition to the numbers obtained directly through addition and reduction, there is frequently another number-and-card concept indirectly connected with your birth date, which I call your "Hidden Factor" or "Teacher Card." The Constellations Chart (on page 41) will help you determine this number. A tarot constellation consists of all the cards with the *same "Root Number"* (the single-digit numbers, 1 through 9), as well as all the other Major Arcana whose numbers reduce to that root number. Their energies constellate, or come together, based on similar principles, that is, on vibrational essences of like quality.

The chart aligns all the Major Arcana numbers above the Root Numbers to which they reduce. For example, in the 19-10-1 column, each of those numbers reduces to the Root Number 1. Each of the nine groups or constellations thus formed also includes all the cards from the Minor Arcana of the same Root Number.

Let's go back to the first birth date used as an example, that of Frida Kahlo: Her Personality Card is the Hanged Man (12) and her Soul Card is the Empress (3). By combining these numbers, we are able to refer to her as

Chart 4: Constellations Chart

19 10 1	20 11 2	21 12 3	22 13 4	14 5	15 6	16 7	17 8	18 9	MAJOR ARCANA
10s/1s	2s	3s	4s	5s	6s	7s	8s	9s	MINOR ARCANA
1	2	3	4	5	6	7	8	9	ROOT NUMBER

a "12-3." Now look at the Constellations Chart and notice that there is one other Major Arcana number listed in her constellation, namely 21. Since she did not get a 21 in the calculations, it is a hidden aspect of her birth vibrational essence. This, then, is her Hidden Factor Card: the World (21). *It is the number that did not appear when we did the calculations, but which is also in her constellation.* All the 3s of the Minor Arcana also belong to her constellation.

Variations of Hidden Factor

One Hidden Factor—20, 21

The first variation is similar to the one above and is exemplified by the forty-fourth president of the United States, Barack Obama (born August 4, 1961):

Month (August, the eighth month of the year) =	8
Day =	4
Year =	+ 1961
	1973

1 + 9 + 7 + 3 = 20 (Judgment)
2 + 0 = 2 (The High Priestess)

Barack Obama's Personality Card is Judgment (20) and his Soul Card is the High Priestess (2); he is a 20-2. Therefore, his Hidden Factor Card is Justice (11), since 11 is the only number in his constellation not directly appearing in the birth date reduction. The 2s of the Minor Arcana also belong to his constellation.

JUDGEMENT.   THE HIGH PRIESTESS   JUSTICE.

One Hidden Factor—Single 5s through 9s

Mick Jagger has the Hierophant (5) as both his Personality and Soul Card (see page 38), so Temperance (14) is his Hidden Factor Card. The 5s in the Minor Arcana are part of his constellation.

No Hidden Factor—the "Nighttime Cards"

The next variation occurs in the constellations 5 through 9, involving the Personality-Soul Patterns 14-5 through 18-9. I call these the "Nighttime Cards."

For example (using Marilyn Monroe's birth date, June 1, 1926):

Month (June, sixth month of the year) =	6
Day =	1
Year =	+ 1926
	1933

$1 + 9 + 3 + 3 = 16$ (The Tower)
$1 + 6 = 7$ (The Chariot)

Marilyn Monroe is therefore a 16-7, with the Tower (16) as Personality Card and the Chariot (7) as Soul Card. There is no number not accounted for in her constellation and therefore no Hidden Factor Card. Thus this combina-

tion (and that of the 14-5s, 15-6s, 17-8s, and 18-9s) includes the Hidden Factor within itself.

The cards Temperance (14) through the Moon (18) are called the Nighttime Cards because they follow the Death card (13) and precede the dawning of the Sun (19). All are depicted at night. In the Waite-Smith deck, Temperance (14) depicts sunset; the Devil (15) is in darkness; and the Tower (16), the Star (17), and the Moon (18) are definitely images of the night. These cards inherently possess a "dark," or ignored, unrecognized side. I want to caution you, though, not to think of the dark side as bad, evil, or valueless; after all, in our journey through the dark (without the distractions of the light), we come to feel who we really are.

No Hidden Factor—The 19-10-1s

Because the Wheel of Fortune (10) was involved in the computation, it is not "hidden." It does not manifest the "shadow" quality normally associated with the Hidden Factor Card.

Two Hidden Factor Cards—Single 1s through 4s

People who are a Single 1, 2, 3, or 4 (that is, having Personality-Soul Patterns of 1-1, 2-2, 3-3, or 4-4) have *two* Hidden Factor Cards, as shown by the chart. For instance, a Single 4 (4-4) has the Fool (22) and Death (13) as Hidden Factor Cards. These patterns are pretty rare, occurring mostly around the turn of the second millennium (in fact there are no Single 1s since 998 CE).

The Hidden Factor Card as Shadow Card

Your Hidden Factor Card indicates aspects of yourself that you fear, reject, or don't see, and thus it can also be called the Shadow Card. The "shadow," a term used and defined by psychologist Carl Jung, refers to unknown or little-known parts of the personality. They are aspects of ourselves that we deny and thus can't see directly. However, we remain sensitive to these qualities and therefore tend to see them in others via the psychological mechanism of projection.

These shadow qualities are dualistic, having a dark side and a bright side. What is called the "dark shadow" refers to those qualities we mistrust and dislike, the little "sins." They contain tremendous psychic power that we can use if we contact them without fear. The "bright shadow" refers to the qualities that we admire (appearance, creativity, assertiveness) and actually have the potential to manifest, but, again, we cannot see them in ourselves. Often these inner impulses pop out at inappropriate times and in unexpected ways, because they are not under the control of our conscious mind.

The Shadow Card functions in much the same way that Saturn does in one's astrological chart. Saturn is the outermost personal planet and, as such, establishes the limits beyond which we cannot go without expanding into transpersonal and metaphysical experience. The card thus represents a doorway into that transpersonal and metaphysical realm, the inner planes. Most of us, though, experience this card as a mirror in which we see fears and fascinations. In it we are confronted with our limitations, our obsessions, our anxieties—the sources of stress. Often the Hidden Factor points out "invisible beliefs": those that lie out of sight behind other beliefs. For instance, one such belief is that you are responsible for your lover's happiness, which for some people lies invisibly behind the belief that if your lover isn't happy, it's your fault and you must do something to fix it.

The Hidden Factor Card as Teacher Card

I've found that the Hidden Factor Card acts as your Shadow most strongly during your younger years. The planet Saturn takes twenty-eight to thirty years to complete a circuit of the zodiac; that is, to return to where it was in the sky when you were born. This approximate twenty-nine-year cycle of Saturn is known as your "Saturn Return." As I mentioned before, Saturn—which represents many of the qualities of your shadow and which has much the same significance as the Hidden Factor—has to face itself every twenty-nine years.

By the time they are thirty years old, most people recognize these shadow characteristics in themselves and now realize that they have learned their greatest lessons from their shadow issues. Carl Jung declared that *the shadow is your greatest teacher*, and that only by getting to know your shadow can you achieve individuation. At the second Saturn Return, between the ages of fifty-seven and sixty, the shadow aspects are revisited at a new level and may require letting go of the outer abilities and responsibilities that that you had learned to rely on, so that in the second half of life you can focus on developing more inner qualities.

With people over thirty, I tend to call their Hidden Factor Card their "Teacher Card," because they are ready to work actively and consciously with its principles. I'm not saying that you can't do this before your first Saturn Return. Many people become aware of their Hidden Factor issues much earlier and experience this Saturn Return as a time of liberation and joy. Most people, at least intermittently, confront their fears, inner restrictions, and limitations. All of these can relate to the Teacher Card. *If you have a Nighttime Card (a Personality Card between 14 and 18), then that card will include in its characteristics some of the Hidden Factor qualities.*

If you are a 19-10-1, you have no Hidden Factor Card; instead, you have the Wheel of Fortune (10) as your Teacher Card. In this pattern, the shadow qualities are not emphasized; rather, you consciously feel that life brings you the experiences you need to achieve your purpose. At worst, lacking the determination developed from dealing with your shadow, you tend to drift through life, never challenged to use your abundant talents.

Your Hidden Factor Card always challenges you to go beyond your usual experiences. Often it represents what you strive to understand and develop in yourself and in the world around you.

Chart 5 lists all twenty-two Personality and Soul Patterns and their associated Hidden Factor Cards.

Chart 5: Hidden Factor Chart

Personality and Soul Card Patterns	Hidden Factor (Teacher) Cards
1-1 10-1 19-10-1	10, 19 19 10 (Teacher)
2-2 11-2 20-2	11, 20 20 11
3-3 12-3 21-3	12, 21 21 12
4-4 13-4 22-4	13, 22 22 13
5-5 14-5	14 *
6-6 15-6	15 *
7-7 16-7	16 *
8-8 17-8	17 *
9-9 18-9	18 *

Personality Cards 14 through 18, as Nighttime Cards, include the Hidden Factor within themselves and therefore have no separate Hidden Factor Card.

Lessons and Opportunities Cards

Based on your birth date, you also have cards from the Minor Arcana with the same number as your Soul Card. Therefore, if your Soul Card is the Hierophant (5), for example, you also have all the 5s in the Minor Arcana as your "Lessons and Opportunities Cards." These cards define the kinds of situations in which you are most likely to encounter your blocks and challenges as well as your personal gifts and opportunities. Through the experiences indicated by these cards, you learn the *lessons* necessary to develop your personality and the *opportunities* most likely to express your soul purpose.

If you are an Emperor-Fool (22-4), for instance, all the 4s of each suit in the Minor Arcana are your Lessons and Opportunities Cards. The exception is the Sun–Wheel of Fortune–Magician (19-10-1), in which you have both the aces and the 10s of each suit.

Your Zodiacal Lesson and Opportunity Card

Each of the Minor Arcana number cards (except the Aces) discussed in chapters 5 through 13 includes a range of dates associated with it. The card associated with your specific birthday is called your Zodiacal Lesson and Opportunity Card.

The Hermetic Order of the Golden Dawn assigned each of the thirty-six Minor Arcana Number cards to ten degrees of the zodiac, known as the "decans." In 1941, Muriel Bruce Hasbrouck published a book called *Pursuit of Destiny* in which she credited *Perdurabo* (Aleister Crowley) and "Paul" (Paul Foster Case) with guiding her tarot studies. In 1932 she had come upon Crowley's *The Equinox* that included the Golden Dawn teaching paper "Book T" that delineated the ten-day decan correspondences that she uses in her book.

Hasbrouck describes the Destiny Card as psychological birth conditioning based on this ten-day-cycle formula. It reveals people's "fundamental, natural response to the basic challenges of life."[11] While one's destiny suggests one's *destination*, she counsels, "we are free to choose for ourselves what use we will make of the weapons furnished to us as our birthright . . . [in] the pursuit of destiny."[12]

If you wish, skip ahead to read about your personal Lifetime Cards or continue on to Chapter 4.

Chart 6: Your Lifetime Cards Chart

My Soul (single-digit) Card is _____.

My Personality (double-digit) Card is _____.
(Can be a repeat of your Soul Card.)

My Hidden Factor/Shadow/Teacher Card is _____.

My Lessons and Opportunities Cards in the Minor Arcana are:

      _____ of Wands   _____ of Cups

      _____ of Swords   _____ of Pentacles

My Zodiacal Lesson and Opportunity Card in the Minor Arcana is _____.

The Tarot Constellations

CHAPTER 4

The Tarot Constellations

In the preceding chapter you learned how to find your Personality, Soul, and Hidden Factor Cards, and that they all are in the same constellation. This chapter provides a detailed overview of the constellations and also shows you several ways to use the information given in the individual constellation chapters. The next nine chapters (chapters 5 through 13) describe what your cards mean in each of the nine constellations.

The Constellations: What They Are

Your Personality Card is a major signpost along your life's journey, while your Soul Card reveals the goal or purpose of your being. These cards can be paired together in twenty-two combinations that I call the Patterns of Personal Destiny (or destiny patterns), constellated around nine basic principles of the journey. These patterns and their associated constellations are the heart-matter of this book. Also constellated around the nine principles are the associated cards from the Minor Arcana, which provide further landmarks on the map of your spiritual travels. If you are unfamiliar with the four suits of the Minor Arcana, there is a description of their primary traits later in this chapter.

The tarot constellations express nine major principles or archetypes underlying our metaphysical makeup. The basic archetypes, though in themselves impossible to pinpoint, are actually unconscious trends that cause certain motifs to appear in all human cultures. The Soul Card of the tarot constellations gives us nine representations of the most common and essential motifs of the Self. These are shown in Chart 7 on page 50.

Each of these nine basic motifs is further amplified by the other cards in its constellation. The constellations that are especially yours, because they correspond with your Birth Cards and Name Cards (the latter will be explained later in the book), tell you the archetypes constellated for you at your birth. These then are particular energies and principles that you will

Chart 7: Soul Card Archetypal Motifs Chart

Magician	Consciousness; Outer Sense of Self; Persona
High Priestess	Unconscious; Inner, All-Knowing Self; Psyche
Empress	Feminine; Fertile, Creative Mother
Emperor	Masculine; Ordered, Structured Father
Hierophant	Spirit; Teacher; Morality
Lovers	Choice: Union/Separation; the Twins—Duality
Chariot	Hero; Warrior; Quest; Power-Over
Strength	Heroine; Enchantress; Animal Helper; Power-Within
Hermit	Old Wise One; Journey to the Underworld

express, explore, and develop in your life as well as the challenges you will have to meet to understand them. They point to your purpose in being here, and to particular qualities you can manifest in this lifetime.

The Constellations and Their Principles

This section contains a summary of the constellations and their principles that should be used and expanded upon.

The Constellation of the Magician

Includes Personality-Soul Patterns 1-1, 10-1, and 19-10-1
The Principle of Will and Focused Consciousness
Soul Archetype: Consciousness; Outer Sense of Self; Persona
The *Aces* indicate the opportunity to begin new things and reveal your four basic skills.
The *10s* demonstrate the developed skills with which to meet challenges and the results of taking the principles to their extremes.

Chart 8: Tarot Constellations Chart

Constellation	Principle	Personality and Soul Card Patterns	Hidden Factor (Teacher) Cards	Minor Arcana cards
Magician (Sun, Wheel of Fortune, Magician)	Will and Focused Consciousness	1-1 10-1 19-10-1	10, 19 19 10 (Teacher)	10s, 1s
High Priestess (Judgment, Justice, High Priestess)	Balanced Judgment through Intuitive Awareness	2-2 11-2 20-2	11, 20 20 11	2s
Empress (World, Hanged Man, Empress)	Love and Creative Imagination	3-3 12-3 21-3	12, 21 21 12	3s
Emperor (Fool, Death, Emperor)	Life Force and Realization of Power	4-4 13-4 22-4	13, 22 22 13	4s
Hierophant (Temperance, Hierophant)	Teaching and Learning	5-5 14-5	14 *	5s
Lovers (Devil, Lovers)	Relatedness and Choice	6-6 15-6	15 *	6s
Chariot (Tower, Chariot)	Mastery through Change	7-7 16-7	16 *	7s
Strength (Star, Strength)	Courage and Self-Esteem	8-8 17-8	17 *	8s
Hermit (Moon, Hermit)	Introspection and Personal Integrity	9-9 18-9	18 *	9s

Personality Cards 14 through 18 have no Hidden Factor.

✹ The Constellation of the High Priestess

Includes Personality-Soul Patterns 2-2, 11-2, and 20-2
The Principle of Balanced Judgment through Intuitive Awareness
Soul Archetype: Unconscious; Inner, All-Knowing Self; Psyche
The 2s represent the four ways in which judgments are made.

✹ The Constellation of the Empress

Includes Personality-Soul Patterns 3-3, 12-3, and 21-3
The Principle of Love and Creative Imagination
Soul Archetype: Feminine; Fertile, Creative Mother
The 3s indicate the opportunities and challenges to creatively demonstrate love.

✹ The Constellation of the Emperor

Includes Personality-Soul Patterns 4-4, 13-4, and 22-4
The Principle of Life Force and the Realization of Power
Soul Archetype: Masculine; Ordered, Structured Father
The 4s indicate the opportunities to consolidate and complete something in preparation for renewal.

✹ The Constellation of the Hierophant

Includes Personality-Soul Patterns 5-5 and 14-5
The Principle of Teaching and Learning
Soul Archetype: Spirit; Teacher; Morality
The 5s indicate the challenges faced when learning through experience.

✹ The Constellation of the Lovers

Includes Personality-Soul Patterns 6-6 and 15-6
The Principle of Relatedness and Choice
Soul Archetype: Choice: Union/Separation; the Twins—Duality
The 6s indicate the challenges of maintaining and sustaining relationships and of taking responsibility for your choices.

The Constellation of the Chariot

Includes Personality-Soul Patterns 7-7 and 16-7
The Principle of Mastery through Change
Soul Archetype: Hero; Warrior; Quest; Power-Over
The 7s test whether mastery and control can be sustained through change.

 ### The Constellation of Strength

Includes Personality-Soul Patterns 8-8 and 17-8
The Principle of Courage and Self-Esteem
Soul Archetype: Heroine; Enchantress; Animal Helper;
Power-Within
The 8s indicate the gifts and challenges in developing the self-confidence to follow a vision.

 ### The Constellation of the Hermit

Includes Personality-Soul Patterns 9-9 and 18-9
The Principle of Introspection and Personal Integrity
Soul Archetype: Old Wise One; Journey to the Underworld
The 9s indicate the challenges to be faced by looking within and discovering your own wisdom.

The Suits of the Minor Arcana

The following chapters on each of the constellations contain meanings for the suit cards of the Minor Arcana, which can be applied to any reading. If you are unfamiliar with the four suits, this discussion will introduce them to you, or serve as a review.

The four suits of the Minor Arcana are based on the four elements. Using the Golden Dawn system, Wands are Fire, Cups are Water, Swords are Air, and Pentacles are Earth. You contain these four suits and elements within you in a combination that is constantly in flux, never in perfect balance. When you read these tarot cards, they tell you what is happening on these four levels, or within these four aspects of yourself. (If you use different elemental correspondences, you will need to adapt the following information to your own system.)

In the descriptions of the constellations, you'll find that each Minor Arcana card is labeled, in accordance with the Golden Dawn system, with a range of dates, ten degrees within a zodiac sign, and that sign's defining characteristics: its element and quality.

+ The 2s, 3s, and 4s in each suit are the *Cardinal* signs of each element. Aries, Cancer, Libra, and Capricorn initiate a season and demonstrate the assertion and drive of that element.

+ The 5s, 6s, and 7s are the *Fixed* signs Taurus, Leo, Scorpio, and Aquarius. They demonstrate the depth, maintenance, and persistence of the suit and element.

+ The 8s, 9s, and 10s are the *Mutable* signs Gemini, Virgo, Sagittarius, and Pisces. They demonstrate the flexibility and adaptability of the element as they prepare for the completion that precedes a new initiation.

Additionally, as mentioned in the previous chapter, each card represents a ten-day subdivision of the zodiac sign associated with that card. The 10 of Wands, for instance, is the third decanate of Sagittarius (Mutable Fire), which includes the dates December 13 to 21. Thus, your birthday (month and day) corresponds to one of the Minor Arcana cards, which is known as your Zodiacal Lesson and Opportunity. Its function as one of your Lifetime Cards is discussed in chapter 3.

Using the Constellations

The information on the constellations in the following nine chapters can be used in a variety of ways:

1. Look up your Personality, Soul, and Hidden Factor/Teacher Cards.

2. Dialogue with the figures in your Personality, Soul, and Hidden Factor Cards (see chapter 2); find out what they have to say to you directly.

3. Include an overview of the querent's Lifetime and recent Year Cards in your readings for others.

Chart 9: Minor Arcana Suits Chart

Symbol	Suit and Element	Meaning of the Suits
	WANDS Fire	Self-growth. Spirit. Inspiration. Energy. Creativity. Initiation. Enthusiasm. Desire. Passion. Perception. Action. Movement. Optimism. Intuitive Function.
	CUPS Water	Feelings and Emotions. Unconscious. Imagination. Being psychic. Dreams. Visualization. Inner processes. Relationships. Receptivity. Reflection. Feeling Function.
	SWORDS Air	Thoughts. Struggles. Conflict. Decisions. Wit and cunning. Analysis. Discussion. Communication. Mental processes. Acuity. Criticism. Pessimism. Thinking Function.
	PENTACLES Earth	Results. Actualization. Sensation. Security. Grounding. Centeredness. Manifestation. Skills. Craftsmanship. Rewards for accomplishment. Fruits of labor. Tradition. The Physical and Material. Sensation Function.

4. Offer your querents a specialty consultation in which you examine their Lifetime Cards and those of members of their family tree (see below), plus a description of significant points in their Year Cards (see chapter 14).

5. Use the constellation descriptions for interpreting individual cards in any reading. These interpretations emphasize the principles you are accessing, as well as the lessons and challenges presented. Use the descriptions to focus your reading on the potentials available and the purpose of the experience. They tell you what energies are presently active.

6. Whenever a card is particularly important in a reading, or if three or more cards from one constellation appear in a spread, consider how the

basic principle of that constellation applies. Examine all the cards in that constellation to find ways to work with the energy in your life.

7. Determine the Lifetime Cards of your family and friends. If you wish, write out your family tree as far forward and backward as you can and add each person's cards. Consider the relational patterns formed and what this suggests about lineage, relationships, and interactions that are part of your family heritage (thanks to Carrie Paris, who suggested the family tree).

8. Read about the famous people in your constellation. (The Internet makes it easy to look them up.) Look for any interesting similarities and coincidences among them. Remember that the cards won't describe what the subjects did so much as *why they did it*. For writers and philosophers, this is often reflected by the key issues in their books. For what quotations are they remembered?. Ask yourself how the significant themes in their lives might apply to your own. Note that a particular destiny pattern can contain quite different "types," as these themes may be expressed across a broad spectrum of behaviors and professions.

9. Take the cards in your constellation and spread them on the floor or table. Move them around in various ways until you find a pattern that seems to make sense to you. Ask yourself the following questions:

   + How are the cards similar and how are they different?

   + How do the Minor Arcana express the qualities of the Major Arcana of the same constellation?

   + How do these Minor Arcana express beneficial and inspiring characteristics, and how do they express limiting and problematic ones?

   + What do the corresponding Major Arcana recommend you do about the challenges presented in the Minor Arcana?

- What kinds of situations, as described by the Minor Arcana, will teach you to actualize the potentials inherent in the Major Arcana?

- In what ways are the Minors the tests and resources of the Majors?

10. If you teach tarot, use the Lifetime and Year Cards as an especially relevant way to introduce the Major Arcana to your students. In larger classes, have students break into small groups based on their birthday constellation and discuss how the cards seem relevant to each person. Then have each constellation group share their discoveries with the whole class.

Who Are You
In the Tarot?

Your association with one of the constellations based on your birth date describes you in terms of the cultural beliefs and mores of the Western world that uses this calendrical system of solar cycles. The characteristics described are general tendencies. Everybody finds their own unique way to express the possibilities that fate deals them. Use these sketches of the territory only as a starting point for your own contemplation and insight.

The Constellation of the Magician

CHAPTER 5

The Constellation of the Magician
19–10–1

The Sun (19)
The Wheel of Fortune (10)
The Magician (1)

Ace and 10 of Wands	Ace and 10 of Cups
Ace and 10 of Swords	Ace and 10 of Pentacles

The Principle of Will and Focused Consciousness

The Magician

Astrological Correspondence:	Mercury
Card Functions within the Constellation:	Unity of Self; The Individual

Wheel of Fortune

Astrological Correspondence:	Jupiter
Card Functions within the Constellation:	Unity in Diversity; The Individual in Society

Sun

Astrological Correspondence:	Sun
Card Functions within the Constellation:	Unity in Spirit; All as One

Soul Archetype: Consciousness; Outer Sense of Self; Persona

Keywords: Communication. Self Consciousness. Individualization. Self-Expression. Initiative. At-one-ment. Originality.

If you are a 10-1, read the following sections in this chapter:

The Magician (1) as Soul Card
The Wheel of Fortune (10) as Personality or Teacher Card
The Sun (19) as Hidden Factor
Famous 10-1s
The Minor Arcana Aces and 10s

If you are a 19-10-1, read:

The Magician (1) as Soul Card
The Wheel of Fortune (10) as Personality or Teacher Card
The Sun (19) as Personality Card
Famous 19-10-1s
The Minor Arcana Aces and 10s

The Magician (1) as Soul Card

(This applies whether you are a 19-10-1 or a 10-1.)

Unity of Self, the Individual

The Magician represents focused consciousness and will. As a card relating to Mercury, it indicates that you are a communicator and a skilled craftsperson, able to direct others and make things happen.

The symbols of the four suits on the table indicate your ability to work with all four elements as your tools.

As a Magician, you work creatively using your hands as well as your mind. You are capable of great mental focus and are self-initiating in your activities. You are good at influencing others and controlling your environment. Logical analysis comes easily to you, and you use this ability to manipulate anything under the sun.

It may be hard for you to work for other people because you want to concentrate on your own ideas. You channel all your energies into your tasks. This helps you believe in and communicate your ideas, but your tendency toward egocentricity doesn't always leave room for others, unless they are willing to follow you. You are an individualist. You are not very patient and expect instant gratification.

To develop your highest abilities, you need to realize that you can be a channel for a higher consciousness. If you open up to Spirit and let the divine Will move through you, you may join the company of 19-10-1s who are outstanding healers, teachers, leaders, innovators, inventors, and communicators of all kinds.

You have an innovative mind and think quickly on your feet. Correspondingly, you are also easily sidetracked by new ideas; it may help to have a coworker who completes the task at hand. You tend to identify with your work and your creations, experiencing them as an integral part of yourself, and are thus sensitive to criticism of your projects.

You have the magical ability to transform and change yourself and to transform mundane, ordinary events into magical ones. You understand yourself as the consciousness that gives meaning to synchronicities, as the actor without whom no action can take place.

At your worst, you can become a con man, or fast-talking trickster with the ability to convince others that they can get something for nothing. You play games and create illusions to achieve your personal ends. You are then something different to every person you come in contact with, appearing just as that person wants to believe you are. With an affinity for fascination and charm, you are at your best with an audience who appreciates your entertaining qualities.

Magicians are also liable to have what is called the Peter Pan complex—not wanting to grow up and accept adult responsibilities. Although you easily retain a sense of fun and play, an urge toward self-gratification is characteristic. You mean what you say at the moment but don't want to be held to anything later. If you are a woman and repress this happy-go-lucky side of yourself, you may project it onto your men, whose refusal to grow up reflects your own hidden desires.

The Magician acts only as a Soul Card, and therefore you will never experience it as a Personality, Hidden Factor, or Year Card. The number 1 has not appeared by itself since January 1, 998 CE and won't reappear until December 31, 9957 CE, when dates will again begin to add up to 10,000 (if our calendar should last that long).

Wheel of Fortune (10)
as Personality or Teacher Card

(This applies as a Personality Card if you are a 10-1, and a Teacher Card if you are a 19-10-1. It has not been possible to have the Wheel of Fortune as a Hidden Factor Card since 998 CE.)

Unity in Diversity, the Individual in Society

The Wheel of Fortune represents change, movement, and expansion of ideas. It is a card of luck, both good and ill. As the wheel turns, new opportunities appear and old projects reach a new turn of the spiral. The wheel bordered by the four figures in the corners stands for a sacred circle protected by the superhuman spirits of the four directions and elements.

Jupiter is most often associated with this card and thus expands the thinking of the Magician to a new level, adding a philosophical perspective. You have a sense of choice that comes from being able to see the sum of the whole—an overview. Your beliefs and hopes either sustain you or plunge you into despair (although probably not for long). Your ideas are favored to reach the public through publishing or other forms of media and communication, as indicated by the books held by the corner figures (in our contemporary culture, they might hold video cameras or computers), and connecting this card back to the mental qualities of the Magician.

The Wheel of Fortune brings the potential for rewards from the creative projects that the Magician initiates. If you have a Wheel Personality, you learn through change. You gamble and take risks for the challenges they present you. You experience the effects of your work in the world and often see them come back to you at a later time, transformed and implemented in ways you may not have imagined. Thus, you may have to face the results of the occasional thoughtlessness of your Magician soul. It is important to you to feel that you control your own destiny.

On the problematic side, you can easily drift along without exerting yourself, being lucky and quick-witted enough to keep on your feet and moving. Sometimes ambition is negated as new and interesting situations arise with intriguing avenues to explore. It seems that if you just wait long enough, everything you need will come to you. You then lack persistence and can be impatient with details, tending to leave many projects by the wayside. This drifting and dilettante attitude could keep you from achieving your highest potential.

Above all, though, the Wheel of Fortune shows flexibility and the ability to grasp opportunities when they happen. You are easygoing, magnanimous, and forgiving. You ride the low points with as much ease as you ride the crests, knowing that such extremes are temporary and you will endure.

The sphinx stands guard at the gateway to further development, asking if you are willing to be spun on the wheel of fate, thus to arise again with greater understanding.

The Sun (19) as Hidden Factor

(This applies if you are a 10-1.)

The Sun, in a 10-1 Personality-Soul Pattern, ironically is your Shadow Card. However, your particular shadow is what Jungians call a "bright shadow." This means you probably have some difficulty acknowledging your good qualities and accomplishments. Look around you: Is there someone you wish you could be like? You may not sufficiently value your own worth, feeling "outshone" by others.

Alternatively, you overcompensate, thinking that you are so unique that no one else is similar to or can understand you. Wanting to have your individuality acknowledged, you long to be the center of someone's universe, which is difficult since you tend to keep your own light hidden. Part of your task is identifying a central goal or focus that lights up your life and gives it meaning. Until then, you might find yourself endlessly circling, trying out too many things while you look for a purpose. Focus will come when you realize your purpose is simple—whatever truly matters to you.

In your youth, you might find it difficult to be open with others. You are essentially a loner and feel more comfortable working by yourself on your own projects. You don't let others get too close, finding it hard to put your trust in someone else, since with the instability of life they could be here today and gone tomorrow. Later, with the Sun as your Teacher Card, you will slowly open yourself to discover the joys of friendship. One of your greatest lessons is to learn trust—to trust yourself to do well, and to trust others with your deepest feelings. When you lack trust, you experience doubt in your projects, yourself, and the value of your friendships. With the shape-changing qualities of the Magician as your Soul Card, your identity is elusive, changing to meet every new circumstance. The Sun challenges you to recognize yourself as the creator of your own reality.

Famous 10-1s

Philosopher René Descartes based his "proof" of God on the fact that we doubt, and if we doubt, we think, and therefore must be fashioned after a thinking being: "I think, therefore I am." But, to Descartes, mind and matter were totally separate substances—one above (Spirit), the other below (the physical world).

> René Descartes (philosopher) 3/31/1596
> Tiger Woods (golfer) 12/30/1975
> Kaká (Brazilian footballer) 4/22/1982
> LeBron James (basketball player) 12/30/1984
> Lady Gaga (musician) 3/28/1986
> Miley Cyrus (actor, musician) 11/23/1992

The Sun (19) as Personality Card

(*This applies if you are a 19-10-1.*)

Unity in Spirit, All as One

The Sun represents wholeness, achievement, and the revelation that comes when the full light of the sun shines and there is nothing to hide. Walt Whitman, a 19-10-1, wrote: "Give me the splendid silent sun, with all his beams full-dazzling!" With a Sun personality, you are basically optimistic and cheerful. Like the sunflowers, you are always looking for the light side of things. The wall in the card indicates awareness of your limitations. You are learning to acknowledge your achievements, and if you have been successful on the inner path of the Wheel, then you realize you can fully reveal yourself and your motivations to others.

Like a child, you take innocent delight in the small things in life and have found that you can ride your instincts, since without hidden motivations they will lead you true. You radiate your belief that others can also accomplish their dreams, and therefore you are an inspiration to them. Your trust brings out their best.

Most tarot decks picture two children dancing under the light of the sun. This emphasizes that you love to share your experience with others. Thus this is the card of cocreativity. You need someone to share your ideas and to work and play with. As the sun is always paired in myth and story with the moon, so too you feel the need to pair, to have a complement. With the Magician as your soul essence, you identify so strongly with your work that it is hard to be in a relationship with someone who is not also interested in what you do. It's a "love me, love my work" kind of situation. You cannot separate yourself from your projects and ideas, so it helps to have a partner who is just as involved and interested as you, or at least who is willing to listen. Because you are a leader and idea person, your "other half" should be a supporter and finalizer. You like to be in the limelight. You'll have a great partnership if your partner takes on the sustaining tasks; otherwise there could be too much competition.

If you have a job in which you cannot be creative or cannot work independently, you will never consider it your "calling," but just a job. You will therefore need another outlet through which you can "shine."

Famous 19-10-1s

As you can see from the list, 19-10-1s are leaders and inventors and many stand out as individualists. They initiate new movements and have many "firsts" to their credit. More than any other group, they stand out as figureheads for their followers and spokespeople for the causes or movements with which they become identified.

> George Washington (U.S. president) 2/22/1732
> Napoleon Bonaparte (French emperor) 8/15/1769
> Karl Marx (social philosopher) 5/5/1818
> Walt Whitman (poet) 5/31/1819
> Herman Melville (writer) 8/1/1819
> Susan B. Anthony (reformer, feminist) 2/15/1820
> Leo Tolstoy (writer) 9/9/1828
> Nikola Tesla (inventor, electrical engineer) 7/10/1856
> Maria Montessori (educator) 8/31/1870
> Carl Jung (psychiatrist) 7/26/1876
> George Gurdjieff (metaphysician) 1/13/1877
> Ernest Hemingway (writer) 7/21/1899

Walt Disney (animator, filmmaker) 12/5/1901
Werner Heisenberg (physicist) 12/5/1901
Simone De Beauvoir (existentialist writer) 1/9/1908
L. Ron Hubbard (writer; founder, Scientology) 3/13/1911
Billy Graham (evangelist) 11/7/1918
Martin L. King Jr. (clergyman, activist) 1/15/1929
Rupert Murdoch (media magnate) 3/11/1931
Salman Rushdie (writer) 6/19/1947
O. J. Simpson (football player) 7/9/1947
Bruce Springsteen (musician) 9/23/1949
Michael Moore (filmmaker, political commentator) 4/23/1954
Steve Jobs (founder, Apple) 2/24/1955
Yo-Yo Ma (cellist, composer) 10/7/1955
Tom Cruise (actor) 7/3/1962
Jimmy Wales (founder, Wikipedia) 8/7/1966

The Minor Arcana Aces

The Aces (or 1s) indicate the levels of consciousness at which you operate. They are also your four basic skills and the four areas into which you can focus your energies. In order to truly focus your consciousness and energy, you must commit yourself to an endeavor. The aces represent that beginning point, the seed ideas, the recognition of opportunity offered you by the hand of Spirit pictured on each card. They also represent a progression that is necessary for any new project to get off the ground. They mark the beginning of focus and concentration of energy. At any point, if one of the ace energies is weak, the project may fail and have to begin anew.

Ace of Wands: The Root of Fire

The Ace of Wands represents inspired consciousness, the point at which an idea catches fire. With this ace, you grasp an opportunity firmly. Like a lighted brand or brilliant idea, it blazes forth with energy and the light of enthusiasm. You warm to the task at hand. You have the spirit to begin and want your ideas to grow and prosper. This ace gives you the first impulse and the passionate will to begin.

Ace of Cups: The Root of Water

The Ace of Cups represents love consciousness. With it, you open yourself to your feelings and acknowledge your resistances. You must be receptive to all the hopes and doubts that arise when you pursue any goal. Do you feel an inner connectedness with this project and a willingness to nurture it along? If not, it will lack value and be discarded once your initial enthusiasm wears off. The abundance pouring over the edge of the cup represents your ardor for your idea, which gives it the sustenance it needs to grow. With this ace, your emotional acceptance is available for any project to develop and flourish.

Ace of Swords: The Root of Air

The Ace of Swords represents reasoning and focused consciousness. With it, you analyze what needs to be done, using logic and discrimination to take the necessary steps. You judge the pros and cons of various methods. You research and synthesize the information needed. The sword symbolizes cutting away unnecessary details, keeping you focused on the point. With this ace, you first dare to develop the idea systematically.

Ace of Pentacles: The Root of Earth

The Ace of Pentacles represents crystallizing consciousness. It provides you with the stability and skills to get results. You stubbornly keep at the process because you want to see the final form and experience the fruits of your labor. The hand holds the product of your efforts, which becomes the seed of a new project. With this ace, you silently visualize your hoped-for results and decide how to use them in a new way.

The Minor Arcana 10s

The 10s are the end of any cycle and the beginning of the next cycle. They remind us that all 1s (aces) are really the result of a previous process. It is in contemplating the 10s that we get the image of the Ouroboros—the snake with its tail in its mouth—and realize that life is a continuous process. So, like the Wheel of Fortune, 10s mark a transition and bring change. Usually the change is helped or hindered by the kind of conditions shown on each of the suit cards. The 10s represent the result of all we have completed through the 9s. They also represent the logical result of following through with the energies of each suit.

For those people in the constellation of the Magician, 10s are gifts or challenges to your communication and individuation process.

10 of Wands (December 13–21, 20°–30° Sagittarius, Mutable Fire)

The 10 of Wands shows what happens when you start too many new projects. It shows that creativity is stifled when you take on too much. Dynamic change will seem impossible if you are burdened by a great a load or too many responsibilities. You don't have time for yourself if you take on everyone's cares and projects. Your vision can be blocked by immediate concerns and day-to-day drudgery.

On the other hand, the 10 of Wands shows the importance of developing a sense of responsibility. When you fulfill your obligations and agreements, you develop the maturity essential to all social relationships; you find faith in yourself and in your ability to accomplish your goals.

10 of Cups (March 11–20, 20°–30° Pisces, Mutable Water)

The 10 of Cups indicates that you have the gift of bringing light and good cheer to those around you. Your family and relations are important to you, and without them you don't feel whole. You need other people with whom to communicate your inspirations and ideas, and their reactions matter to you. Even though individuality is your main characteristic, you need a highly social environment in which to express it. This is what prosperity means to you.

As a challenge, the 10 of Cups can indicate pie-in-the-sky fantasies and unrealistic dreams. The rainbow represents the promise, but the actuality has to be worked for. Still, your dreams of social harmony and global coexistence, or personal hopes for a happy family, must first be clearly envisioned before they can be realized.

10 of Swords (June 11–20, 20°–30° Gemini, Mutable Air)

The 10 of Swords indicates that you feel most blocked when you think your friends are against you or you can't get a project off the ground. The image is that of being stabbed in the back. This can be deadly to your sense of self-worth.

One of your greatest challenges is to know when to give up—when to turn away from ungrateful friends or abandon a futile endeavor. It is like a nightmare in which "something" is chasing you but you can't run; as if with a severed spinal cord, you are paralyzed and unable to move. You may need to quit trying, to stop fighting a losing battle. Once you surrender, you'll find that a change occurs; there's a release and you can run, or you discover that the monster isn't so bad after all. It's the "down so low the only way is up" card. The black clouds are lifting and a new day is beginning. As a gift, the 10 of Swords indicates that you examine things from every angle and are very thorough in trying to pin down all aspects of a situation. You stretch yourself in your search for knowledge and, with diligence, you will develop wisdom.

10 of Pentacles (September 12–22, 20°–30° Virgo, Mutable Earth)

The 10 of Pentacles indicates that you can use the wealth of your resources and talents to build lasting structures in the world. You are challenged to make this a better place to live and to leave something solid and tangible behind you. You are also challenged to support with your gifts those traditions that are meaningful to you. Like the 10 of Cups, this card indicates that you gain valuable support from your friends, relations, and heritage. Most people with the Wheel of Fortune as one of their Lifetime Cards are never penniless, as this picture affirms.

The magical signs on the robe of the old man, the wand leaning against the arch, and the Qabalistic Tree of Life placement of the 10 pentacles are indicators that this is, in reality, a card of magic. The old man is the Magician, now an ancient wizard after having gone through the experiences of life. Although you leave to those who come after you what knowledge you can, in your wisdom you realize that each new child must repeat the journey.

The Constellation of the High Priestess

CHAPTER 6

The Constellation of the High Priestess
20–11–2

Judgment (20)
Justice (11)
The High Priestess (2)

| 2 of Wands | 2 of Cups |
| 2 of Swords | 2 of Pentacles |

The Principle of Balanced Judgment through Intuitive Awareness

The High Priestess	
Astrological Correspondence:	Moon
Card Functions within the Constellation:	Personal Knowledge; Inner Truth
Justice/Adjustment	
Astrological Correspondence:	Libra
Card Functions within the Constellation:	Social Wisdom; Social/Public Truth
Judgment/Aeon	
Astrological Correspondence:	Pluto
Card Functions within the Constellation:	Cosmic Understanding; Spiritual Truth

Soul Archetype: Unconscious; Inner, All-Knowing Self; Psyche

Keywords: Intuition. Self-Sufficiency. Self-Trust. Independence. Duality. Self and Other. Choice. Analysis. Struggle. Division. Reflection. Clairvoyance. Counterpoise or Contraposition. Equilibrium. Adjustment.

If you are a Single 2 (2-2), read:

> The High Priestess (2) as Personality or Soul Card
> Famous Single 2s
> Justice (11) as Hidden Factor
> Judgment (20) as Hidden Factor
> The Minor Arcana 2s

If you are an 11-2, read:

> The High Priestess (2) as Personality or Soul Card
> Justice (11) as Personality Card
> Judgment (20) as Hidden Factor
> Famous 11-2s
> The Minor Arcana 2s

If you are a 20-2, read:

> The High Priestess (2) as Personality or Soul Card
> Judgment (20) as Personality Card
> Justice (11) as Hidden Factor
> Famous 20-2s
> The Minor Arcana 2s

If you see 11 as Strength, read:

> Strength as the Number 11

The High Priestess (2) as Personality or Soul Card

(*This applies if you are a Single 2, 11-2, or 20-11-2.*)

Personal Knowledge, Inner Truth

The High Priestess represents the wisdom, independence, and self-sufficiency of the inner mind, or psyche. As a card astrologically relating to the Moon, she represents its waxing and waning phases and the ebb and flow of the tides. She mirrors our present circumstances as reflections of previous events and memories, coded in symbols and projected to us (as on the veil behind her) through our dreams and feelings. Although she is also referred to as the Virgin Priestess, we must go back to the original significance of the word *virgin* to find that it means "whole unto herself" or "not belonging to any man." She was a priestess dedicated to the Goddess, keeper of the knowledge of the mysteries of birth and death, of our past and future lives, and of our purpose in this lifetime. M. Esther Harding, in *Woman's Mysteries*, virtually describes the High Priestess in this passage:

> The woman who is virgin, one-in-herself, does what she does—not because of any desire to please, not to be liked, or to be approved, even by herself; not because of any desire to gain power over another ... but because what she does is true.[13]

As the 2nd card of the tarot Trumps, following the concept of the unity of Self, the High Priestess represents your realization of "the other," of duality. She is like the infant who begins to realize that everything is not a part of itself, that it is separate from its mother. And so, as the interplay of the palms and the pomegranates (significators of sexuality and fertility) indicates, this card also represents the apparent duality of Self and other, male and female, dark and light, etc.

As a High Priestess, you make choices intuitively and change them often. This is not because you are fickle, but because you recognize that circumstances are always changing, that energy ebbs and flows. You move with an inner rhythm that you have come to rely on and that cannot be hurried. Your ability to be calm is soothing to others, who often find themselves drawn to your serene demeanor. Other people talk freely to you about themselves and their worries because you are a good listener; you seem to know their innermost thoughts. In your nonjudgmental acceptance, they see their ideas and feelings mirrored back to them.

You are empathic and psychic, aware of the subtle undercurrents in a situation. You often experience something in your body before you know it in your mind. Being receptive to these impressions can create rapid mood changes. Often you experience other people's feelings as well as your own. The Justice card can help you separate your energies from those of others.

Being near water is essential to your mental and physical well-being. If nothing else, a warm bath with salt and soda in it will help clear your energy field. Your power is of water and the Moon: cool, dark, and fluid. It needs to be contained.

Feminine qualities are highly developed, and women friends, mentors, and teachers are very important to High Priestesses. Since men often feel the need to repress this side of themselves, they may project their inner High Priestess qualities onto someone else. Therefore men with a High Priestess Soul Card have highly developed animas—inner images of the feminine—that they are always looking for in the outer world. The problem is that no real woman can live up to the perfection of this ideal image.

You are independent and self-sufficient. Solitude is important to you as an opportunity to reconnect with your spiritual source. You don't often reveal your true feelings and therefore attract others who find you mysterious and wise. Your feelings and emotions motivate you. Your mind compares and associates current situations with remembered ones from the past; your responses are strongly emotional.

If you have repressed your intuitive and psychic experiences, you may be skeptical of metaphysical beliefs—so much so that Shakespeare's line "The Lady doth protest too much" comes to mind. You will then find it hard to trust your intuitive feelings and attempt to justify everything you do with "reason."

Your dreams can be very important to you—write them down. They are an excellent means for accessing your intuition and getting advice from your inner Self. By looking into your deep unconscious, you can come to know yourself.

The problematic side of the High Priestess comes from her essentially paradoxical nature. You can be pleasantly intriguing, or become involved in intrigue and lies. You can be flexible or fickle. You can be distrustful of logic, affecting disdain for it, or just the opposite, distrustful of intuition, creating a facade of logic and sophistry. You can pride yourself on your emotional sensitivity, or keep coolly distant from anything that affects your inner peace.

If you are a Single 2, with the High Priestess as both your Personality and Soul Cards, then both Justice and Judgment are your Hidden Factor Cards; read the descriptions of these cards next.

Famous Single 2s

There is only a short window of time when Single 2s could have been born.

Mariah Carey (singer, songwriter) 3/27/1970

Justice (11) as Personality Card

(*This applies if you are an 11-2.*)

Social Wisdom, Social/Public Truth

Justice represents our social and cultural laws, which we create to maintain order and to compensate those who have been injured. The figure represents such goddesses of truth as Ma'at in Egypt and Themis and Athena in Greece, who seek to maintain the balance of nature and rhythm of life. Outer laws must accord with our inner nature in order to be just.

This card indicates that you believe it important to adjust yourself to others. You take responsibility for the way your judgments and decisions affect both yourself and others. You are aware that every action necessitates a reaction for which you must be responsible, so you look ahead to see the potential results of your impulses and actions. Or you look back to see what you did to warrant a specific result.

As a Personality Card, Justice refers to the need to be true to yourself, for neither justice nor mercy are possible without self-honesty. You learn through your mistakes by carefully evaluating the people, situations, and beliefs you trust. When these no longer have validity, nor bring appropriate results, you are able to sever your connections and free yourself from outmoded dependencies. With your sword, you sacrifice the illusions, pretensions, and dreams that are in error. But you will strongly defend those ideas that represent to you the basic truths of existence. At the extreme, as Sallie Nichols points out in *Jung and Tarot*, you can get so caught up in wanting everything to be fair that you spend all your time "in court," or berating the system rather than working on yourself.

Your logical way of looking at the world means you pay close attention to the law of cause and effect and prefer to rely on deductive reasoning. Yet with the High Priestess as a Soul Card (note the two pillars appearing in both High Priestess and Justice), you must learn to use both logic and intuition to balance your judgments (symbolized by the pillars being blended to gray). The Justice card tells you to apply the wisdom of the High Priestess when acting in the world.

You expect to pay for your transgressions, as well as benefit from your good deeds. When making decisions, you weigh all the pros and cons carefully, as in a set of scales, to be sure that balance is achieved. You seek harmony and stability by observing the rules. Be mindful that it is only through an awareness of the pain of chaos that equilibrium can be appreciated.

You make the most of memories, weighing and balancing them to achieve inner harmony. For this reason, many famous 11-2s are connected to children. They explore the relationship of childhood experiences to psychological development, or use the sword as pen to write down and seek the meaning in the memories and feelings of youth.

As an 11-2, you strive to maintain an even keel when buffeted by emotional tensions and unexpressed feelings. You might find writing to be a good outlet for those feelings and for your concerns about justice.

Judgment (20) as Hidden Factor

(*This applies if you are Single 2 or an 11-2.*)

Judgment as your Hidden Factor indicates that change and transformation are essential but difficult. You feel the weight of order and authority judging you. You can be very critical of others and of yourself. You'd like to be in control, yet you see others as more powerful than you, and perhaps you feel only able to react and not initiate action. You may seek to obtain power in a situation by passive resistance.

Your heightened sensitivity to major global and Earth changes can become personally uncomfortable and, in extremes, terrifying, resulting in a feeling that natural justice is aiming to reassert balance through destruction.

You can learn from this teacher that *you* are the initiator of your own change and development; you are responsible for yourself. Furthermore, you have a responsibility to all humanity and to the planet. Trying to hold on passively only makes changes more difficult. Changes you originally felt to be destructive you can eventually see as liberating. You work to assuage fears and right injustices through the exposure of the truths that were formerly hidden or unacknowledged, especially those fears and injustices that you yourself once experienced.

In learning to take responsibility for transforming your life, the acceptance of your personal power opens new vistas of possibility. You eventually awaken to the social and/or spiritual significance behind individual and often isolated incidents.

Famous 11-2s

In this small group of 11-2s, you'll find several people who have physically defended basic ideas of truth and freedom: Davy Crockett, Lord Byron, and Benjamin Spock. Crockett said in his autobiography, "I leave this rule for others when I'm dead: Be always sure you're right—then go ahead." Byron is known for the line "Truth is always strange—stranger than fiction" (from *Don Juan*, canto XIV). Several of these people studied early child development and wrote books for and about children.

> J.M.W. Turner (artist) 4/23/1775
> Davy Crockett (frontiersman) 8/17/1786
> Lord Byron (poet, adventurer) 1/22/1788
> Hans Christian Andersen (writer) 4/2/1805
> Beatrix Potter (children's writer, illustrator) 7/28/1866
> Harry Houdini (magician, escape artist) 3/24/1874
> A. A. Milne (children's writer) 1/18/1882
> Marc Chagall (modernist artist) 7/7/1887
> Benjamin Spock (pediatrician, peace activist) 5/2/1903
> Stephanie Meyer (writer) 12/24/1973
> Prince William (Duke of Cambridge) 6/21/1982

Judgment (20) as Personality Card

(*This applies if you are a 20-2.*)

Cosmic Understanding, Spiritual Truth

Judgment represents resurrection or "awakening" in all the various forms of this card. In the Waite-Smith and most other decks, Judgment shows the resurrection of the dead from their coffins while an apocalyptic angel sounds the trumpet of life. In Crowley's Thoth deck, the corresponding Aeon card shows Isis (called "Giver of Life") with Osiris ("God of Death"), reminding us how Isis found Osiris spread across the waters of the Nile and brought him back to life. To complete the constellation's symbolism, the High Priestess is clearly Isis, and Crowley's Justice card (called Adjustment) represents the Goddess Ma'at, who showed Isis the way to Osiris. This kind of mythic awareness of a constellation can add depth to your own life-story, helping you to see the greater picture and purpose in everyday events.

As a 20-2, you are aware that although the past has made you who you are, you can transcend those limitations. You will have many such awakenings in your life: jolts or "epiphanies" in which you suddenly recognize a purpose behind the events.

Judgment is the card of synchronicities—that is, events that seem like "coincidences" but may have strong personal significance. The meaning is always there, only most of the time we don't bother to look. With Judgment as your Personality Card, you will find that these synchronicities call attention to points of decision when your path branches in several directions.

Those who are 20-2s seek to transform and take control of things around them. You are similar to the Plutonian people described by Robert Hand in his book *Horoscope Symbols:* "They embody the forces of death and resurrection inherent in society . . . [taking] advantage of energies stirring within the culture." You are often involved directly in your generation's struggle for consciousness and identity. You see yourself embodying values that need to be brought into the world and shared.

Those who are 20-2s can be healers, therapists, and those who teach techniques of self-transformation, or gurus and religious leaders who stress the roles of death and rebirth. You have an intuitive insight into the mass unconscious of your time, but especially of your generation.

This card represents the process of perfecting yourself and therefore the necessity of leaving behind gross or imperfect elements that can hold you back. Like the revolutionary writer 20-2 Thomas Paine, you believe in going all the way: "Moderation in principle is always a vice."

The lesson you must learn is to use your personal power and influence on others, not for personal ends but to assist them in their own transformations. Those who are 20-2s have the potential to communicate with all parts of themselves, as shown by the three figures usually pictured rising from the coffins. In Eric Berne's Transactional Analysis, for instance, they would represent the Parent, the Adult, and the Child; in Jungian terms, the Self, the Shadow, and the Ego. As a 20-2, you can reach others, as well as various parts of the Self, with your understanding and vision. Most often you keep your visions quietly to yourself, affecting others through the integrity of your actions. You are socially oriented and good at bringing people together. You can be a valued friend and loyal partner, while maintaining a strong sense of your own independence and self-worth.

With your strong Pluto-Moon relationship, you are highly psychic, but because our culture does not value psychic development, you may deny this aspect of yourself and determinedly focus on the rational qualities of Justice, which is your Hidden Factor. (By hidden, in this case, I mean connected with repressed aspects of the unconscious and possibly liable to eruptions of inappropriate behavior.) Males in our culture tend to have problems acknowledging their intuitive feelings. If this is you, your avowed rationality may be an illusion. Many 20-2s have heard an inner call, responding to an intuitive vision of what a harmonious world could be like.

Justice (11) as Hidden Factor

(This applies if you are a Single 2 or a 20-2.)

Justice most often appears as a Hidden Factor Card. It indicates that you must learn to accept reason and responsibility when called to do so. You have a highly developed sense of personal right and wrong and can be overcritical of both yourself and others. Your judgments can separate you from others and destroy friendships. Paradoxically, you are very sensitive to criticism, even when unintentional.

You consider all sides of an issue or conflict, weighing the pros and cons carefully before acting. You feel it is important to be logical, even if inappropriate to the situation. In your desire to be fair, you may rely on the "facts" alone, without acknowledging extenuating circumstances. Remember that most judgments are actually a matter of intuition. Reasons come afterward. Justice indicates that your actions depend on understanding the past as remembered by your inner High Priestess and using her intuitive knowledge in a practical way. Memories are your most instructive resources. Communication between your conscious and unconscious selves leads you to equilibrium.

Since your Hidden Factor Card is ultimately your teacher, you will find that by adjusting to circumstances and acknowledging the results, you can develop wisdom. By taking responsibility for your actions, you develop mercy, and by accepting that each person's values and needs are as valid as yours, you develop compassion. You must face the imbalances in your life and evaluate which side is true to your own nature. Only you can judge which memories to foster and which to deny, which actions to honor and which to castigate, which beliefs to uphold and which to cast down. Thus you can control the balance.

Strength as the Number 11

If you see the Strength card as embodying the number 11, then the focus of this constellation is on how the feminine responds both inwardly and outwardly to the call to resurrection or a new life of the Spirit. It indicates that good judgment is having the strength to act outwardly on your inner wisdom. It takes faith (the High Priestess) to hold fast to our natural instincts when challenged by Judgment. Strength is the power and resolve that is needed when the High Priestess answers a higher calling or responds to a time of great crisis and change. Strength represents the laws of Nature—"tooth and claw"—rather than the human law represented by Justice. This alternate view suggests that rather than intuition and reason being united, the focus is on body and soul uniting as is prophesied for the Last Judgment.

Famous 20-2s

You'll find people in this list who answered a call to devote themselves to establishing world harmony. There are many human rights workers like Thomas Paine, Elizabeth Cady Stanton, Rosa Parks, and Julian Bond. (Not included below are several famous psychics and two creators of round, feminist tarot decks.) You'll also find many imaginative romantics: Mozart, Poe, Jules Verne—people who were able to actualize their inner visions. Most surprising are the number of politicians who appear to have some kind of innate sensitivity to the group unconscious and have provided us with the images needed by the masses but not always with the substance.

Elizabeth I (Queen of England) 9/17/1533
Antonio Vivaldi (musician, composer) 3/4/1678
Thomas Paine (writer, human rights activist) 2/9/1737
Wolfgang Amadeus Mozart (musician, composer) 1/27/1756
Edgar Allen Poe (mystery writer) 1/19/1809

Elizabeth Cady Stanton (feminist) 11/12/1815
Jules Verne (science fiction writer) 2/8/1828
Ramakrishna (Hindu mystic) 2/18/1836
Claude Monet (artist) 11/14/1840
Nikolai Rimsky-Korsakov (musician, composer) 3/18/1844
Claude Debussy (musician, composer) 8/22/1862
Amelia Earhart (aviator) 7/24/1897
Karl Popper (philosopher, critical rationalist) 7/28/1902
Bob Hope (comedian) 5/29/1903
Ronald Reagan (U.S. president) 2/6/1911
Rosa Parks (civil rights activist) 2/4/1913
L. I. Brezhnev (Russian leader) 12/19/1906
Peter Hurkos (psychic) 5/21/1911
Edith Piaf (singer) 12/19/1915
Joe Louis (boxer) 5/13/1919
Jack Kerouac (writer) 3/12/1922
Norman Mailer (writer) 1/31/1923
Maria Callas (opera musician) 12/2/1923
Richard Burton (actor) 11/10/1925
Jackie Kennedy Onassis (U.S. first lady, society figure) 7/28/1929
Yuri Gagarin (Soviet cosmonaut) 3/9/1934
Jim Brown (athlete, actor) 2/17/1936
Julian Bond (civil rights activist, politician) 1/14/1940
Pelé (Brazilian footballer) 10/23/1940
Bobby Fischer (chess champion) 3/9/1943
Bill Clinton (U.S. president) 8/19/1946
Andrew Lloyd Webber (composer, musical theatre) 3/22/1948
Al Gore (politician, environmentalist) 3/31/1948
Prince Charles (Prince of Wales) 11/14/1948
Rush Limbaugh (radio host, political commentator) 1/12/1951
Tony Blair (U.K. prime minister) 5/6/1953
Barack Obama (U.S. president) 8/4/1961
Michael Jordan (basketball player) 2/17/1963
Michelle Obama (U.S. first lady) 1/17/1964
David Beckham (soccer player) 5/2/1975

The Minor Arcana 2s

The 2s represent your lessons and opportunities, your gifts and whatever blocks you from expressing the highest qualities of the High Priestess.

When dealing with any aspect of the constellation of the High Priestess, you are often faced with a decision. The Minor Arcana show how you might handle that choice-making process: blending them together (Cups), choosing one over the other (Wands), remaining indecisive (Swords), or choosing them both (Pentacles).

Angeles Arrien uses the 2s to represent types of intuition: Swords are telepathic, Cups are empathic, Wands are perceptual, and Pentacles are kinesthetic.

2 of Wands (March 21–30, 0°–10° Aries, Cardinal Fire)

The 2 of Wands indicates that when you are in charge, you are comfortable making decisions and will stand by them. Although you may not be able to give logical reasons for your decisions, you feel confident enough to act on them. You seldom turn to someone else for direction, preferring to use your own values for assessment, but also taking responsibility for the outcome.

You need equilibrium between mind and body, so you don't act until you need to. This self-discipline, combined with your intuition, can bring success to your enterprises. Boredom—lack of a new direction or stimulus—is your greatest problem here. Your faults include ignoring the assessments of others and believing that your decisions are right for everyone.

2 of Cups (June 21–July 12, 0°–10° Cancer, Cardinal Water)

The 2 of Cups indicates that you are a compassionate and caring person. You understand the healing powers of love and the importance of relating with others. The two entwined snakes and the strange red-winged lion head suggest a spiritual dimension to your passion and a passionate drive toward spiritual expression. Acceptance of your own inner masculine or feminine Self (the opposite of your physical gender) is one of your primary tasks.

This card shows that your conscious and subconscious dimensions can work together and that seeming oppositions can be reconciled. Your faults can include becoming overly sentimental and empathizing with others so strongly that you forget whose feelings are whose. Sometimes it is better to quell your urge to comfort and heal everyone with whom you come in contact.

2 of Swords (September 23–October 22, 0°–10° Libra, Cardinal Air)

The 2 of Swords indicates that in your desire to be a peacemaker, you can be reluctant to express an opinion or make a decision unless forced to. Wanting order and stability can lead you to blind conformity and rigidity. Although you seek to maintain calm through balanced rationality, it also makes you deny your intuitions. When you are uncertain of your objectives, you procrastinate. Conflicts between your own opinions and those of others can cause stalemates and indecision.

When you are unable to see your options, rationality (Swords) is of no help. Don't try to force things to happen prematurely. By listening to the swell of your emotions, you will know when the tide turns and that it is time to act.

2 of Pentacles (December 22–30, 0°–10° Capricorn, Cardinal Earth)

The 2 of Pentacles represents your ability to handle two or more situations at once but may make it difficult to treat each with due seriousness. Travel and change can regenerate you, but too much makes you feel restless and unstable. Being near water is very healing for all 2s, as is time out for recreation. Take time to remember your childhood and let yourself play. Being flexible and venturesome provides scope for your intuition.

You are adaptable and easygoing with friends and associates but in danger of being easily influenced by individuals or mass opinion. When you feel that life is pushing you around, and you don't know where you're going, look around for synchronicities; you may discover a deeper meaning to your experience and find new direction.

THE WORLD.

THE HANGED MAN.

THE EMPRESS.

The Constellation of the Empress

CHAPTER 7

The Constellation of the Empress
21–12–3

World (21)
The Hanged Man (12)
The Empress (3)

3 of Wands   3 of Cups
3 of Swords   3 of Pentacles

The Principle of Love and Creative Imagination

The Empress	
Astrological Correspondence:	Venus
Card Functions within the Constellation:	Personal Love; Giving Birth to Body
The Hanged Man	
Astrological Correspondence:	Neptune
Card Functions within the Constellation:	Unconditional Love, Giving Birth to Soul
The World	
Astrological Correspondence:	Saturn
Card Functions within the Constellation:	Universal Love, Giving Birth to Spirit

Soul Archetype: Feminine; Fertile, Creative Mother

Keywords: Creativity. Nurturance. Sacrifice. Surrender. Form. Relatedness. Fertility. Limitation. Imagination.

If you are a Single 3 (3-3), read:

> The Empress (3) as Personality or Soul Card
> Famous Single 3s
> The World (21) as Hidden Factor
> The Hanged Man (12) as Hidden Factor
> The Minor Arcana 3s

If you are a 12-3, read:

> The Empress (3) as Personality or Soul Card
> The Hanged Man (12) as Personality Card
> The World (21) as Hidden Factor
> Famous 12-3s
> The Minor Arcana 3

If you are a 21-3, read:

> The Empress (3) as Personality or Soul Card
> The World (21) as Personality Card
> The Hanged Man (12) as Hidden Factor
> Famous 21-3s
> The Minor Arcana 3s

The Empress (3) as Personality or Soul Card

(*This applies if you are a Single 3, 12-3, or 21-3.*)

Personal Love, Giving Birth to Body

The Empress is related to the goddesses Demeter and Ceres—bountiful, fertile, growth-producing. She represents the union of the first two cards in the Major Arcana, the Magician and the High Priestess. Their combination is the Empress, shown pregnant with a totally new being, that is, something more than the sum of the parts. As a card relating to Venus, she signifies love and beauty. She is the feminine energy that provides a nurturing environment for the growth and well-being of those around her. She is the archetypal Earth Mother and seeks to connect all opposites, to banish disharmony.

With the Empress as your Personality or Soul Card, your sense of aesthetics, harmony, and balance is innate. You recognize and enjoy beauty in all its forms. Thus you will be drawn to hobbies or jobs that let you express these talents. You can be fertile with creative ideas, yet you may lack the discipline necessary to give them practical form, or the aggression necessary to market them. Your power comes from love, and you rule through understanding the needs of others.

You thrive in comfortable surroundings, finding ugliness distasteful and, from your point of view, unnecessary. Food is a possible metaphor for the expression and fulfillment of your qualities—growing it in gardens, aesthetically preparing it, and nurturing others with it. But because you enjoy the delights of a well-prepared meal so much, watch your weight. If food is not your métier, notice what other arts you use to please and nurture yourself and others.

Mothering is another central issue. You may have close ties with your own mother; she was probably the more significant parent in the formation of your basic character. Whether you are a man or woman, you want to "mother" others. If this is not expressed through actual childbearing or child rearing, then you will project that instinct onto other people, projects, and interests in your life. Or you will be drawn to coaching or mentoring others and helping them bring their creative projects to life.

You have a deep regard for the relatedness of all things. You experience this as a feeling of allegiance with the Earth, with Spirit, your country, your group, your work, or with individuals. Although you can be very regal and commanding, you feel you can sway others best through love. Your primary task is to make connections. Through your creative imagination, you find new solutions that bring people and things together.

You have a strong sense of reality, functioning primarily through your physical senses. You like to touch and handle situations directly. You want to know where your food and clothes come from, for instance, to assure that they are healthful or well-made.

Negatively, you fear letting go of those you feel connected to. You can be smothering and even devouring in your care. Jealousy and vindictiveness are among your less pleasing traits, but these come from a need to preserve your home and loved ones, or from not wanting to entrust them to another. You feel devalued when you are not "needed."

If you are a Single 3 (that is, with the Empress as both your Personality and Soul Card), then both the Hanged Man and the World are your Hidden Factor Cards. Read descriptions of these cards next. They are found later in this chapter.

Famous Single 3s

Like the Single 2s, there was only a small window of opportunity for Single 3s to be born. I've only identified three.

Brooke Shields (model, actor) 5/31/1965
Christian Bale (actor) 1/30/1974
Rihanna (musician) 2/20/1988

The Hanged Man (12) as Personality Card

(*This applies if you are a 12-3.*)

Unconditional Love, Giving Birth to Soul

The Hanged Man has appeared, from the end of the 19th century until the late 20th century, most frequently as a Hidden Factor Card. More recently, people have been born with the Hanged Man as a Personality Card.

As a 12-3, you can devote yourself so completely to your work, art, or cause that you become oblivious to yourself. Hanged Man personalities can merge totally with their calling. When you sacrifice yourself with confident abandon to the requirements of your chosen path, you unify with its spirit. You give without thought of receiving. Others may feel you have lost your mind; you seem to have given up common sense, but you are only seeing something that escapes others, and with this vision you can accomplish wonders.

You might do things diametrically opposed to other people and thus find yourself in conflict with the world (as indicated by the World card being your Hidden Factor). Your actions may be misunderstood and misinterpreted. The Hanged Man corresponds to Neptune, sensitizing you to the wrongs of the world and the injustices done to humankind. However, you express your realization in ways that may seem extremist and disorganized.

You must learn to give up all expectations and sidestep the rules. Even during periods of enforced inactivity when nothing seems to be happening, try to understand that vital growth is taking place within. Accept your circumstances with humility and you will discover new possibilities. Your interludes of loneliness and helplessness allow you to value love and relationships.

Ironically, 12-3s find their inspiration in the depths of helplessness. Realization of your own powerlessness spurs you to deep reflection and eventual action. When you are truly bereft, you finally must turn to some greater power and allow it to work through you.

You experience time subjectively, depending on whether you are totally involved in what you do or just hanging around waiting for something to happen. The Hanged Man as the number 12 symbolizes both the clock (hours) and the year (months). You realize you are fated to obey not your own will, but the impersonal dictates of time.

This is the card of the mystic, the shaman, the dreamer, and 12-3s see things that are not of this world. You gather in the impressions of your imagination and surrender to your vision. You can act for others by uniquely expressing through your own life the inner needs and dilemmas of the masses. By describing what you see through writing, film, or paintings, or through some other creative medium, you give others a new perspective on their own experience.

Taken to the extreme, 12-3s can totally sacrifice themselves for their loved ones or a beloved cause. They may blind themselves to the imperfections of others, or feel incapable of withdrawing from a difficult situation. Sometimes this leads to imprisonment, or bondage to a person, lifestyle, or ideal. Thus, 12-3s need to be wary of whatever fascinates them.

The World (21) as Hidden Factor

(*This applies if you are a Single 3 or a 12-3.*)

The World as your Hidden Factor Card indicates that you fear restriction of any kind. Form and structure tend to limit you, and you deliberately try to escape from them. Time, as a kind of form, is an enemy holding you back; later in life, as the World becomes your Teacher Card, you learn that time can be used with grace and precision.

You fear your life being out of control. You want to "dance" freely but are somehow restricted from doing so, and thus freedom becomes a major issue. You feel incomplete in yourself, and a sense of wholeness eludes you in the physical world. It is only through transcendent mystical experience, or the immersion of yourself in your work, that you find a sense of wholeness.

The wreath encircling the dancer in the World card represents containment of energies to prevent their dissipation. With the World as your Hidden Factor, a lack of boundaries is dangerous: It leads to confusion, like that experienced by undisciplined mystics or psychics who cannot tell whether their images and emotions are their own or another's. Thus, 12-3s may have trouble with their identity, although struggling with this problem helps formulate a strong and unconventional sense of Self.

Famous 12-3s

The Hanged Man theme seems especially strong in this group—either through a life of sacrifice and suspension or through the imagery in their works. Dalí's surrealist paintings depict his dreams with bizarre images and wild techniques—one of his most famous, *The Persistence of Memory*, deals with time in the form of melting clocks. He was also fascinated by religious subjects, especially the crucifixion theme. Nat Turner was a deeply religious, natural preacher who believed himself divinely appointed to lead his fellow slaves to freedom. Alfred Hitchcock was known for his suspense movies (in which everyone is suspended, hanging on to their seats). Charles Dickens felt the sorrows and imprisonment of his fellow beings strongly and through his imagination let others experience them, too. The childless Emma Goldman was selflessly dedicated to her cause of anarchy and overturning the power structure yet was known to close friends as "Mommy." Eva Braun is a classic example of a tragic 12-3, a helpless dreamer and captive of cheap novels and trashy films. Hitler's chauffeur said "she spent most of her life waiting for Hitler." On the other hand, Frida Kahlo immortalized in paintings the lifelong pain she experienced from having been speared by an iron rail as a girl.

Jane Austen (writer) 12/16/1775
Nat Turner (slave leader) 10/2/1800
Charles Dickens (writer) 2/7/1812
Emma Goldman (anarchist) 6/27/1869

Colette (writer) 1/28/1873
Alice Bailey (metaphysician) 6/16/1880
Alfred Hitchcock (writer, film director) 8/13/1899
Salvador Dalí (artist) 5/11/1904
Frida Kahlo (artist) 7/6/1907
Eva Braun (Hitler's mistress) 2/6/1912
Daniel Radcliffe (actor) 7/23/1989
Dakota Fanning (actor) 2/23/1994

The World (21) as Personality Card

(*This applies to 21-3s.*)

Universal Love, Giving Birth to Spirit

The World card literally indicates your strong connections to the Earth. Nature thus gives you a profound love of beauty and sensitive aesthetic appreciation.

As a Personality Card, the World indicates that you must learn to work within structure. The card shows a woman suspended in air, a braided wreath forming a ring around her; I call this learning to dance on your limitations. As the card is associated with Saturn (known as the Great Liberator), the wreath can be seen as the boundary of the personality, which manifests as the structures within which we live. Many of those structures, such as genetic inheritance and our language and culture, we cannot change. Nevertheless, these frameworks do not limit our experience of freedom; they only channel it. In like manner, you find that your need to develop your potential self-expression, although circumscribed by your society, is not necessarily limited by it.

You learn to know the medium that you work with so well that it does not hamper your creativity. For instance, as a musician, you learn the notes, scales, and fingering of your instrument in order to create and improvise with complete freedom. The same with painting; you have to know the possibilities and limitations of your brush, colors, and surface before you are truly free to create with them.

If 21-3s wish to accomplish something, they need to establish personal discipline. Only in this way can you use your penchant for being drawn to many different areas of endeavor to become a well-rounded individual. Remember that discipline, combined with what 21-3 John Wayne called his "favorite four-letter words: *hard work*," gives you the basic tools with which to express your creative imagination and give it form.

The figures in the corners of the card represent the four fixed signs of the zodiac—Scorpio (eagle), Aquarius (angel), Taurus (bull), and Leo (lion)—and also symbolize the four directions, four winds, four seasons, etc. They represent your ability to locate yourself in space and time. You synthesize the holistic thinking of the intuitive with the four-square rationality of the scientific thinker. This synthesis can also be apparent in a career that combines two different aspects into a new expression.

Just as your Soul Card, the Empress, represents physical birth, so the World represents your ability to give birth to yourself and your ideas, in this world. The scarf flowing around the figure, which has been called both winding sheet and birthing sheet, conceals the dancer's hermaphroditic qualities, which are also indicated by the double-tipped wands and infinity signs on the wreath (like those of the Magician and Strength). Your ultimate creation, represented by this, the last trump, is your ability to integrate masculine and feminine characteristics within yourself, giving birth to the wholeness of being human.

Many 21-3s use holistic thinking that enables them to sense the larger picture. This is also why you may focus your "mothering instinct" on planetary or even cosmic issues. Because they focus on functioning within limitations, 21-3s stretch our concepts of what is humanly possible in all fields. Also, many 21-3s break through the previously accepted ideas of what is appropriate for their gender, such as Amelia Earhart and Indira Gandhi for women, and Bill Cosby, who embodied the role of man as nurturer.

Since 21 is the last number in the Major Arcana (the Fool is an unnumbered card), it is also a card of completion. In this case, completion implies freeing yourself from inhibitions and seeing things from that holistic perspective. Once you conceive what is possible and see it in all of its dimensions, the process of actualization becomes automatic.

The Hanged Man (12) as Hidden Factor

(*This applies if you are a Single 3 or a 21-3.*)

The Hanged Man represents self-sacrifice and submission of the Self to higher ideals. For many people with an Empress need to mother, this represents the desire to hold on to someone; for instance, it can represent a person who talks about their sacrifices in order to receive recognition of love. You need to ask yourself, How and why am I being a martyr? Lessons to learn include humility and letting go.

If not already focused on family and children, you may devote yourself to an equal or greater cause. However, this devotion can be overwhelming, turning a normal life upside down and becoming greater than any personal relationship.

The Hanged Man literally represents your "hang-ups," things you try to hang on to and whatever you are hung up on. You fear being alone and powerless. Yet it is often through bafflement and confusion that spiritual growth can take place. Mythologically, the figure on the card represents the Goddess's son/lover, who is sacrificed yearly after impregnating Her. It is also the scapegoat, which was historically an actual goat on which was symbolically placed all the blame for old feuds, angers, and anything that went wrong during the year. When it was killed, all blame died with it, so that the community was cleansed and renewed and made sacred again. Some 21-3s seem to take on the woes of the world, or act out the myths and dreams of the masses. When such a role becomes too great to handle, you may turn to drugs, drink, or overwork to escape the pressure, which ultimately only intensifies the problems. These Neptunian qualities of the Hanged Man may also emerge in flights of fancy and imagination or in becoming lost in illusion.

In its teacher aspect, the Hanged Man shows you how to make noble and unconditional sacrifices. You will be forced to release your preconceptions, especially in Hanged Man Years. It is also the pattern breaker, turning upside down any habits that limit you from realizing your highest Self.

Famous 21-3s

Among the 21-3s are several people whose lives express the fantasies and dreams of specific groups of people: Arthur Rimbaud represents, for poets, the extremes of passion reached in giving oneself over to the Muse. Queen

Victoria, Empress Dowager Cixi, Margaret Mead, Indira Gandhi, and Hillary Clinton are women who have shown great ability but paid a great price for it. We have Neil Simon, whose plays examine the details of love in contemporary relationships. Bill Cosby was not afraid to be identified with children and food and thus has become an image of the male ability to nurture. The work of many of these people shows their ability to be highly disciplined and creative in several fields.

Johann Goethe (poet, playwright) 8/28/1749
George Sand (writer) 7/1/1804
Queen Victoria (Queen of England) 5/24/1819
Cixi (Tz'u Hsi) (Dowager Empress of China) 11/29/1835
Arthur Rimbaud (poet) 10/20/1854
William B. Yeats (poet, occultist) 6/13/1865
F. Scott Fitzgerald (writer) 9/24/1896
Margaret Mead (anthropologist) 12/16/1901
John Wayne (actor) 5/26/1907
Henri Cartier-Bresson (photographer) 8/22/1908
Wernher von Braun (rocket scientist) 3/23/1912
Indira Gandhi (Indian prime minister) 11/19/1917
Farley Mowat (environmentalist) 5/12/1921
Judy Garland (singer, actor) 6/10/1922
Fidel Castro (Cuban leader) 8/13/1926
Neil Simon (playwright) 7/4/1927
Alejandro Jodorowsky (filmmaker, tarotist) 2/7/1929
Anne Frank (diarist) 6/12/1929
Ted Kennedy (U.S. politician) 2/22/1932
Bill Cosby (comedian) 7/12/1937
Mir-Hossein Mousavi (Iranian politician) 3/2/1942
Werner Herzog (film director) 9/5/1942
David Bowie (musician, actor) 1/8/1947
Hillary Rodham Clinton (U.S. politician) 10/26/1947
Starhawk (Miriam Simos) (witch, writer, political activist) 6/17/1951
Paul Krugman (economist) 2/28/1953
John Travolta (actor) 2/18/1954
Jackie Chan (martial artist, actor) 4/7/1954
Kate Middleton (Duchess of Cambridge) 1/9/1982

The Minor Arcana 3s

The 3s are the gifts, challenges, and opportunities of the principle of love and creative imagination. They represent four aspects of the creative imagination and are the tests of love.

3 of Wands (March 31–April 10, 10°–20° Aries, Cardinal Fire)

The 3 of Wands indicates that you have the ability to envision new possibilities, often long before they become actuality. Your mind is fertile and receptive to new things and foreign ideas. You travel further in your mind than some people ever do in physical reality, and therefore you have many unusual experiences—perhaps even astral traveling. You require a broad perspective and a sense of the entire terrain before you begin anything. You get excited by your vision and are able to communicate your enthusiasm to others. However, determining the specific steps necessary to actualize your creative ideas is difficult for you. Sometimes you remain too distant from where things are happening, with no conception of how to get down to work or put your ideas into action.

In love relationships, this is the test of time and distance. You may already have a partner yet still want the freedom to look around. It shows an ability to love more than one person at once. One of the dangers of the 3 of Wands is that by always wanting something out of reach, you may fail to appreciate fully what is close at hand. Even with your need for free expression of your feelings, you are still steadfast and dependable. Like a mother waiting up for her children or watching over their lives from a distance, your love and care for the people in your life is strong.

3 of Cups (July 2–11, 10°–20° Cancer, Cardinal Water)

The Three of Cups indicates the gifts of friendship and hospitality. You are social and love a party as an opportunity to get together with others and celebrate your mutual accomplishments. You work well with other people and can bring out the best in them, so that they reveal aspects of themselves that they normally couldn't share. Your natural grace, rhythm, and harmony make you enjoyable to be around. Like the Muses, you inspire others with your belief in them and their capabilities.

As a challenge, this card can represent dissipation and overindulgence. Like the fabled grasshopper who is interested only in frolicking, you may find bleak and difficult times when winter sets in. The lessons of discipline come hard but are essential. The Empress must learn to cultivate her garden, or many potentials will be sacrificed to the wild growth of weeds.

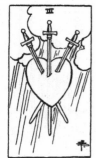

3 of Swords (October 3–12, 10°–20° Libra, Cardinal Air)

The 3 of Swords indicates the gift of sorrow. It is the ability to experience your emotions fully, even pain and heartbreak, so that you don't get blocked. It is the cleansing and purifying process of grief, through which you let your feelings wash over you and release any anguish that has built up. It says that even in the most loving of relationships there are times of conflict, hurt, and separation.

It also represents painful memories, usually of old hurts triggered by fears in current relationships. Jealousy, the ultimate block to love and creativity, is actually a mental (Swords) process in which you use your creativity to imagine the betrayals of a loved one, or to play back old scenes. You may either quietly bear your pain as a martyr or get hung up in your jealousy, whether based on reality or in the imagination. The card also shows how conflicting ideas may seem to cancel each other out, making you think all your heart's labor is for naught; your center is pierced. Often this stage of despair comes just before a major creative breakthrough.

Your opportunity with the 3 of Swords is to express your feelings of hurt or pain through some creative form. Also, as they've discovered with posttraumatic stress disorder (PTSD), talking (in the right environment) offers the best chance of recovery. This deals with old issues in a new way, releasing their constraining energy so that healing is possible.

3 of Pentacles (December 31–January 9, 10°–20° Capricorn, Cardinal Earth)

The 3 of Pentacles indicates love of your work. It is a card of the craftsperson, and its gift is in working together with others. It shows the harmony that can result when you use your best skills in cooperation with other capable partners. This card also shows your ability to create and work out practical plans for any project. You are able to advance step by step when you recognize and value the role of each person in the endeavor, and you ground your vision in the practical world through physical effort. You have the discipline to work long and hard when you understand the overall plan; otherwise you get caught up in the drudgery of meaningless exertion, or hung up in the details. Stand back periodically to take a look at the whole and form a mental picture of the completed project.

The major challenge in this card is in thinking you can do everything. This leads to workaholism, which is just as devastating to love and creativity as any other excess, and you'll end up sacrificing many things for the sake of one. Your opportunity with the 3 of Pentacles is to demonstrate and share your work with others, which satisfies your need for feedback and approval, and it allows the expression of your own nurturing qualities. Whatever your vocation, you go further with the active support and encouragement of those around you.

DEATH.

THE EMPEROR.

THE FOOL.

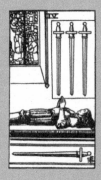

The Constellation of the Emperor

CHAPTER 8

The Constellation of the Emperor
22–13–4

The Fool (22 = 0)
Death (13)
The Emperor (4)

4 of Wands	4 of Cups
4 of Swords	4 of Pentacles

The Principle of Life Force and Realization of Power

The Emperor	
Astrological Correspondence:	Aries
Card Functions within the Constellation:	Realization of Paternal and Worldly Power, Physical Force, and Generation
Death	
Astrological Correspondence:	Scorpio
Card Functions within the Constellation:	Realization of Life Power, Vital Force, and Release
The Fool	
Astrological Correspondence:	Uranus
Card Functions within the Constellation:	Realization of Eternal Power, Spiritual Force, and Regeneration

Soul Archetype: Masculine; Ordered, Structured Father

Keywords: Completion and Transition. Establishing and Building. Releasing. Mortality and Immortality. Stability and Instability. Rites of Passage.

If you are a Single 4 (4-4), read:

The Emperor (4) as Personality or Soul Card
Famous Single 4s
The Fool (22) as Hidden Factor
Death (13) as Hidden Factor
The Minor Arcana 4s

If you are a 13-4, read:

The Emperor (4) as Personality or Soul Card
Death (13) as Personality Card
The Fool (22) as Hidden Factor
Famous 13-4s
The Minor Arcana 4s

If you are a 22-4, read:

The Emperor (4) as Personality or Soul Card
The Fool (22) as Personality Card
Death (13) as Hidden Factor
Famous 22-4s
The Minor Arcana 4s

The Emperor (4) as Personality or Soul Card

(*This applies if you are a Single 4, 13-4, or 22-4.*)

Realization of Paternal and Worldly Power, Physical Force, Generation

The Emperor represents power that comes with establishing, building, and doing. As a card relating to Aries, you are at the forefront of new projects and activities, but as a 4, you seek to establish a structure and order for them. Relying on reason and "using your head," you are primarily fact oriented. You also take pride in "fathering" things—in inventing, initiating, and promoting them. You want to immortalize yourself through your creations. You are assertive, positive in outlook, forceful in your beliefs, and dynamic about getting things done.

As an Emperor, you like the security that can be found in rules of order and underlying structures. Once order reigns, you begin to find yourself bored and confined. It is the act of discovering principles, defining laws, and mapping domains that interests you. You seek to understand and comprehend the forms in Nature. By naming things, you feel you gain the power to use them constructively.

Because you strive to master your situation, it is difficult for you to work under others. Most Emperors eventually find themselves either in business for themselves, or if they work for others, they need to be in charge or in positions of authority. Since you understand the purpose of rules and corporate gamesmanship, you can move quickly up the ladder of success if you apply yourself.

If you are a Single 4, you feel comfortable within your boundaries. You need security and stability in your life and want to act with power and authority. If your social situation makes you relatively powerless, you might tend to project your images of power onto the authority figures in your life, thus giving parents, political leaders, employers, or cultural idols more importance than warranted. You are most fulfilled by being a leader, even if over a small and personal domain. You need to "wield the scepter" in order to feel a sense of achievement.

Your greatest problem could be your need to find a reasonable explanation for anything before accepting its validity or even its reality. You want to rule situations by discovering an order in them. In the extreme you can become dictatorial.

With Death and the Fool as your Hidden Factors, you seek immortality through the creations you "father" and the structures you produce. Change, disruption, lawlessness, humor that pokes fun at the things you stand for, and the "unexplained" all confuse or even frighten you, and yet they offer your best opportunities for growth and self-understanding. You always seek a method in the "madness" around you and perhaps will find real solutions to some of humankind's problems. You deny there are any limits to reason and therefore continually push back those limits to pioneer new frontiers. You can be an architect of the spirit, a builder of new worlds.

If you are a Single 4 (with the Emperor as both your Personality and Soul Card), then both Death and the Fool are your Hidden Factor Cards. Read the descriptions of these cards that appear later in this chapter.

Famous Single 4s

There are only two Single 4s on my list of famous people, although we should be seeing more of them in the next few years.

Mike Tyson (boxer) 6/30/1966
Will Smith (actor, rapper) 9/25/1968

Death (13) as Personality Card

(*This applies if you are a 13-4.*)

Realization of Life Power, Vital Force, Release

Death represents an end but is also a new beginning, a cutting away that leads to new growth. It is destruction and renewal, immortality and regeneration, as well as dismemberment and severing. Relating it to its sign, Scorpio, it eliminates anything restrictive or no longer of service. I like to think of it as the "compost card," the decaying dead matter out of which comes rich, fertile soil that encourages new growth.

As a Personality Card, Death refers to letting go of old ways and thoughts in order to be transformed or renewed. "It is enough" were the last words of 13-4 philosopher Immanuel Kant. Most 13-4s tend to learn by facing their mortality, even taunting it, orchestrating their lives to take them to the very brink of death or discorporation. Krishnamurti, a 13-4, welcomed the dying process as a way of life. He said, "Each day I die a little."

You plunge deeply and totally into your experiences, putting such passionate feeling into your beliefs that you are not always aware of the consequences of your actions. As Benjamin Franklin said, "Experience keeps a dear school, but fools will learn in no other."

Your natural leadership attracts followers to you, and you must eventually come to terms with your desire for power for its own sake. You bring passion and depth to whatever you do, for nothing is taken lightly.

You are a transformer, working to dismember outworn policies, to set free new human possibilities, to liberate potentials. You have no qualms about dissociating from whatever states cannot continue to exist. Your sexuality is either very active and passionate or consciously sublimated into your work. "Intellectual passion drives out sensuality," said Leonardo da Vinci, a 13-4.

The Fool (22) as Hidden Factor

(This applies if you are a Single 4 or a 13-4.)

The Fool as your Hidden Factor indicates fear of being considered foolish and immature. And you will, at times, feel you are living your life foolishly, throwing away your potential, or working on something that others deem a waste. It may be hard for you to see yourself as an unlimited being. But confronted by the spirit within, you learn to trust your own natural abilities. You fight to maintain independence, although you are often, incongruously for a fool, cast into the role of leader. You admire freedom of thought above all else. Ignorance is limitation to you, and so you always seek the meaning or purpose behind things. Others may think you've lost your reason or gone mad, but you are simply discovering your infinite potential.

You seem to have either no ambition or no sense of fun and play. People who know you in one state may not recognize you in the other. Your fascination with diverse topics makes you seem scattered, but you should trust that your natural instincts are steering you right. You need to understand, not necessarily control, your own desire for anarchy.

Because the Fool has no real number value, you fear being counted as insignificant, as *nothing*; yet, just as adding the a 0 to the number 1 results in the number 10, you increase whatever you combine with the Fool's 0. Therefore, while you fear loss of Self, your abilities can combine well with those of others, helping them to achieve their own potentials.

As your teacher, the Fool helps you let go of other people's opinions and trust in your own processes. The Fool shows you vistas that others rarely see and encourages you to take risks, plunge off into the unknown, and enjoy every minute to its fullest.

Famous 13-4s

Famous 13-4s have been responsible for shocking revelations of deeply hidden things—for revealing the undercurrents of passion, power, and the potential for good and evil in us all. Several, such as Harriet Beecher Stowe, with *Uncle Tom's Cabin* (credited with starting the Civil War); J. R. Oppenheimer, with the atomic bomb; or Immanuel Kant in philosophy; exploded the myths of their time, resulting in worldwide reconstruction of the basic assumptions by which we live. Many have used death as the theme of their greatest works, such as J. D. Salinger in *Catcher in the Rye*, the English poet Shelley and the German composer Richard Wagner. Some have courted death, even flaunting it, such as William S. Burroughs with his drug sagas or Thor Heyerdahl, sailing the high seas in a tiny reed raft. Immanuel Kant was so concerned about dying that he never varied his rigid physical regimen and never married. He is known for his *Critique of Pure Reason* (a very Emperor topic) and for developing the theory that individual freedom lies in obedience to moral law within, a perfect example of Emperor and Fool.

Leonardo da Vinci (artist, inventor) 4/15/1452
Immanuel Kant (philosopher) 4/22/1724
Marie Anne Lenormand (fortune-teller) 5/27/1772
Percy B. Shelley (poet) 8/4/1792
Joseph Smith (founder, Mormon Church) 12/23/1805
Harriet Beecher Stowe (humanitarian, novelist) 6/14/1811
Richard Wagner (composer) 5/22/1813
Henri Matisse (artist) 12/31/1869
Amedeo Modigliani (artist) 7/12/1884
J. Krishnamurti (philosopher) 5/12/1895
M. C. Escher (artist) 6/17/1898
René Magritte (artist) 11/21/1898
J. R. Oppenheimer (atomic bomb project leader) 4/22/1904
William S. Burroughs (writer) 2/5/1914
Thor Heyerdahl (anthropologist, explorer) 10/6/1914
Harold Wilson (U.K. prime minister) 3/11/1916
J. D. Salinger (writer) 1/1/1919

The Fool (22) as Personality Card

(*This applies if you are a 22-4.*)

Realization of Eternal Power, Spiritual Force, Regeneration

The Fool represents your childlike, spontaneous nature. As your Personality Card, it indicates that you will develop great trust, innocence, and lightheartedness. You will gain wisdom only when you realize how much you don't know.

As a 22-4, you always live with the paradoxical nature of wisdom and foolishness. Your purpose is to establish self-control and set the standards in your field, yet you must be prepared to admit ignorance, cast your fate to the winds, and make wild leaps of divine inspiration. As Sallie Nichols says in *Jung and Tarot*, "The job of the fool is to remind us of our folly and keep us from hubris—overwhelming pride." But few 22-4s have the wisdom to play the fool with grace and humility.

One of the problems of 22-4s is their belief that they are exempt from the rules they make. They will accept no discipline from without and can be irresponsible and even amoral. Often, 22-4s have the attitude, if not appearance, of youth and vigor. In old age, they are constantly surprising others with their ability to integrate the new, unexpected, and strange.

Emperor-Fools can be quite different at different stages of their lives. There is the stage of being totally the Fool—usually when you are young—of doing things on a whim, of being the vagabond. Then you settle down and become the Emperor, very organized and practical, establishing businesses and a home. But occasionally you need to break out and be footloose again in order to rejuvenate yourself. When these two qualities are combined, you can be creative and even innovative. You take risks but get results. You are the pioneer, the inventor. But when this inner contrast is not well integrated, you want to be the Emperor yet are afraid you are the Fool. You are then unable to let go of inhibitions and cannot truly look at yourself or your own processes. You must learn to laugh at yourself for taking your situation too seriously.

As a 22-4, you may have a finely developed sense of humor based on the ironies of life and a poignant appreciation of human foibles. You know all too well the situations into which we are led by unruly passions, but you can see their comic side.

The Fool represents your spirit before manifestation, between incarnations. The cliff on the card represents your jump-off into life, into the manifested world of the Emperor. Death represents being released again so that you can freely experience your limitless Self. After accepting Death as your teacher, you realize the polarity of wisdom and folly and recognize that death is only a mechanism of eternal life.

When I first wrote about Birth Cards in the early 1980s, I claimed that the Emperor was the Personality Card and the Fool was the Soul Card. Over time and knowing a great many 22-4s, I realized that Emperor-Fools tend to resist all categorization, so I work with them both together. In tarot philosophy, the Fool is to be found nowhere and everywhere.

Death (13) as Hidden Factor

(This applies if you are a Single 4 or a 22-4.)

Death as your Hidden Factor indicates that you deny death, experiencing it as an idea that limits and binds you. One outcome is that you strive (perhaps a bit fanatically) to produce works (or children) that will live after you are gone, so as to carry on your name and perpetuate your existence. You can be a dictatorial parent, demanding that your child follow in your footsteps. Or you may feel that in the face of death life becomes meaningless, and thus you suffer from existential angst.

Death becomes a thing to fight, something against which to prove yourself. Humans are the only creatures aware of the fact that they die, and thus death can become the measure by which all action and creations are judged. But the more you hate death, the more you will hate the life around you. Death means totally losing your sense of ego, so many people with Death as a Hidden Factor will work to make their ego strong and well-known—an indelible identifying mark. As 22-4 Mark Twain wrote in a famous telegram, "The reports of my death are greatly exaggerated."

Since death, in symbolic and vernacular terms, has long been considered a metaphor for orgasm—"the little death"—4s and 22-4s may experience their fear of the loss of Self through sexual release. It used to be said that each orgasm shortens one's life by a day. You will either "foolishly" and joyfully embrace that death, or run from it. Fascination with this subject is evidenced by the famous 22-4 Sigmund Freud. Death becomes the Teacher Card when you realize that coming to terms with death is true liberation. You can then die to those rules that constrict your freedom of spirit.

Famous 22-4s

There are several threads to follow when looking at famous Emperor-Fools. Many of them were revolutionaries or radicals or were not afraid to take tremendous risks to achieve their ends. Some were charged with unconventional behavior and insensitivity to criticism. Another major tendency of

Emperor-Fools seems to be the urge for immortality as a driving force, to prove themselves physically and to reach the peak of their respective fields. There are numerous humorists and even professional fools: the great mime Marcel Marceau, Woody Allen, Mark Twain, Ed Sullivan, and Ingmar Bergman, who always blended humor with his death-wish imagery. Woody Allen is a model 22-4. He once cited *The Denial of Death* by Ernest Becker as the most important book he had ever read. Also, one of his great lines is about wanting to achieve immortality, not through his work, but by not dying.

Marie Antoinette (Queen of France) 11/2/1755
Mark Twain (writer, humorist) 11/30/1835
J. P. Morgan (financier) 4/17/1837
Annie Besant (social reformer, theosophist) 10/1/1847
Sigmund Freud (psychiatrist) 5/6/1856
Marie Curie (chemist, discovered radium) 11/7/1867
Frank Sinatra (musician, actor) 12/12/1915
Ingmar Bergman (filmmaker) 7/14/1918
Marcel Marceau (mime) 3/22/1923
Margaret Thatcher (U.K. prime minister) 10/13/1925
Hugh Hefner (publisher of *Playboy*) 4/9/1926
Miles Davis (musician) 5/26/1926
Alejandro Jodorowky (filmmaker, tarotist) 2/17/1929
Clint Eastwood (actor) 5/31/1930
Charles Manson (cult leader) 11/12/1934
Tenzin Gyatso (fourteenth Dalai Lama) 7/6/1935
Luciano Pavarotti (opera musician) 10/12/1935
Woody Allen (filmmaker, humorist) 12/1/1935
Paul McCartney (musician) 6/18/1942
Newt Gingrich (U.S. politician) 6/17/1943
Arnold Schwarzenegger (actor, politician) 7/30/1947
Eckhart Tolle (inspirational speaker, writer) 2/16/1948
Oprah Winfrey (TV host, philanthropist) 1/29/1954
Nicolas Sarkozy (French president) 1/28/1955
Bill Gates (founder, Microsoft) 10/28/1955
Bono (Paul Hewson) (musician, activist) 5/10/1960
Brad Pitt (actor) 12/18/1963
Eminem (Marshall Mathers) (rapper) 10/17/1972

The Minor Arcana 4s

The 4s represent stabilization after the creative interaction of the 3s, a time to consolidate what has come before. In metaphysical philosophy, 4s represent completion, similar to that of the 10s (because 1 + 2 + 3 + 4 = 10). Like the Emperor, they deal with your ability to locate yourself in time and space. The 4s are the gifts or challenges relating to your personal power. They represent opportunities to release outworn modes and stabilize change. They picture the situations you experience when developing leadership abilities and establishing a firm base for your continuing activities.

4 of Wands (April 11–20, 20°–30° Aries, Cardinal Fire)

The 4 of Wands indicates the sense of completion and welcome renewal that comes when opposing energies harmonize, for instance, at the change of seasons, or when day and night are equal. You treat such times as rites of passage: cleansing, celebrating, and being generous with the fruits of your labor. You show appreciation for those who have supported you, you give thanks for your bounty, you enjoy what you harvest.

The first gift of the 4s is, therefore, your ability to celebrate life. This card pictures the rewards that come from moving through each developmental stage in your life and your acceptance of responsibility at new levels.

4 of Cups (July 12–21, 20°–30° Cancer, Cardinal Water)

The 4 of Cups is both gift and challenge. You have the ability to let things take their course, trusting the cycles of change. You recognize the need for letting situations lie fallow in order to regenerate. By resting and meditating, you receive new insights and messages from your unconscious.

As a challenge, though, the 4 of Cups represents the inertia that develops when you lack focus or a sense of purpose. Indulging in your feelings, as in the 3 of Cups, often leads to dissatisfaction, lethargy, or exhaustion. Go slowly in emotional matters. You get bored only when your curiosity has not been piqued or when self-indulgence has become meaningless. Take time to be with Nature, observing its natural rhythms, and you will be rejuvenated.

4 of Swords (October 13–22, 20°–30° Libra, Cardinal Air)

The 4 of Swords indicates that stress is a large factor in your health. Because of the weight of your responsibilities, there are times when you need to ask for advice, either from your Higher Self or from a professional counselor. Taking everything on yourself makes matters worse.

When you feel burdened or stressed, pull back into solitude in order to consider the details calmly. Put your thoughts in order and determine priorities. Suspend action on all issues but one, which you can then ask your unconscious to address, and sleep on it. Through centering and meditation practices, you can create the objectivity required to see all sides of an issue. From this experience, something useful and powerful can emerge.

4 of Pentacles (January 10–19, 20°–30° Capricorn, Cardinal Earth)

The 4 of Pentacles indicates that you have the gift of drawing to you the resources you need. You consolidate your power so that you can act with assurance. You need to feel secure in your sense of worth, for *only* then can you have a sense of humor about yourself.

This card also represents the dangers of grasping material accumulations too tightly. This is the constipating aspect of a fear of Scorpionic Death. Miserly protectiveness of your possessions closes you off to personal development. The transitions pictured in the 4 of Wands can no longer take place, nor can the new experiences in the 4 of Cups or the release from the stresses of responsibility in the 4 of Swords. Think about the positioning of the pentacles in the Waite-Smith image, which illustrates the posture of personal power or miserliness.

To experience the power pictured in the card, balance a pentacle above your head, ground your feet firmly on the two pentacles below, and finally center the last pentacle in your hands. When you feel completely centered and stable, bring the last pentacle inside your body—this is your point of personal power. Having found your security within, you no longer need to hold on to anything out in the world.

TEMPERANCE.

THE HIEROPHANT

The Constellation of the Hierophant

CHAPTER 9

The Constellation of the Hierophant
14–5

Temperance (14)
The Hierophant (5)

5 of Wands	5 of Cups
5 of Swords	5 of Pentacles

The Hierophant

Astrological Correspondence:	Taurus
Card Functions within the Constellation:	Social/Cultural Education; Freedom of Choice; Learning from Authoritiy

Temperance

Astrological Correspondence:	Sagittarius
Card Functions within the Constellation:	Spiritual Education; Freedom of Action; Learning by Experience

---

The Principle of Teaching and Learning

Soul Archetype: Spirit; Teacher; Morality

Keywords: Testing. Counseling. Training. Assimilating and Integrating. Healing. Guidance. Bridging. Translating. Interpreting. Channeling. Arbitrating.

If you are a Single 5 (5-5), read:

The Hierophant (5) as Personality or Soul Card
Temperance (14) as Hidden Factor
Famous Single 5s
The Minor Arcana 5s

If you are a 14-5, read:

The Hierophant (5) as Personality or Soul Card
Temperance (14) as Personality Card
Famous 14-5s
The Minor Arcana 5s

(Note: If a card from 14 through 18 is your Personality Card, you will not have a separate Hidden Factor. As a "Nighttime Card," the shadow aspect is contained within the Personality Card itself.)

The Hierophant (5) as Personality or Soul Card

(*This applies if you are a Single 5 or a 14-5.*)

Learning from Authority, Freedom of Choice, Social/Cultural Education

The Hierophant represents teaching and learning the laws set down by the Emperor. *Hierophant* means "Shower of Mysteries." In this capacity, you become a spokesperson for the powers that be and in effect translate information to make it accessible to the general public. For instance, if you are a scientist with specialized knowledge, you communicate it to others who would not otherwise understand. Artists like van Gogh and Cézanne (both 5s) saw the world in a very particular way, yet were able to give us some insight into what they saw through their "interpretations" on canvas. You are a bridge maker. As Hierophant, you communicate what is mysterious or strange to others so that they will have the opportunity to experience it, too. Many 5s are known as storytellers. Any incident can become an adventure in your eyes.

Like the two acolytes pictured in the card, you are either an active learner, searching and questioning the validity of what you learn, or you are the submissive learner, accepting what you are taught by those considered to be authorities. Often Single 5 Hierophants will rebel against authority while they're young, but as they grow older they become authorities themselves; they have discovered their niche—what they have chosen to stand up for.

Whether you officially do any teaching or training, you love to give advice and help people with problem solving. As a matter of fact, people often come to you for assistance because they respect your expertise and knowledge and know that you are willing to help them. You are able to separate complex directions into simple components, and you don't give information that is extraneous or too difficult to understand. In problem-solving situations, you choose between going to an authority and following instructions or testing techniques for yourself, trusting your intuition for guidance.

You can be a good listener, recognizing that what's on the surface does not tell all. The figure on the card has two fingers of the right hand upright, indicating what is said, while the three closed fingers indicate understanding of what is not said. The Bishop's cross demonstrates the four levels (including the top circle of Spirit) of every statement. There are also four ways to teach or learn anything (hearing, doing, reading words, and seeing pictures or diagrams). You are the fifth element, the one who understands. You can adapt your teaching to the needs of those you teach.

Your greatest problem is when your knowledge becomes codified into dogma that may no longer be appropriate in current situations. When you refuse to continually question your beliefs, they become that dogma and thus limit your possible experiences. While beliefs are important to everybody, it is harder for 5s to separate their subjective beliefs about what things "should be" from what they simply "are."

Just as your adherents swear by your teaching, so you in turn admire and even idolize the teachers and models you trust. The danger in this is in accepting what they say as "God's own truth." The need to believe in something is so strong that you may turn to gurus or spiritual leaders who you think can give you access to something on which you can pin your hopes. As teachers themselves, Hierophants come to expect submission and adherence to the doctrines they teach.

Single 5s are often afraid of making mistakes. Thus, you want to be sure before you do anything. Rather than being ridiculed, you would prefer not to try at all if you think you might fail. You believe there is a right and wrong way of doing things and blame yourself when something goes wrong. Yet Hierophants learn best through their mistakes. One of the challenges for Single 5s is to learn to value your own authority, based on realizations arrived at through trial and error, experimentation, and experience. You will face this lesson over and over until you develop the flexibility to accept your problems and mistakes as your teachers. Being "wrong" can be good if it points out the need for readjustment or alternate methods that work better. An equally strong sense of pragmatism helps with this.

Fives have highly developed consciences; a strong sense of morals and values (the "shoulds" and "oughts") determines your actions. Watch your tendency to be self-righteous.

You search for a purpose that is larger than our mortal order. You yearn for a quintessential truth that ties everything meaningfully together. Oswald Wirth, in *The Tarot of the Magicians*, says, "In your own way formulate your own knowledge and in your heart conceive the religion which convinces you." With the Hierophant as your Soul Card, your purpose is to develop your own authority via an inner Self that speaks with the innocence of a child and the wisdom of your inner High Priestess. When you act in accord with your highest potential, you transmit information from the Higher Self into the physical world.

Temperance (14) as Hidden Factor

(*This applies if you are a Single 5.*)

With Temperance as your Hidden Factor, you can be rigid and temperamental. Especially when you are young, you think that mistakes are wrong, and you judge yourself to be wrong if you make them. This can hamper your willingness to take risks and try things out. Single 5s always want to do things the "right" way and tend to follow the directions as learned. Alternatively, they question and rebel against everything. By coming to terms with Temperance as shadow, you learn give-and-take and the importance of trial-and-error learning from your mistakes. The challenges of life may appear as "problems" until you temper your nature through learning patience and good timing.

Balancing the "shoulds" and "oughts" of a moral universe with the realities of life as it is requires great understanding, adaptation, and compassion.

Compassion is the greatest teaching of this card. Along with healing, they represent this constellation's "bright shadow" aspects. You may find it difficult to value your spiritual resources or trust your natural empathy. Out of fear of appearing wishy-washy, you will hold to a position even after it no longer seems tenable. You feel that sensitivity and displays of emotion are weaknesses. Thinking of yourself as a pragmatist, you disguise what you may think of as sentimentality with cynical humor and wisecracks. With maturity, as you accept Temperance as your teacher, you become more flexible, easing up on your judgments of yourself and others. Eventually you discover what you can do best to aid in alleviating suffering in yourself and the world around you.

Famous Single 5s

Famous Single 5s are somewhat difficult to classify because they are quite different from each other. Still, they have more than their share of idealism and require perfection of themselves and their models. An example is Bertrand Russell, who describes the beauty of mathematics in his essay "The Study of Mathematics" as "without appeal to any part of our weaker nature, sublimely pure, and capable of stern perfection." Blake could have said this. While many are revolutionaries and iconoclasts in their youth, they tend to quickly find an ideal they can believe in and spend the rest of their lives in the role of "authority," promoting, teaching, and following that ideal.

William Blake (artist, poet, mystic) 11/28/1757
Paul Cézanne (artist) 1/19/1839
Pierre-Auguste Renoir (artist) 2/25/1841
Vincent van Gogh (artist) 3/30/1853
Arthur Conan Doyle (writer) 5/22/1859
Bertrand Russell (philosopher) 5/18/1872
James Joyce (writer) 2/2/1882
Malcolm X (religious leader, revolutionary) 5/19/1925
Michael Dummett (philosopher, tarot historian) 6/27/1925
Willie Nelson (country musician) 4/30/1933
Werner Erhard (founder, est) 9/5/1935
Rudolf Nureyev (dancer) 3/17/1938

Mick Jagger (musician) 7/26/1943
Steven Spielberg (film director) 12/18/1946
Kareem Abdul Jabbar (basketball player) 4/16/1947
Mikhail Baryshnikov (dancer) 1/27/1948
J. K. Rowling (writer) 7/31/1965
Pierre Omidyar (founder, eBay) 6/21/1967
Dave Eggers (writer, publisher) 3/12/1970
Angelina Jolie (actor) 6/4/1975
Beyoncé Knowles (musician, actor) 9/4/1981
Mark Zuckerberg (founder, Facebook) 5/14/1984
Blake Ross (founder, Firefox) 6/12/1985
Michael Phelps (Olympic swimmer) 6/30/1985

Temperance (14) as Personality Card

(*This applies if you are a 14-5.*)

Learning by Experience, Freedom of Action, Spiritual Education

Temperance represents healing, tempering, adjusting, and redistribution. As a 14-5, you seek to creatively combine contrary forces into a new whole that is more than the sum of its parts. For these reasons, the figure on this card is often called the Alchemist. After the dismemberment and blackening melancholy of Death (the "nigredo" stage of alchemy) comes the creative reconstitution or the purified Self. Temperance believes there is a solution to every problem.

As a 14-5, you look inward to find personal resources and creative materials with which to aid not only your own growth but also that of others. You are a humanist, filled with compassion for the feelings and failings of others because you recognize them first in yourself. Many 14-5s actively seek to describe the human condition in new ways, uncovering and delving into the shadowy realms that are rarely acknowledged socially in order to bring these forgotten parts back into ourselves. You work actively to promote the circulation of ideas.

To 14-5s, teaching is healing. Illness is the deterioration of a perfect whole that needs to be reassembled and understood on an entirely new level. Your problems don't exist in a void but are connected to everything else in your life. You assist others in seeing the whole picture and finding the connections among the parts. You heal others (individually and socially) not only by lending your own strength, but also by your loving acceptance of who they are, with sympathy for their plight. You seek to heal both physical and psychic wounds.

When you trust the deeper currents of life and value your inner experiences, they bring new insights and reveal new dimensions of experience. Yet you must always work to reconcile the world of your dreams with that of your daily life, to mix inner knowledge with the appropriate physical expression.

In the extreme, you desire to purify by wiping out undesirable qualities, or to simplify things to their essence (like Mao Tse-Tung, Georgia O'Keeffe, Yukio Mishima). You are a purist. Those who are 14-5s are often not moderate. Hitler, a 14-5, is well-known for his excessive desire to purify the Aryan race, summed up in this remark: "I shall stop at nothing and crush anyone who opposes me." You may need to learn moderation and to temper your idealism in order to deal with contingencies. But learn you will.

As if washed in the fountain of youth, 14-5s maintain a certain impetuosity, often accompanied by a tendency to look and act younger than their age.

Right timing is essential to problem solving, and 14-5s often achieve their greatest successes by being in the right place at the right time. You recognize the importance of seasonal change and renewal and of yielding when appropriate. If the time is not propitious, you will still seek the right gradient or catalytic agent and trust that through trial and error you will eventually arrive at a workable solution.

But, because 14-5s carry their own shadow within them (Temperance is a "Nighttime Card"), you are just as likely to be in the wrong place at the wrong time. You must recognize timing as being the key to manifesting results on the physical plane. Otherwise you may be unsure of what you stand for, or perhaps feel out of place, born too soon or too late. You are caught between the land and the sea. You may be unrealistic about where to focus your talents and energies, squandering them in time-consuming and fruitless tasks. You may also be giving up your own autonomy and personal ideals in order to live by the dictates of those you consider your superiors (bosses, religious and secular authorities, etc.), living by their standards rather than your own.

If such is the case, you need to recognize that your beliefs form the basis of the reality you experience, whether valid or not. Like the two cups the

Temperance angel holds, they are the only things you have to juggle with. You create your world in the image of your thoughts. This idea was stated as a scientific theorem by consciousness researcher John C. Lilly (a 14-5): "What one believes to be true either is true, or becomes true within limits to be determined experimentally." Opportunity therefore comes when you are confronted with conflicting beliefs that you normally experience as stress. Instead, treat them as a creative challenge: Make something more out of them than either belief would warrant by itself. You can accomplish whatever you set out to do, and you are capable of solving intricate problems. Believe in yourself. Take care not to get scattered; keep yourself focused on the task at hand and on your image of success.

Famous 14-5s

There is a tendency for famous 14-5s to step out of the world of the mundane and into the metaphysical, although always with the purpose of exploring and describing the human condition. They often tap into such deep, numinous sources that they become spokespersons for, or even representatives of, archetypes of the time. There are notable freedom fighters here, and fascination with the macabre and mysterious. Many have found that out of bones and decay comes a purity of truth and beauty undiscerned by others.

> Benjamin Franklin (statesman, journalist, inventor) 1/17/1706
> Allesandro di Cagliostro (occultist) 6/2/1743
> Simón Bolívar (Latin American political leader) 7/24/1783
> Abraham Lincoln (U.S. president) 2/12/1809
> Charles Darwin (naturalist) 2/12/1809
> Frédéric Chopin (musician, composer) 3/1/1810
> Soren Kierkegaard (ethical philosopher) 5/5/1813
> Helen Keller (activist, spokesperson for the blind and deaf) 6/27/1880
> Georgia O'Keeffe (artist) 11/15/1887
> Adolf Hitler (German leader) 4/20/1889
> Louis Armstrong (jazz musician) 8/4/1901
> Marlene Dietrich (actor) 12/27/1901
> Haile Selassie (Ethiopian emperor, spiritual leader) 7/23/1892
> Mao Tse-Tung (communist Chinese leader) 12/26/1893
> William Faulkner (writer) 9/25/1897
> Jorge Luis Borges (writer, magical realist) 8/24/1899

John Steinbeck (writer) 2/27/1902
Tennessee Williams (writer, playwright) 3/26/1911
Albert Camus (writer) 11/7/1913
Alan Watts (mystic, writer) 1/6/1915
John C. Lilly (neuroscientist, psychoanalyst) 1/6/1915
Diane Arbus (photographer) 3/14/1923
Yukio Mishima (writer) 1/14/1925
Che Guevara (revolutionary) 6/14/1928

The Minor Arcana 5s

The 5s upset stability and stagnation. Each of the 5s gets us out of the rut of the 4s by overthrowing complacency and creating challenges to be met creatively, in the spirit of adventure. It is through such testing of our fears that we learn to activate our potentials.

Wands present you with the test of ideas, in which you must face your fear of strife that results in stress. Cups present you with the test of love, in which you must face your fear of disappointment that results in sorrow. Swords present you with a test of will, in which you must face fear of defeat that results in defensiveness. And Pentacles present you with a test of belief, in which you must face the fear of insecurity that results in worry.

The 5s teach you temperance, that is, combining your abilities and being sensitive to right timing.

5 of Wands (July 22–August 1, 0°–10° Leo, Fixed Fire)

The 5 of Wands indicates you find your ideas tested through conflict and disagreements. Question authority! Such arguments or discussions can be invigorating and give you the opportunity to contribute your ideas and teach what you know. Temperance stresses the need to balance and temper individual ideas until something new can be formed out of the variety of experiences—a broader picture than just one individual (or point of view) can offer. This kind of synergistic process is one of the major ways in which to learn.

When this confrontation of differing ideas takes place within you, like an inner committee with five different voices rattling on in your head, producing too many things to think of at once, it can create confusion over what to do. You may find that the problem is based in conflicting beliefs. The Temperance card suggests finding a concept or overview that will bridge varying beliefs, allowing for each to coexist with the others.

5 of Cups (October 23–November 1, 0°–10° Scorpio, Fixed Water)

The 5 of Cups shakes you from the complacency of the 4 of Cups. You don't sufficiently appreciate something until you have lost it. Cups teach you about grief and how to transcend loss. When something you put your heart into has not worked out, you experience disappointment. The three spilled cups can represent a loss of harmony, or beliefs that used to sustain you. This can be a friendship turned sour, a physical loss, or plans overturned. You wrap a black coat of sorrow about you and turn inward with your grief. This is appropriate for a time. The two cups remaining are in the hands of the Temperance angel; thus healing can take place when you finally throw off sorrow and pick up the remaining cups. Renewing your interactions with loving friends, focusing on a new project, and "crossing bridges when you come to them" are ways out of grief and disappointment.

The Temperance angel reminds you that nothing is really ever lost. All energy continues, taking on new forms. The eternally pouring water symbolizes the continuity of the life force. When you experience disappointment, remember there is a time and season for everything. Let your tears flow; realize that time will bring healing and that creation itself is never ending. Ask yourself what you can learn from this experience.

5 of Swords (January 20–29, 0°–10° Aquarius, Fixed Air)

The 5 of Swords represents difficulty in communicating your ideas to others. Thinking is fragmented and decisions are difficult, bringing confusion and doubt. Others try to impose their ideas on you, but you must rely on your own inner voice. Or perhaps your thinking is so rigid that there is no room for other opinions. Avoid willful confrontations. Accept input from others but do not let it destroy your own perspective. This is not a situation of right or wrong but of needing to look at all possibilities and rejecting none. The preceding 4 of Swords retreats from such issues and attempts to deal with them in solitude. Here, in the 5 of Swords, you are ready to clash with others.

Such circumstances are no-win situations. Or you win the battle but lose the war; you make your point but lose your best friends. Trying to prove that you are right is not going to change their minds. Arguments and stormy scenes arise from a dogmatic stance.

When you have been injured and hurt from such an encounter, you need to heal. When you are fragmented like the scattered swords, you need to be made whole again. Don't let such experiences limit you to a desire for revenge. Instead call on the angelic, spiritual being inside you for guidance. Most of the great healers gained their gift from a personal wounding that they transcended. Then they assisted others in this process.

5 of Pentacles (April 21–30, 0°–10° Taurus, Fixed Earth)

The 5 of Pentacles represents the challenges of deprivation, insecurity, and exclusion. It is everything that the 4 of Pentacles is holding out against. It shows the upset of every effort toward stability. As a 5 or a 14-5, you learn by being denied everything you wanted to hold on to. This technique is sometimes deliberately used in spiritual teachings to help you recognize the transitory nature of physical and material desires. Such austerity and even poverty is felt to channel all your thoughts into your spiritual development.

But you can also find yourself in such a situation through your iconoclastic questioning of the powers that be. In rebelling against the norms of society, you may choose to live the life of the "outsider"—upholding the beliefs that you value with a few like-minded friends.

When your home, work, or other form of security is threatened, you have to choose how to handle it. If you feel powerless, you might seek sanctuary or accept welfare—perhaps an appropriate first step. But, as the equivalent card in the Motherpeace Tarot deck, the 5 of Disks (a woman kneading clay or bread), and Temperance card both suggest, you can work at your situation slowly and steadily, trying different things until you get a combination that holds together. Despite the hardships, this is a card of progress toward a goal. The reward will be as great as your belief in what you can achieve.

The Constellation of the Lovers

CHAPTER 10

The Constellation of the Lovers 15–6

The Devil (15)
The Lovers (6)

| 6 of Wands | 6 of Cups |
| 6 of Swords | 6 of Pentacles |

The Principle of Relatedness and Choice

The Lovers

Astrological Correspondence:	Gemini
Card Functions within the Constellation:	Urge to Unite; Choice to Love; Ourselves in Relation to Others

The Devil

Astrological Correspondence:	Capricorn
Card Functions within the Constellation:	Urge to Separate; Choice to Fear; Ourselves in Relation to the World

Soul Archetype: Choice: Union/Separation; the Twins—Duality

Keywords: Attraction and Division. Synergy and Separation. Exchange. Sharing and Relating. Reciprocity. Vitality. Sensuality. Connectedness. Ability to Discriminate between Good and Evil. Temptation. Obsession.

If you are a Single 6 (6-6), read:

The Lovers (6) as Personality or Soul Card
The Devil (15) as Hidden Factor
Famous Single 6s
The Minor Arcana 6s

If you are a 15-6, read:

The Lovers (6) as Personality or Soul Card
The Devil (15) as Personality Card
Famous 15-6s
The Minor Arcana 6s

The Lovers (6) as Personality or Soul Card

(This applies if you are a Single 6 or a 15-6.)

Urge to Unite, Choice to Love, Ourselves in Relation to Others

The Lovers represents synergy, reciprocity, and learning from others. This card has very different pictures in the French and English schools. The French school shows a man standing between an older woman and a young woman, thought to represent vice and virtue, or his mother and his wife. From a cloud above the people, Eros shoots his arrow at them. In the English school, beginning with the illustrations by Pamela Colman Smith, the picture is of Adam and Eve in the Garden of Eden with the snake of wisdom and the fiery archangel Michael above.

Both designs focus on an initiation—a choice being made to experience knowledge that was previously unknown or unavailable. This knowledge is traditionally couched in carnal terms. We see the severing of the previously unquestioned protective restrictions and an acceptance of the resultant power of procreation—to allow you to become a god, a creator in your own right. The individual leaves the mother and/or father, to cleave to the lover. Unity is broken, and from the separation comes the desire to reunite in order to create something new that is different from the originator.

As a card relating to Gemini and thus to the Jungian archetypal motif called "The Journey of the Twins," it shows two sides to yourself that you must attempt to reconcile. This can be the split perceived between the "good" and "bad" parts of yourself, the reflective and the dynamic, the passive and the active, the masculine and feminine, or your personal independence and your desire to relate.

Ultimately, your task is to unite these two aspects of yourself. When these two parts work together in harmony, you experience tremendous power and pride in your knowledge and abilities. You can then bring intuitive awareness and focused consciousness into relationships and, ultimately, be able to perceive the truth that transcends them both.

With the Lovers as either your Personality Card or your Soul Card, personal relationships are of primary importance to your own development. You learn most about yourself through the people with whom you are in relationship: your family, friends, coworkers, lovers. Be aware that occasionally it is a cause, work, or gadgets, rather than people, that attract or even obsess you.

Unrestricted and honest communications are vital. You look for a partner with whom you can communicate your deepest feelings and aspirations and will prefer people with interests similar to your own. The central issue for you is, What do I want and need in relationships? Relationships of all kinds tend to fascinate you, so you are always figuring out and tinkering with how people and things are related to other people and things, and you even see associations where none may exist.

Many 6s work with or share a hobby with a partner they consider to be their best friend. If you are "unattached," you are probably attracted as much by conversation and friendship as anything else. Consider whether someone who is "just a friend" could be a person with whom you could share more.

With the Lovers, the people you relate to mirror your own self-image. The best way to see yourself is to look at who you have drawn into your life. The qualities you cannot see in yourself, often called your shadow, you project onto others; you are unusually sensitive to, annoyed by, or envious of these traits in others. While this happens with everyone, for Lovers this is a major way in which you learn about yourself. Your relationships reflect this self-image until you learn to take back and claim for yourself all your projected traits. The Lovers is a card of choice, symbolic of separating ourselves from the Garden of Eden, from our parents, from our security bases, in order to choose our own experiences and thus achieve knowledge. For Lovers, though, the choices are based on the two core emotions of love and fear, from which all others arise. At every junction in the path, you must ask yourself which of these is determining your choice. Is your action motivated by love or to avoid what is fearful? This question is related to another of your characteristic dilemmas, that of choosing between your belief in freedom and your need for attachment. Because you tend to think in terms of "we" rather than "I," the influence of others is felt in all your decisions, drawing you even further into relationships.

The Devil (15) as Hidden Factor

(*This applies if you are a Single 6.*)

The Devil as your Hidden Factor indicates that you tend to hide your untamed instincts, even from yourself. Thus your sexuality in particular, and your vivacity in general, can feel overwhelming to you at times. You either see yourself as a basically sexual creature motivated by your desires and obsessed with your needs, or you repress these feelings in yourself with accompanying inhibitions and taboos.

If you grew up in an environment with rigid standards that allowed you little freedom, you may harbor doubts about your self-worth. If you experienced your situation as oppressive, you may have felt punished for transgressing in ways you did not understand. You may have internalized some personal qualities as being "bad" because of these repressive attitudes. For instance, you might have felt or been told that sex was forbidden or repulsive. If you were a "good" child, you tried to make sure you never did anything to be ashamed of, hiding even from yourself thoughts and feelings that were not sanctioned.

Single 6s as children open themselves to others with total trust. You intensely desire relationship and reach out freely to others. When this trust is betrayed, you end up feeling the guilty and responsible one. You may have been abused either physically or mentally by someone exerting power and control over you. Girl children accused of being flirts or teases, for instance, are particularly susceptible to self-blame.

You then grow up either feeling guilty about sex, repressing your natural instincts, and sublimating them into a need for power, or you see sexuality as an expression of your personal power. Being sexually desirable can become a way of proving your own importance and self-worth. You may feel you have things to hide—some "dirty" secret. If anyone found out, they couldn't possibly love you. Alternatively, you may turn this feeling into suspicion of others and their motivations. At the extreme, unable to face your own sense of guilt or blame, you may project it onto others. You find scapegoats for your own sense of powerlessness, or try to manipulate your relationships as the only way of getting what you need.

Within the Golden Dawn tradition, the key to this card is mirth! Don't take manipulation and other people's power trips seriously. See the humor in the situation. This is how to break through obsession, manipulation, and overweening pride. Nietzsche, who was a Single 6, said, "Man alone suffers so excruciatingly in the world that he was compelled to invent laughter." Bedevilment shakes you out of a fixed way of seeing things and allows for new perspectives. Like the tricksters and coyotes of myth, you shake things up; you emphasize new connections instead of accepting previous divisions and discrimination. You need to learn there are no sins, only errors—and these are rectifiable. Union with Self comes through learning to forgive yourself.

After your Saturn Return (about age thirty), as the Devil becomes your teacher, you become more comfortable with the natural power and magnetism that draws others to you. You discover that you can activate tremendous creativity when you trust your instincts and face the things that terrified you previously. This can become a desire to explore hidden traditions, places, and taboo subjects, or it can be a fascination with the powers of the dark and mysterious.

Eventually you realize that ultimate power lies in being able to choose your own values. You find that all those secrets and manipulations assumed power over you by obsessing you. By admitting your fears and taking them from the shadows, you gain the personal power to laugh away constrictions and liberate your full creative potential.

Famous Single 6s

Among the well-known Single 6s, John Lennon, Charles Schulz, Stephen King, and H. G. Wells, all use satire and humor to expose the hidden fears of the human species. Stieg Larsson revealed the hidden dimensions of violence in racism and crimes against women. Einstein's research released the power and, in his term, "menace" of the atomic bomb, but he also said (rightly or not), "It may intimidate the human race into bringing order into its international affairs, which, without the pressure of fear, it would not do." Nietzsche, expressing the Devil side, believed in the full expression of our ruthlessness, courage, and pride in order to access our true power. John Lennon epitomizes the Lover in his lyric "In the end, the love you take is equal to the love you make."

> Friedrich Nietzsche (philosopher) 10/15/1844
> William Randolph Hearst (publisher) 4/29/1863
> Edvard Munch (artist) 12/12/1863
> H.G. Wells (writer) 9/21/1866
> Vladimir Ilyich Lenin (Russian leader) 4/22/1870
> Sergei Rachmaninoff (composer) 4/1/1873
> Albert Einstein (physicist) 3/14/1879
> Charles Schulz (cartoonist) 11/26/1922
> Sandra Day O'Connor (Supreme Court justice) 3/26/1930
> John Lennon (musician) 10/9/1940
> Kim Jong-il (North Korean leader) 2/16/1941
> Jesse Jackson (civil rights activist) 10/8/1941
> George W. Bush (U.S. president) 7/6/1946
> Stephen King (writer) 9/21/1947
> Meryl Streep (actor) 6/22/1949
> Stieg Larsson (journalist and writer) 8/15/1954
> Michael Jackson (musician/entertainer) 8/29/1958
> Eddie Murphy (actor, comedian) 4/3/1961
> Jeff Bezos (founder, Amazon.com) 1/12/1964
> Sarah Palin (politician) 2/11/1964
> Kim Hee-sun (actor) 2/25/1977
> Justin Timberlake (musician, actor) 1/31/1981
> Britney Spears (musician, actor) 12/2/1981
> Rafael Nadal (tennis player) 6/3/1986

The Devil (15) as Personality Card

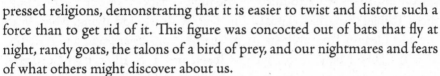

(*This applies if you are a 15-6.*)

Urge to Separate, Choice to Fear, Ourselves in Relation to the World

The Devil represents raw, untamed power and creativity. This lord of the material world, feared as dangerous to Self and society, is represented by the devil in a composite image taken from the gods of suppressed religions, demonstrating that it is easier to twist and distort such a force than to get rid of it. This figure was concocted out of bats that fly at night, randy goats, the talons of a bird of prey, and our nightmares and fears of what others might discover about us.

Therefore the Devil represents what you as a 15-6 try to keep hidden or repressed. Characterized as a card associated with the earth sign Capricorn, you prefer to find a structured form that can contain your fears and thus keep them separate from your sense of Self. This card also represents the part of yourself considered "worldly," base, or material—the part that Western culture has tried to separate from the spiritual, and with which, since your Soul Card is the Lovers, you will always strive to unite.

You can be ambitious and willing to go to both the heights and depths of experience in the service of that ambition. You sacrifice your own needs and those of others you love to the ideals that obsess you, making yourself difficult to live with. You work hard and play hard. You appear distant and cold, presenting an air of formality to those who are unaware of the passionate commitments you hold. Your pride is beneficial in that you recognize your abilities, and it is harmful in that it promotes artificial distinctions between yourself and others. Robert Browning, a 15-6, recognized this when he wrote "as if true pride / Were not also humble!"

Feeling ultimately alone in your freedom to choose a purpose for your life, you either become a bold romantic, upholding a strict moral ethic as a method of keeping society together, or you struggle with the despair and bewilderment of a meaningless universe that neither rewards nor punishes you and therefore makes all action absurd.

You probably grew up within a rigid but satisfyingly structured view of the world, in which certain behaviors were correct no matter what was actually happening beneath the surface. Later you became painfully aware of the contrast between this world of social etiquette and the real world, with its underlying deceit and lack of deep connectedness in personal relationships. "Human kind / Cannot bear very much reality," said 15-6 T. S. Eliot.

You may see yourself as some sort of dupe or clown who tries to imagine yourself free when you know yourself to be constricted by the boundaries of Self, society, and the natural world—things outside your control. You dissect social conditions and human character in an attempt to discover who you are. You feel that if only you can have control over a situation, you will be free.

Often, 15-6s work to uncover the hidden aspects of our culture. Elizabeth Kübler-Ross has exposed our fear of death and dying. Mike Wallace and Eleanor Roosevelt strove to uncover consumer fraud and state our human rights. Many 15-6s, such as Ibsen and T. S. Eliot, have portrayed humans as responding to life in a constricted world with a sense of separateness by labeling lack of responsibility as freedom—thus ultimately sinning through our failure to love.

The central question for 15-6s is in their relationship to the universe. What is the place of human beings? How do we fit into the structure? At various times we have perceived ourselves differently: sometimes we think we are as gods, sometimes we see ourselves in the image of a devil or monster, and sometimes we are even aware of our foolish self-importance in thinking that we are made in the image of anything, rather than by just pure chance. What is the nature of man—to be god or beast? Ram Dass, a 15-6, in his book *Grist for the Mill*, concludes, "We are in training to be nobody special. And it is in that nobody-specialness that we can be anybody."

You either take yourself too seriously or you see yourself ironically, laughing at your all-too-human foibles and the hidden beastliness that keeps you from being somebody.

For 15-6s, the challenge is to maintain godly honesty and inner freedom in relationships, while being devilishly surefooted in the world.

Famous 15-6s

At the top of the list are the famous lovers, Elizabeth Barrett Browning ("How shall I love thee, let me count the ways . . .") and Robert Browning. Note how many 15-6s have written for theatre and film, with a special emphasis on "Theatre of the Absurd," which portrays our existential dilemma of having choice in a meaningless universe. Coppola and Bradbury explored the darker side of literature, nor should we forget the more delicate portrayals of evil by Agatha Christie. The ability to explore evil through art is especially interesting.

Elizabeth Barrett Browning (poet) 3/6/1806
Robert Browning (poet) 5/7/1812
Henrik Ibsen (playwright) 3/20/1828
Lewis Carroll (writer, mathematician) 1/27/1832
Eleanor Roosevelt (U.S. first lady, humanist) 10/11/1884
D. H. Lawrence (writer) 9/11/1885
T. S. Eliot (poet, playwright) 9/26/1888
Agatha Christie (mystery writer) 9/15/1890
Buckminster Fuller (design engineer) 7/12/1895
Jean-Paul Sartre (philosopher, playwright) 6/21/1905
Samuel Beckett (playwright) 4/13/1906
Jean Genet (playwright) 12/19/1910
Jackson Pollock (artist) 1/28/1912
Michelangelo Antonioni (filmmaker) 9/29/1912
Richard Nixon (U.S. president) 1/9/1913
Mike Wallace (TV commentator) 5/9/1918
Aleksandr Solzhenitsyn (writer) 12/11/1918
Isaac Asimov (biochemist, sci-fi writer) 1/2/1920
Federico Fellini (filmmaker, writer) 1/20/1920
Ray Bradbury (sci-fi writer) 8/22/1920
Elizabeth Kübler-Ross (writer on dying) 7/8/1926
Harold Pinter (playwright) 10/10/1930
James Dean (actor) 2/8/1931
Ram Dass (Richard Alpert) (spiritual teacher) 4/6/1931
Francis Ford Coppola (filmmaker) 4/7/1939

The Minor Arcana 6s

The 6s show how to sustain relationships. They are the gifts and challenges that those in the constellation of the Lovers must face in relating to others and the world around them. All the Minor Arcana 6s, which, in the Golden Dawn system, represent the best of their suit, seek a reciprocal balance of energies.

6 of Wands: Fixed Fire, 10°–20° Leo; August 2–11

The 6 of Wands represents the gift of victory that can come from working with others to achieve a goal. Both the leader and the followers are victorious. From the struggle of ideas in the 5 of Wands there emerges a dominant theme and a leader. But the leader can do nothing without the support and backing of the followers. This shows the necessary reciprocal relationship that exists between any leader and followers, between the chairman and the committee, if they are to succeed.

This card shows the self-confidence and pride that comes from creatively solving a problem. When your work is recognized, you feel elevated above those around you. But your pride can make you forget where you came from and those who helped you get where you are.

When you have skills or influence that can assist others, you have a responsibility to be of service to them, using your abilities to bring victory to all concerned. In making your choices, you need to consider whether you act out of love, which takes you to freedom through understanding, or out of fear, which takes you to guilt and bondage.

6 of Cups (November 2–12, 10°–20° Scorpio, Fixed Water)

The 6 of Cups represents the exchange of love and pleasure that two people can bring to each other. You take advantage of your opportunities to let dear ones know how you feel. Don't hold back, or you will regret it at some later time.

You are a romantic who will always fall for the hearts-and-flowers routine. You enjoy being showered with love and are hungry for tender words and a caring touch.

After the disappointment and hurt of the 5 of Cups, the 6 of Cups poses the real test. Are you willing to accept an apology, forgive, and let go of your pain? Can you be the one to ask first for forgiveness? Are the memories of your happiness together strong enough to sustain you through separations? Those with the Lovers for their Personality or Soul Card must learn to love with the trust and receptivity of a child.

6 of Swords (January 30–February 8, 10°–20° Aquarius, Fixed Air)

The 6 of Swords represents the gift of support in adversity. It is the ability to stick with someone when their luck has run out, or to help them through difficult times and transitions to new phases. It is also the challenge of maintaining personal perspective and mental tranquility during times of turmoil.

This card indicates that you must be willing to "cross the water" to see the other person's point of view. In resolving arguments you must "lay all the swords on the table" in order to achieve clarity and unruffled communications. When caught up in the obsessions, fears, and panic of the Devil, you need to make your way to someplace (inner or outer) where you can clear your mind and order your thoughts. In situations in which there has been mental or physical abuse, you need distance and support to gain perspective. With distance it is possible to rise above the particular situation so that you can begin to see the larger pattern and determine some meaning behind it and what actions are necessary. There are times when you must leave others behind, to break through relationship patterns that obsess and bind you.

6 of Pentacles (May 1–10, 10°–20° Taurus, Fixed Earth)

The 6 of Pentacles offers the gift of success in relationships, achieved through generosity of spirit and sharing your resources. Each person's wants and needs must be considered equally. At its best, love gives you a feeling of abundance that you share magnanimously, with no fear of running out. Benevolence is an infinitely renewable resource.

Many of our personal as well as global relationships are based on dynamics between those who have and those who don't. Doling out your attentions, promises, "sexual favors," or finances can be a manipulative means of keeping people bound to you. Your challenge is to give with no conditions, according to your ability, and contrariwise, to receive what is freely given. Only then will you find true stability and security in your relationships.

When success is measured in terms of what you give, everyone shares in it. When it is measured in terms of what you get, then you are chained to the need for more.

THE TOWER.

THE CHARIOT.

The Constellation of the Chariot

CHAPTER 11

The Constellation of the Chariot
16–7

The Tower (16)
The Chariot (7)

7 of Wands	7 of Cups
7 of Swords	7 of Pentacles

The Principle of Mastery through Change

The Chariot

Astrological Correspondence:	Cancer
Card Functions within the Constellation:	Mastery; Controlled and Directed Energy

The Tower

Astrological Correspondence:	Mars
Card Functions within the Constellation:	Breakthrough; Illuminating Energy Unleashed

Soul Archetype: Hero; Warrior; Quest; Power-Over

Keywords: Starting. Causing. Stimulating. Controlling. Breakthrough. Self-Development. Insight. Building Up and Letting Go. Conflict and Trials.

If you are a Single 7 (7-7), read:

> The Chariot (7) as Personality or Soul Card
> The Tower (16) as Hidden Factor
> Famous Single 7s
> The Minor Arcana 7

If you are a 16-7, read:

> The Chariot (7) as Personality or Soul Card
> The Tower (16) as Personality Card
> Famous 16-7s
> The Minor Arcana 7s

The Chariot (7) as Personality or Soul Card

(This applies if you are a Single 7 or a 16-7.)

Mastery, Controlled and Directed Energy

The Chariot represents self-mastery and control and thus victory. It is a card relating to Cancer, but Aleister Crowley calls it Mars in Cancer, which gives a better description of the contrary energies found here. The Chariot is like the crab in his shell, armored and protected so that his soft inner emotions and intuitions are not exposed. On the other hand, he is posed outwardly as the dynamic protector of others, the warrior who fearlessly drives to meet his opponent. With the Chariot, you are both the warrior and the crab.

You take your job and other personal roles very seriously. For instance, if you are a businessperson, you cloak yourself in an executive suit as if it were the charioteer's armor. After work, you change clothes to portray yourself as a party or sports person. You are not afraid of danger but rather of someone getting under your skin. You have an outward appearance that says you can take care of yourself. However, you're prone to being annoyed or distracted and may have a chip on your shoulder, as the moons on the charioteer's shoulders suggest.

You like being in the driver's seat, exerting control over situations, ready to conquer. With your mind firmly fixed on your destinations, you move quickly and surely toward them. Without a sense of purpose, you can get mired down and become inflexible. Unexpected events and emotional scenes are disrupting. You wear your armor to protect yourself from a fall or from criticism or to keep others from knowing your true feelings.

You have high ideals and can elevate your consciousness above the mundane. Your motivating force comes from your questioning mind, just as the sphinx was known to question travelers. You are always looking to find the answers. Your emotions and instincts are often in conflict about which direction to take, so it is only through the firm use of your will, focused on your goal, that you are able to harness your conflicting perspectives to move forward. Sometimes it seems as though your conflicts and feelings could tear you apart.

With Cancer as your astrological Significator, you have strong roots in your family, your people, and your country. You see yourself as their defender. Although you like to travel, you still keep connected to your source. Your roots provide nurturance, security, and a comforting flow of feelings. Yet you must move outward to prove yourself and develop your own mastery. So while part of you wants to keep the values and ideals of your origins, another part urges you toward self-development and individuation.

Many of your tasks involve tearing up old foundations that are inconsistent with new ideas, or confronting and destroying whatever stands in the way of "progress."

As a 7, you have a "breakthrough" consciousness, the ability to see old things in exciting new forms and thus revive their usefulness. You tear down whatever cannot be shaped into new concepts. Your sphinxes (or horses in some decks) pull in two different directions, perhaps between the desire for progress and the desire to leave things intact. You are not passive when challenged, but will fight back and move forward with audacity.

Eventually you need to establish equilibrium, so that all parts of yourself are properly harnessed, with your will holding the reins. Your task is to develop a firm identity keyed to an inner guiding principle. Some form of meditation or centering practice, perhaps a martial art, will help you in doing this.

The Tower (16) as Hidden Factor

(*This applies if you are a Single 7.*)

With the Tower as your Hidden Factor, you are afraid of being thrown off course, losing control, or otherwise being left vulnerable and unprotected. Changes in midcourse or abandonment of plans can shake you to your very roots. Then you dig in until you can assess the damage. You either lose your temper frequently to let off steam or control your feelings so tightly that you think you never get angry.

You may be afraid of your own fury and what you might do if you express it. On the other hand, you may have unconsciously discovered that displaying your anger is an effective way of breaking up resistance, although you would deny it is a *modus operandi*. Sometimes 7s have an out-and-out violent temper, released when their normal controls are affected by drinking, drugs, or emotional upheaval.

When opinions or work have to be thrown out, you might lose your temper, but it also clears the way for you to begin building anew. You are afraid that people may see through your armor, possibly exposing you as a hypersensitive wimp. As the Tower becomes your teacher, you will welcome the opportunity to rebuild a more appropriate "front."

You keep sexual release tightly under control and can learn to direct and focus energies through tantric practices. Or contrariwise, you prove your virility by directed sexual prowess. War and sex, anger and passion stimulate you, but your task is to direct them always to a higher purpose. Learning patience with your own impetuosity is important.

Ultimately, you learn to respect power and recognize the need to release it through anger or lightning insights. Attempting to stop these disintegrative forces will only lead to personal disaster or to becoming totally rigid. Because you are goal focused, you may not realize the extent to which you built up an inflexible inner structure. Then you need either a flash of insight or some kind of shock that releases you from the prison of yourself.

As the Tower becomes your teacher, you learn to channel its light as a healing force. You also learn to accept your defeats and clear out the debris of what is no longer necessary. Whether you do this through a cleansing fast, a housecleaning, by throwing out old clothes that represent old roles and personalities, or by letting go of people and places that are not good for your continuing development, it is necessary to further your quest for self-mastery.

Often, it is a devastating Tower experience, either for yourself or others, that gets you angry and riled up enough to become a warrior for a cause, a spokesperson for or protector of a person or situation in need. Such a situation can prove to be your finest hour.

Famous Single 7s

You might say a key phrase for this relatively small sampling is "no one tells me what to do." On my list there are two members of the Hermetic Order of the Golden Dawn (GD), whose tarot tradition this book follows. Hermann Hesse stands out for his archetypal quest novels. Most of these people were notorious for their disruptive attitudes and shattering of social conventions, as well as for their highly individualistic lifestyles. Johnny Depp admitted to identifying strongly with his pirate character, Captain Jack Sparrow, a disruptive but masterful adventurer if there ever was one.

Erik Satie (composer) 5/17/1866
Marcel Proust (writer) 7/10/1871
Gertrude Stein (writer, patron of arts) 2/3/1874
Aleister Crowley (occultist, tarotist) 10/12/1875
Hermann Hesse (writer) 7/2/1877
Paul Foster Case (occultist, tarotist) 10/3/1884
Rocky Marciano (boxer) 9/1/1923
Niki de Saint Phalle (artist, filmmaker, tarotist) 10/29/1930
Saddam Hussein (Iraqi president) 4/28/1937
Nancy Pelosi (politician) 3/26/1940
Bruce Lee (actor, martial artist) 11/27/1940
Deepak Chopra (writer) 10/22/1946
Hajo Banzhaf (tarotist) 5/15/1949
James Cameron (filmmaker) 8/16/1954
Diana Spencer (Princess of Wales) 7/1/1961
Johnny Depp (actor) 6/9/1963
Julia Roberts (actor) 10/28/1967
Carrie Underwood (country singer) 3/10/1983
Taylor Swift (country singer) 12/13/1989

The Tower (16) as Personality Card

(*This applies if you are a 16-7.*)

Breakthrough, Illuminating Energy Unleashed

The Tower represents insight that strikes your crown and shatters whatever is rigid and unyielding. It represents the natural disasters in your life that move you to constantly build new and more appropriate structures or to find a haven out of the storm. As a 16-7, you weather these storms well, because you have to. You often find yourself up against great odds and acting counter to public opinion, and yet you continue with determination. As 16-7 Dostoevsky scornfully said, "Taking a new step, uttering a new word, is what people fear most." You have strong force of character, are willing to be an individual, and can take abuse without letting it dissuade you from your task. You take upsets in stride. You are looking for the big breakthroughs and know that if you shirk your task, they will never happen.

Often major changes in your life circumstances catapult you into a whole new direction or change the circumstances of your life. Your way is filled with adrenalin and emotional ups and downs that the Chariot Self tries to control.

You are able to cut through all opposition, and you burn through your tasks. Like Thomas Huxley, a 16-7, you believe that "The great end of life is not knowledge but action" (from his essay "Technical Education"). You are not afraid to show anger and don't bother to hide your temper, realizing that its expression is healthy and clears the air quicker than holding it in.

With a nighttime Personality Card, 16-7s contain their own shadow in the qualities of the Tower. Your shadowy aspects are pride, arrogance, and a belief that you are beyond the rules that govern others. Your towering intellect and drive to the heights of ambition are fraught with the risk of setting you up for a fall. You might come to feel yourself a victim—innocent but punished nonetheless. Your personal intensity and passion and your urge to "burn the candle at both ends" can exhaust you, leaving you depressed and alienated.

Still, you have the potential to learn to use the force of light for healing. And you can be a ray of inspiration, a beacon for others to follow.

Famous 16-7s

Examples of famous 16-7s include many scientists who've tried to plumb the depths of the unseen universe: Pasteur, Huxley, Rhine, Reich, and Hawking. Daguerre tried to "fix" the flash of light that creates a photograph. Others were concerned with the relationship between individual and cultural neurosis and how to release pent-up energies without pathological or destructive results. Thomas cried out in a poem to his father, "Do not go gentle into that good night / Rage, rage against the dying of the light." Then there is the strange trinity of Arthur Miller, Marilyn Monroe, and John F. Kennedy.

Christopher Columbus (explorer) 10/31/1451
Louis Daguerre (inventor, photographer) 11/18/1787
George Eliot (writer) 11/22/1819
Fyodor Dostoevsky (writer) 11/11/1821
Louis Pasteur (chemist) 12/27/1822
Thomas Huxley (biologist) 5/4/1825
Emily Dickinson (poet) 12/10/1830
William Morris (writer, artist) 3/24/1834
Pyotr Tchaikovsky (musician, composer) 5/7/1840
Paul Gaugin (artist) 6/7/1848
C. C. Zain (tarotist, Church of Light Tarot) 12/12/1882
Walter Gropius (architect) 5/18/1883
Herman Goering (German politician) 1/12/1893
J. B. Rhine (parapsychologist) 9/29/1895
Wilhelm Reich (psychiatrist, biophysicist) 3/24/1897
George Gershwin (composer) 9/26/1898
Ansel Adams (photographer, environmentalist) 2/20/1902
Joseph Campbell (mythographer) 3/26/1904
Dylan Thomas (poet) 10/27/1914
Arthur Miller (playwright) 10/17/1915
John F. Kennedy (U.S. president) 5/29/1917
Marilyn Monroe (actor) 6/1/1926
Andy Warhol (pop artist, filmmaker) 8/6/1928
Johnny Cash (musician, songwriter) 2/26/1932
Stephen Hawking (physicist) 1/8/1942
Muhammad Ali (boxer) 1/17/1942

The Minor Arcana 7s

The Minor Arcana 7s are the gifts and challenges for developing self-mastery, breaking through obstacles, and dealing with anger. Since the number 7 relates to initiation, the minor 7s represent the trials and tests that must be passed to prove yourself. They show how you seek dominion over your environment. They are the ordeals over which you triumph, using the potentials inherent in the Chariot and the Tower.

7 of Wands (August 12–22, 20°–30° Leo, Fixed Fire)

The 7 of Wands represents the need to test your mettle, to prove yourself in combat, against competition, or when facing impediments. Only then will you know whether you have mastered your lessons. Your gift is having the nerve, sense of purpose, and determination to meet such challenges. It is a willingness to stand up to opposition without backing down. When you are fired up about something, you speak your ideas and stand up for your values. You have the courage to face odds and overcome obstacles. Your opponents test your limitations, but you build your mastery.

When you achieve a position of leadership like that pictured in the 6 of Wands, there will always be others who crop up to challenge you. The 7 of Wands depicts such competition: It is the jealousy of others who want what you have. As a warrior, you will encounter situations in which it seems everyone is against you. You need to be realistic about the odds you face and not let rage back you into a corner. Set your sights on where you want to place your next mark.

7 of Cups (November 13–22, 20°–30 Scorpio, Fixed Water)

The 7 of Cups represents your ability to conjure up visions, fantasies, and dreams. You are able to visualize possibilities, seeing them clearly in your mind. This card shows you trying to choose a single goal from among several options—each with their own dangers and rewards. With your skills and abilities so well developed, you now have to decide where to use them. In your mind, you explore the potentials, but you need to beware of slipping into unrealistic dreams.

The challenge lies in allowing yourself to experience your emotions—to know what you really want but at the same time not get caught up in fantasies. At the extreme, you may wallow in indecision or let your emotions swamp you. Your test here is to look at your deepest desires and then choose one upon which to focus. Allowing them all to draw your attention will eventually tear you apart. Or you may choose, only to find your choice vanish like smoke. You need to learn to recognize which goals have enough meaning and power to sustain you.

7 of Swords (February 9–18, 20°–30° Aquarius, Fixed Air)

The 7 of Swords indicates that you have wit and cunning, with the ability to create plans and stratagems. When the odds seem to be against you, you find a way to disarm the enemy. You can also take the potential sting out of a situation by forethought and preparation, using your ability to take care of details.

Since you are able to outthink others, your challenge is to use such abilities honorably. Being so goal oriented, you may come to believe that the end justifies the means. If so, you can then find yourself involved in stealing, lying, scams, and "con jobs," possibly even with the best of intentions. When dealing upfront seems futile, you think it justified to sneak around. When you get angry, you can become vindictive. As a test of your mastery, this card can mean "counting coup": doing something daring that proves your bravery, skill, speed, and cunning. By applying mental energy to every task, you prepare the ground for later action.

7 of Pentacles (May 11–20, 20°–30° Taurus, Fixed Earth)

The 7 of Pentacles indicates that no matter what you do, there is a certain point at which you have to wait for the results. You must allow the fruit to ripen in its own time. While you wait, thoughts arise of sudden storms or other disasters that can destroy all your work. So your challenge is to face and move through the self-doubts that raise your fear of failure and your apprehension that your work will be for nothing.

This card also refers to the responsibility for being the reaper, cutting off the fruit for some personal purpose. Even in the face of such overwhelming odds as man versus Nature, you still seek to submit these elemental forces to your labors and your will. To do this you must calculate the odds and sow the seeds most likely to grow. But, ultimately, you must let go of your expectations and cultivate patience.

THE STAR.

STRENGTH.

The Constellation of Strength

CHAPTER 12

The Constellation of Strength
17–8

The Star (17)
Strength (8)

8 of Wands   8 of Cups
8 of Swords   8 of Pentacles

Principle of Courage and Self-Esteem

Strength	
Astrological Correspondence:	Leo
Card Functions within the Constellation:	Courage of Your Convictions; Acknowledging the Power Within
The Star	
Astrological Correspondence:	Aquarius
Card Functions within the Constellation:	Courage to Be Yourself; Acknowledging the Power from Source

Soul Archetype: Heroine; Enchantress; Animal Helper; Power-Within

Keywords: Self-Confidence. Fate. Perseverance. Power. Force. Kundalini Energy. Hope. Grace. Balance.

If you are a Single 8 (8-8), read:

> Strength (8) as Personality or Soul Card
> The Star (17) as Hidden Factor
> Famous Single 8s
> The Minor Arcana 8s

If you are a 17-8, read:

> Strength (8) as Personality or Soul Card
> The Star (17) as Personality Card
> Famous 17-8s
> The Minor Arcana 8s

If you see 8 as Justice, read:

> Justice as the Number 8

Strength (8) as Personality or Soul Card

(This applies if you are a Single 8 or a 17-8.)

Courage of Your Convictions, Acknowledging the Power Within

Strength represents the balance and integration of opposites. Like the Magician, the woman in this card has the lemniscate (infinity sign) over her head. She is the female magician or witch, sometimes called the enchantress because of her ability to charm the beasts and animals. Her power to do this comes from a recognition of the similarities in their natures rather than the differences. She exemplifies how we can accomplish anything we set our minds to by acknowledging our linkage with the world and working *in harmony with its principles.* Strength represents being attuned to Nature, not denying it.

She demonstrates the belief that Will and Desire are not at odds and shows that they can work together. By gentling the wild animal within rather than "breaking it," its will is not subjugated and its spirit remains free. A quote from the *Tao De Ching* shows the difference between the constellations of the Chariot and that of Strength: "One of courage, with audacity, will die. One of courage, but gentle, spares death. From these two kinds of courage arise harm and benefit." To draw from Hemingway, Strength's courage is "grace under pressure."

As a witch/enchantress with an astrological relationship to Leo, you are an overtly emotional person. Part of your task is to understand your emotions, not suppress them. Your passionate feelings can be used to charge your hopes with the energy that will actualize them. You need to express yourself in your own unique way, allowing the zest, vitality, and vision within you to emerge. This takes courage, for people will try to pressure you into conforming. You have to struggle between your own inner needs and the demands of work and society.

You are a midwife, which means you are "with the wife" at the birth, assisting in that natural, inevitable process. You are also the one in labor. You know that life force moves through you with a great surge of energy, and through your breathing and pushing, you simply work with and become part of those natural forces. You are a healer who assists the body's own mechanisms in maintaining health. You know about working with your own resources and are instinctively aware of your regenerative abilities. Trusting in the power of love and the healing qualities of touch, you do not shy from direct contact with whatever needs your understanding.

As your soul purpose, Strength means that you must engage your heart in whatever you create. Therefore, you must learn self-acceptance and come to terms with your nature. As in the many myths and stories where wild animals come to the aid of a heroine, you need to let your instincts play a part in whatever you do. If you are to have the fortitude to express yourself and use your abilities, you must learn to love what society may call ugly or ungainly in yourself. Face your fears by expressing them. Look bravely at the worst that can happen. Often, once the "worst" is voiced, you can see that behind its dreadful aspect it is endurable, if not beneficial.

You are a survivor. Your inherent lust for life is felt by others as steadfast strength and perseverance, and as never letting the odds get you down. In any struggle, you have the advantage of being able to empathize with your adversaries so that you know what they are feeling and thinking. You also recognize that life's jailers and murderers are your shadow Self and that, by hating them, you become them. By learning to love what you fear in yourself, you begin to befriend it and find the strength to endure.

When you refuse to give voice to your emotions, they burst upon you unawares, breaking bonds in a destructive way or resulting in sins of passion. Your unexamined feelings can swallow you whole, making you fearful of life itself. At its worst, Strength becomes caught in a battle with life that is perceived as overwhelming and frightening. Or, you refuse to take responsibility for the effects of your passions, thinking that your own feelings are all that count, resulting in self-centeredness and isolation.

You can be calm and collected in emergencies, for you possess an instinctive understanding that showing fear is dangerous. Instead, you use firmness and gentleness to handle the situation, first calming the panic, then examining the needs.

While the Chariot focuses on progress, Strength seeks to cultivate and civilize. As with the feeding and pruning of a rose garden, you cultivate your desires and, with perseverance, produce rewarding results. Like using a waterfall to generate electricity, you civilize by changing raw energy into power for work.

Some people can readily identify with the "power of love" and the giving of oneself to the forces of life, but others project this outside of themselves, on to the image of another, seeing that person as "fascinating." This has become part of the myth of the female enchantress. For instance, for men with this image in mind, there is a fear of women and their life-giving power, as well as a fascination: an attraction/repulsion impulse that sees women as either devouring and overwhelming or as soothing and humanizing. This fascination frightens these men so that they want to run away but can't. They either idealize women or characterize them as bitches; if the latter, they fear the feminine within themselves. It is from such paranoia that the horrors of the witch-burnings arose.

Justice as the Number 8

If you see the Justice card as embodying the number 8, then the focus of this constellation is on cooler, more intellectual characteristics such as those found in the corresponding air signs Libra and Aquarius. This is still the constellation of the visionary and innovator. An idealistic desire for social justice is more defined, along with a draw to social activism and humanitarian causes. The Star's vision of universal rights becomes the inspiration for action but may get lost in abstract principles. Truth, justice, and integrity serve as the basis of your convictions and self-esteem. The Star's sense of personal destiny involves turning hopes and ideals into the soul's need for a higher justice. Reason is seen here as the basis of the urge to cultivate, civilize, and conserve, rather than arising from instinct and desire. If you are a Single 8, then issues of justice and injustice and of maintaining one's natural rights become paramount.

Star (17) as Hidden Factor

(*This applies if you are a Single 8.*)

With the Star as your Hidden Factor, you tend to hide your bright shadow from yourself. That is, you don't acknowledge your own abilities and accomplishments, or you fear that you lack purpose. Or, you may go to the other extreme and insist on being the "star of the show." How you handle your charisma or lack of it is a central theme. You could think yourself superior to others and may rage when they don't appreciate your vision and achievements. You feel insulted when called on to perform menial tasks. Nonetheless, perseverance and integrity will keep you going even when you don't yet understand the reason behind it.

Like the witches of history, you may feel you have to hide your true Self and not let your power show (represented by keeping your hair bound and out of sight). You cannot see your own good qualities, believing yourself to be ugly and graceless, while admiring the beauty of others. You may be unsure of your own abilities to heal or to be creative.

You may fear squandering your emotions or wasting your energy. This can manifest as hypochondria—being plagued by ailments because you are unable to see yourself as whole and healthy. You sometimes lack objectivity and distance from your feelings so that your own emotions color everything. You may believe only what your senses tell you, becoming insular and landlocked.

The worst fear associated with the Star as a Hidden Factor is a lack of hope and lack of belief in the future. This is expressed in pessimism and self-doubt. Yet the positive force of the Star is so powerful that most 8s learn to overcome such doubts.

The Star as your teacher shines out in the darkest of times. It becomes a drive to bring hope into the world and a need to help others recognize and develop their highest capabilities. It awakens a rage against injustice and a dedication to preserving life and our natural resources. You come to believe strongly in the future and wish to leave something for the generations that follow. The Star urges you to follow your instincts and embrace your fears.

Famous Single 8s

There are few Single 8s on my list of famous people, but they are becoming more abundant as we progress through the 21st century. Many of them encouraged the development of one's own natural abilities beyond what was thought possible at the time.

> Ludwig van Beethoven (composer) 12/16/1770
> Edgar Cayce (psychic, healer) 3/18/1877
> Orville Wright (aviator) 8/19/1871
> Grace Slick (musician) 10/30/1939
> Joe Namath (football player) 5/31/1943
> Paulo Coelho (metaphysical writer) 8/24/1947
> Condoleeza Rice (diplomat) 11/14/1954
> Maharaji Ji (spiritual teacher) 12/10/1957
> Zac Efron (actor) 10/18/1987

The Star (17) as Personality Card

(*This applies if you are a 17-8.*)

Courage to Be Yourself, Acknowledging the Power from Source

The Star represents hope in a vision of the future. As the card that follows the Tower, it shows the individual freed from all masks and restrictions, being replenished by the waters of the unconscious. It represents the regeneration of life after the Great Flood. The card pictures Isis Unveiled, sky-clad, using the elements to link the purposes of heaven and earth: "As above, so below." She is both Earth and Star Goddess fully revealed, signaling the rise of the waters of the Nile, bringing fertility to the land and hope to the people.

As a card relating to Aquarius, the Star means that 17-8s are innovative. You are way ahead of your time, an inventor and visionary. As an experimenter, you are willing to try anything at least once. As a visionary, you are able to see possibilities far in the future or off in the distance, yet you don't always know how to relate them to the here and now or to your immediate circumstances. For instance, you can envision a way for us to have peace and happiness on the planet but may have trouble keeping peace with your neighbor.

One of your major learning tasks as a 17-8 is to reveal yourself and be receptive. It is only through the uninhibited expression of your hopes and visions, when you are stripped clean of all pretensions, that you can begin living out your destiny unimpaired.

As a 17-8, your sense of destiny or fate is very strong. When you look in the mirror, you see not only yourself but also a reflection of something much larger than yourself, a feeling of personal fate as part of a universal design. William Wordsworth, a 17-8, knew this when he said "There's not a man that lives who hath not known his godlike hours" (in "The Prelude"). When you seek to live in accord with that destiny, finding the inner meaning of the events and disasters in your life, you draw from the patterns a font of strength and a sea of potential with which you can inspire others. You may be willing to work for a long-term goal not accessible in your lifetime.

Although you present a cool, even distant, exterior to others, inside you burns the light of inspiration. You are not swayed by your emotions to the same degree as the Single 8s. You have a scientific, objective mind that seeks expression through causes, and a commitment to reflecting society back to itself. Your sense of Self is strongest when identified with something external to and greater than yourself. While the desire for fame and recognition is strong, and you are very ambitious, you prefer being known for your works and causes rather than your personal life.

As the personality aspect of the Enchantress archetype, you are a ritualist, finding that through repetitive actions and personal discipline you perceive order in your world and can experience serenity and a feeling of connectedness with the universe. For this reason, a regular meditation practice, or the opportunity to get away from it all, is helpful. Nature is a source of comfort and healing to you, and 17-8s return that gift with an involvement in ecology or world peace.

With a talent for seeing the inner light and the possibilities inherent in people, you can be inspiring, although you often expect too much of specific individuals' lives; they may feel unworthy of your image of them. The Star represents the focus of your longing for an unattainable goal of perfect happiness.

You have a personal sense of grace, which, when called upon, can spark into charisma. You believe in yourself and your capabilities. When you have been blessed with the recognition and rewards you feel you deserve, you will try to give back some of your gifts to the world, usually through some altruistic cause. You want to help redistribute wealth and resources and succeed in situations that allow you to do so.

With a Nighttime Personality Card, you carry your own shadow within. This manifests when you get so involved in helping others and with ideals of kinship that you can't connect on an individual level. Your concern with causes is seen as a personal issue, inseparable from your sense of Self. You may be extraordinarily sensitive to other people's opinions of you. Oscar Wilde, a 17-8, made a pertinent comment: "There is only one thing in the world worse than being talked about, and that is not being talked about" (from *The Picture of Dorian Gray*).

Another shadow aspect is to be so convinced that there is an abundance of resources that you squander them, mistakenly believing that they will never run out. Or you may believe they are yours to use because the generations that follow will be able to develop new technologies—perhaps out in the stars. Ultimately your lesson is to open yourself to the gentle voice of intuition, which, like the bird on the card, sings the song of your spiritual destiny. Only then will you find personal resources ever renewed and yourself able to bear the scrutiny of public recognition.

Famous 17-8s

Among the 17-8s we find visionaries and inventors, futurists, and innovators. There are also a surprising number of astrologers, tarotists, and neopagans of whom only a few are mentioned.

John Dee (astrologer, alchemist, occultist) 7/13/1527
Mary Wollstonecraft (writer, social philosopher) 4/27/1759
Mary Shelley (writer) 8/30/1797
Brigham Young (Mormon elder) 6/1/1801
Mary Baker Eddy (founder, Christian Science) 7/16/1821
Andrew Carnegie (industrialist, philanthropist) 11/25/1835
Anna Kingsford (Hermeticist, antivivisectionist) 9/16/1846
Alexander Graham Bell (inventor) 3/3/1847
Oscar Wilde (writer) 10/16/1854

Pablo Picasso (artist) 10/25/1881
Eden Gray (tarotist) 6/9/1901
George Orwell (writer) 6/25/1903
Jonas Salk (physician, developed polio vaccine) 10/28/1914
Nelson Mandela (South African president) 7/18/1918
Timothy Leary (neuropsychologist, futurist) 10/22/1920
Paul Newman (actor, philanthropist) 1/26/1925
Stanley Kubrick (filmmaker) 7/26/1928
Yasser Arafat (Palestinian leader) 8/24/1929
Neil Armstrong (astronaut) 8/5/1930
Elizabeth Taylor (actor) 2/27/1932
Bob Dylan (musician, songwriter) 5/24/1941
Aretha Franklin (singer) 3/25/1942
Barbra Streisand (singer, actor) 4/24/1942
Isabel Allende (writer) 8/2/1942
George Harrison (singer, musician) 2/25/1943
Annie Leibovitz (photographer) 10/2/1949
Robin Williams (comedian, actor) 7/21/1951
Vladmir Putin (Russian prime minister) 10/7/1952
Osama bin Laden (Al-Qaeda founder) 3/10/1957

The Minor Arcana 8s

The Minor Arcana 8s are the gifts and challenges relating to developing self-esteem, accessing your potential, and finding and living your personal destiny. Since 8 is the number of balance and renewal of energies, the minor 8s represent the trials and tests that must be passed in order to transform hope into actuality.

8 of Wands (November 23–December 2, 0°–10° Sagittarius, Mutable Fire)

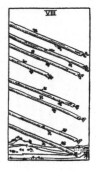

The 8 of Wands represents your ability to express your energies creatively in light of a direction or focus. You dynamically release them toward your goal with the assurance that you will succeed. Your enthusiasm can sweep people off their feet and get them moving with you. Freedom of speech and personal expression is vital to you. When unleashed, your imagination flows unchecked. Such a burst of energy can be felt as an urgency to get moving or as a frenzy of activity. At times you need to gentle these impulses with quiet meditation or an effort of self-control.

To you there is no joy like that of running free or traveling light. You fall in and out of love at the drop of a hat. You probably enjoy new technologies and instantaneous communications. You can get over-enthused and carried away with new ideas or passions, so be careful lest you lose your perspective. Your challenge is to maintain your direction and intent while taking sudden infatuations and new ideas in stride.

8 of Cups (February 19–29, 0°–10° Pisces, Mutable Water)

The 8 of Cups represents the ability to go deep within yourself to regenerate your energies. Your passionate nature and lust for life can lead to overindulgence in sex, alcohol, drugs, or work, to the point of burnout. Then you must find the courage to retreat and heal yourself, even when your loved ones are there to nurture you. You may find that you are dissatisfied with outer fulfillment, recognition, and even demonstrations of affection. You may have plenty of love, care, and support, but there are times when you feel that something is missing, and you don't know what it is. You sense that there is something more that draws you into the unknown. This could be a spiritual search for meaning or for a purpose that is worthy of your total commitment and dedication. Since the Moon is shown full *and* waning (or eclipsed), it seems that you actualized something with the full Moon and now must move on as it fades.

Your basic fortitude and hope for the future are strengths on which others may depend. Some people may be too needy, making you feel manipulated or used without a return of energy. Avoid such a psychic drain; take time out to care for your own needs.

8 of Swords (May 21–31, 0°–10° Gemini, Mutable Air)

The 8 of Swords represents a major challenge to the development of your potentials. You fear success and power, perhaps because of a refusal to accept the beast within. You figuratively blindfold yourself so that you can't see your abilities and then manage to get "tied up" so that your passions won't be loosed. You restrain yourself from activity as a way of avoidance, convincing yourself there are no alternatives.

This card represents a sense of destiny turning into a feeling of choiceless predestination. The swords represent beliefs that keep you hemmed in and reasons why nothing will work. You think you will be swamped by your emotions if you take a step. You hope that a knight in shining armor will rescue you, so you wait. Or you feel only temporarily stuck, or blocked by giving away your power to someone else. The challenge is to realize that you have done this to yourself. The situation shows in a negative way the power of what you can visualize, but you can use that same power to transform the situation. Begin by recognizing *right now* where in your life you *do* have power. Begin with that, for by activating your sense of power in any area, you will be rebuilding self-confidence.

This card indicates tremendous potential for focusing on innovative ideas and then releasing a burst of energy. It is what I call the Houdini card, one that represents backing yourself into a corner. You deliberately get yourself in an apparently impossible situation in order to force a really creative solution. You use your intuition and ingenuity, rather than brute force, to liberate yourself.

8 of Pentacles (August 23–September 1, 0°–10° Virgo, Mutable Earth)

The 8 of Pentacles represents your ability to develop and refine your skill or craft. In the 7 of Pentacles, the work was in doubt; here you are sure of your purpose. When a goal is clearly defined, you keep working on it even if it seems tedious. Some situations call on all your energy to keep going. You might be hoping for things to get better. Still, repetition of activities in a ritualistic way gives you a sense of security. You want to be recognized for your craftsmanship and are willing to undergo an apprenticeship to develop your strengths.

You do things with the belief that they are worth your time and effort. You look forward to the future, plan your moves, and prudently prepare things in advance. This is one form of taking care of yourself and your own needs.

One of the greatest skills of a craftsman is knowing both your medium and your message so well that you work in harmony with their natures, so that they function together at their best.

The Constellation of the Hermit

CHAPTER 13

The Constellation of the Hermit 18–9

The Moon (18)
The Hermit (9)

9 of Wands   9 of Cups
9 of Swords   9 of Pentacles

The Principle of Introspection and Personal Integrity

The Hermit	
Astrological Correspondence:	Virgo
Card Functions within the Constellation:	Completing Karma through Service; Looking Within; The Seeker

The Moon	
Astrological Correspondence:	Pisces
Card Functions within the Constellation:	Completing Karma through Evolution; Journeying Within; The Source

Soul Archetype: Old Wise One; Journey to the Underworld

Keywords: Completion. Perfection. Patience. Integrity. Authenticity. Illusion (Delusions versus Reality). Karma. Culmination. Journey into the Unknown. Prudence. Reason vs. Instinct.

If you are a Single 9 (9-9), read:

The Hermit (9) as Personality or Soul Card
The Moon (18) as Hidden Factor
Famous Single 9s
The Minor Arcana 9s

If you are an 18-9, read:

The Hermit (9) as Personality or Soul Card
The Moon (18) as Personality Card
Famous 18-9s
The Minor Arcana 9s

The Hermit (9) as Personality or Soul Card

(This applies if you are a Single 9 or an 18-9.)

Completing Karma through Service, Looking Within, the Seeker

The Hermit represents introspection, solitude, personal integrity, and prudence. It is a card relating to Virgo and the harvest of the grain. (Some decks include the wheat symbol on the card itself, or show the Hermit as Father Time holding a scythe.) When ripened grain is cut, it is sacrificed so that it can be transformed into bread, feeding and serving others. Yet in spring, the grain, after a dormant period under the earth, will sprout with new life. Thus the Hermit as Soul Card is a metaphor for how you can serve others with the knowledge you have gathered that has ripened and been transformed into a palatable form. Likewise, after the long periods of introspection that you need as a Hermit, you too will emerge with new life.

You need to be alone, to have time to yourself. You feel you must work through your own problems and can only make decisions for yourself, yet you are available to assist others. You always have some feeling of isolation but also an inner strength that comes from facing the unknown alone.

"Showing the way" is your characteristic action, and you will eventually serve as some kind of a teacher or role model for others. Since you are circumspect and discreet, people come to you with their troubles because you don't betray their trust. You know how and when to keep secrets. Your insights into the problems of others help them learn to look within themselves. You teach best by living what you believe in, but you are a perfectionist and may expect others to live up to the same standards. Thus you can be difficult to live with, one of the many isolating factors in your life.

You have strong role models in your own life, and you learn from their actions: not what they say, but what they do. You stand by what you believe in, trusting wisdom that comes from experience and has stood the test of time. This can be a problem if you refuse to take risks or accept anything new. Thus, you can become overcautious, needing to know exactly where you are going, resistant to change, and needing to do things your own way.

Your prudence can make you hesitant with untried solutions and suspicious of iconoclastic behavior. You have no desire to stand out in a crowd or to be flashy or loud. You probably follow social mores and exhibit good manners primarily to escape notice and because it makes the way go smoother. Since you think for yourself, you may actually be quite unconventional, but you are quietly so, preferring to act circumspectly.

Your social detachment and objectiveness draws you to humanitarian service. You project your high ideals into works that will benefit everyone. It is only through such service that you as a Hermit can realize yourself fully. You cannot work successfully for yourself alone, but must act for the benefit of humanity.

Hermits like to travel but usually do so by themselves. Yet your desire for solitude and sobriety hides an exaggerated need for love and personal acceptance. Since you rarely express this need, you may pretend to be emotionally self-sufficient and even rebuff those who attempt to get too close as a test to see if they really care.

You have mediumistic gifts and psychic abilities that are of primary importance to your quest for inner understanding, but you like to appear logical and fact oriented, and you take pride in an analytical approach to problem solving. This is a well-developed and possibly unconscious ploy to cover up an almost instinctive awareness of situations. Although your intuitions cannot be explained, you eventually learn to trust them.

As the last of the prime numbers, 9 represents completion. Thus, Hermits usually have something to complete in this lifetime. You have the wisdom of many previous incarnations, which may emerge as easily developed talents and skills. You have little difficulty understanding concepts and probably appeared "older than your years" as a child. Responsibilities and decision making are thrust on you quite early by your parents—or you impatiently want to be allowed to go your own way. You are here in this lifetime to share what you have learned and thus release it so that you can continue your own development unencumbered by old tasks.

Thus, many Hermits feel that they have a "purpose" and decide on a direction early in life. You have strong creative energies, especially for synthesis, which you apply to definite goals. You plan thoroughly and can clearly visualize the results you want.

You are likely to have friends and relatives whom you feel you've known for more than a lifetime. However, you can also easily release old relationships, so don't be surprised by your ability to make deep connections for a short period and then move on without looking back.

Hermits find it hard to ask others for assistance because their natural tendency is to turn within. Yet by allowing others to assist you, you teach while at the same time letting go of any limiting sense of self-importance.

Periodically, you will need to turn away from the outer concerns of life. This is in order to consolidate knowledge for completing the task at hand. This task involves looking within, no longer projecting onto others, and simply accepting yourself. A 9, mathematically as well as personally, always returns to itself.

The Moon (18) as Hidden Factor

(*This applies if you are a Single 9.*)

With the Moon as your Hidden Factor, you have some deeply hidden emotions and an inability to see part of yourself—perhaps because you fear that your feelings and psychic abilities will overwhelm you. There can be latent alcoholism or dependency on drugs and mind-altering substances, supported by denial of your blind spots. However, Maurice Maeterlinck, a Single 9, accepted this, saying, "Men's weaknesses are often necessary to the purpose of life" (from *Joyzelle*).

Your shadow reveals its presence by the feeling that there is something inside you, something much bigger than yourself—and you are not sure if it even belongs to you. You feel an unfulfilled urge to be doing something. Somewhere, something is calling to you, but you can't see it. By comparison, everyone else will seem to know just where they are going and what they are doing. You will probably feel confused until you chance upon a goal or task that suddenly feels right. Or you may experience what appears to be a series of coincidences and then find yourself moving swiftly in unplanned directions. Eventually you learn to trust this process.

You tend to be suspicious of others and fear that people are talking behind your back or that they don't really like you. Thus, you may affect an exterior attitude of not caring about anything. Actually you are very sensitive. You hunger to be liked and accepted. Wanting to please those about whom you care, you reflect what they are looking for, and then you don't understand if they later say you're not being honest.

As the Moon becomes your teacher, you learn to trust in some inner guiding process. You realize that the walls between you and other levels of awareness are very thin. Finally you come to realize that your earlier suspicions were other people's self-conscious fears and anxieties, acutely sensed, even when not directed at you. Eventually, you develop compassion and understanding for the human condition. You recognize the suffering that others feel and find ways to alleviate it.

You may have a strong interest in the occult and in reclaiming hidden traditions. You intuitively understand symbolism and may have mystic experiences, especially if you are religiously inclined. Your psychic gifts and strong ability to visualize, if developed, enable you to help others access their own inner worlds. You can be a mirror reflecting the hopes, needs, and visions of a group of people. Being very suggestive yourself, you can influence individuals around you, reflecting what they find unable to express. Thus, you can act as a catalyst for people. This is a potent ability that can have unforeseen results when unconsciously activated, but it can be consciously channeled to the public good, especially to bring out unexpressed currents and intentions.

Famous Single 9s

While there are not enough Single 9s below to see clear trends, there is an suggestion of individuals unexpectedly rising out of obscurity to show the world the wisdom and vast potential of the scorned and disenfranchised. There will be far more of these people born during the first half of the 21st century.

Diego Velázquez (artist) 6/6/1599
George Handel (musician, composer) 2/23/1685
Maurice Maeterlinck (writer, playwright) 8/29/1862
Maud Gonne (revolutionary, magician) 12/21/1866
Imogen Cunningham (photographer) 4/12/1883
Zora Neale Hurston (writer) 1/7/1891
Evonne Goolagong (tennis player) 7/31/1951
Hugo Chávez (Venezuelan president) 7/28/1954
Scott Cunningham (witch, writer) 6/27/1956
Lance Armstrong (cyclist) 9/18/1971

The Moon (18) as Personality card

(*This applies if you are an 18-9.*)

Completing Karma through Evolution, Journeying Within, the Source

The Moon represents intuition and delving deep into the unconscious, where the veils between worlds are very thin. With this influence we become aware that reality is a dream, that time and space (as well as our physical bodies) are merely conceptions, and therefore all can be changed. Moon-Hermits don't have abilities that the rest of humanity lacks; they just are more curious about them. As an 18-9, you are fascinated by the unseen and the unknown, the strange and even the macabre.

The Moon relates to past lives, to magic and mystery. It involves working with hidden forces and factors and learning to function in the realm of the subconscious. Imagine yourself at night on a forest path during the dark of the Moon; you can either make your way slowly along the path, stumbling as you go, or, by drawing on your intuitive sense of where you are going, you can run swiftly and surely without needing to see your way. This is activating a sense of inner knowing that Hermits must learn to trust. Your life as an 18-9 tends to revolve in cycles like the phases of the Moon, moving into periods of heightened psychic awareness and a sense of rightness about it and then into periods in which you fear you are being deceived by your insights. You must learn that the cycle has its own natural rhythms. The confusion, illusion, and delusion of the Moon comes in part from trying to do something when it is not the right time in the cycle.

Your purpose as an 18-9 is to evolve into a higher being. You are here to deal with specific karmic responsibilities. These can involve making actual genetic changes to help in the evolution of the human race. This is possible through capabilities biologically and psychically inherent in you as an individual and within the potentialities of all life on the planet. It is through the imagination that you can make subjective experience objective. By mirroring your desire in your mind, you can restructure the particles of energy in order to bring about the outer objective change. You believe, as 18-9 Mohandas Gandhi did, that "the highest law is that we should unremittingly work for the goal of [hu]mankind."

The Moon relates to the use of intuitive functions rather than rational ones. This knowledge is often experienced through the body rather than through the brain. And in ancient writings, the seat of conscious thought was considered to be either in the gut or the heart. Knowledge was something that came from deep within the body—an inner wisdom that people trusted. As the rational faculties developed, intuitive thinking was no longer valued or trained. The Delphic Oracle fell silent. Fewer and fewer people had access to this knowledge, and it came to be distrusted. For the last several thousand years, the world of the unconscious has been seen as a delusional trap. Yet it is only by the marriage of both lunar and solar consciousness that unity of spirit can be born.

The Moon represents divination, whose language is signs and symbols and whose meaning is not always immediately apparent. You need insight and patience, as indicated by your Soul Card, the Hermit. The Moon does not represent deception; it is the "glamour" in which we wrap ourselves that deceives us. You may come to respect the unseen and unprovable experiences of others as valid experiences from which we can learn. And 18-9s have historically unveiled the realities of both our inner and outer lives.

Just as the crayfish in the card devours all that is decomposing and, from this, builds its house, so you realize the importance of digesting your past, your fears, and what you have hidden from yourself in order to experience a moral and psychic regeneration. Accepting your destiny, you leave the crusty shelter that is your past and instinctively take refuge in the pool of your habits. Otherwise you will be caught in nostalgic reveries, in a passive attitude resulting from unfulfilled aspirations. Break out of your shell of old ways of thinking that lock you inside. Pass by your wild desires (the wolf) and your domestic breeding (the dog) and, walking between the towers of lofty thought and human technology, follow the path to the high mountain of spiritual intuition.

Your thinking mind sometimes resists the expansion necessary to take in new concepts. When beyond the control of ordinary perception, there could be a panic reaction that makes you feel as if you're going crazy. This probably indicates entry into new levels of awareness, but it can be most unsettling while you are actually experiencing it. This happens very often to the elderly in our society (who are in a Hermit/Crone developmental stage). They go through rapid changes and expansion in preparation for their crossing, only to be labeled senile as a result.

Famous 18-9s

Diarist Anaïs Nin best characterizes the inner process of an 18-9 in *A Woman Speaks*: "There is the whole mystery of growth, of expansion, of deliverance from the traps which life sets us . . . . Every difficult situation into which you are sometimes thrown has some way of opening somewhere, even if it is only by way of the dream."

You'll find a large number of people with interests in "other realities" and many who became teachers or way-showers through mystical, magical, or psychological realms. There are also a surprising number of writers who could be loosely characterized as "imaginative realists."

Nostradamus (astrologer, physician, prophet) 12/24/1503
Johann S. Bach (composer) 3/31/1685
Dante G. Rossetti (artist, poet) 5/12/1828
John Muir (naturalist) 4/21/1838
Auguste Rodin (sculptor) 11/12/1840
Rudolf Steiner (metaphysician) 2/27/1861

Mohandas Gandhi (Indian leader) 10/2/1869
Frank Lloyd Wright (architect) 6/8/1869
Virginia Woolf (writer) 1/25/1882
Kahlil Gibran (poet) 1/6/1883
Roberto Assagioli (founder, psychosynthesis) 2/27/1888
Robert Graves (poet, writer) 7/24/1895
Henry Moore (sculptor) 7/30/1898
Erich Fromm (psychoanalyst) 3/23/1900
Anaïs Nin (writer, diarist) 2/21/1903
Israel Regardie (metaphysician) 11/17/1907
Mother Theresa (humanitarian) 8/26/1910
Kurt Vonnegut (writer) 11/11/1922
Flannery O'Connor (writer) 3/25/1925
Carlos Castaneda (anthropologist, writer, shaman) 12/25/1925
Allen Ginsberg (poet, publisher) 6/3/1926
Ray Charles (musician) 9/23/1930
Yoko Ono (musician, artist) 2/18/1933
Gloria Steinem (writer, feminist) 3/25/1934
Shirley MacLaine (actor, writer) 4/24/1934
Elvis Presley (musician, actor) 1/8/1935
Bernie Madoff (Ponzi schemer) 4/29/1938
Dustin Hoffman (actor) 8/8/1937
Z. Budapest (witch, writer, feminist) 1/30/1940
Barbara Boxer (politician) 11/11/1940
Jimi Hendrix (musician, singer) 11/27/1942
Angela Davis (revolutionary) 1/26/1944
Bob Marley (musician, songwriter) 2/6/1945
Amory Lovins (environmentalist) 11/13/1947
Benazir Bhutto (Pakistani prime minister) 6/21/1953

Minor Arcana 9s

Minor Arcana 9s are the gifts and challenges relating to developing introspective insight, personal integrity, and completion of our lessons. Since the
number 9 is usually associated astrologically with the Moon or Neptune,
dreams and delusions play a role in these cards.

9 of Wands (December 3–12, 10°–20° Sagittarius, Mutable Fire)

The 9 of Wands presents the opportunity to face your greatest fears with the gift of strength of purpose. You meet your future with an unshakable stance. You are prepared to protect and support others who are in need. You find spiritual strength in facing your fears. With the 9 of Wands, you must complete a spiritual or creative task.

The 9 of Wands also carries a warning that the barriers you have set up to protect you can also become your cage. This concept is a reminder that the Moon corresponds to Pisces, and the symbolic Piscean fish swims both ways.

Rather than completion, this can be a card of following old habits, suggesting inflexibility of outlook. You have risked so much through the previous eight wands that when you come to this one, with its relative safety, you may be afraid to go on. If you fear facing the beasts outside the stockade, you'll be stuck. But the very feeling of being fenced in can force you to the next stage, the 10s, and in the 10 of Wands, the same person has taken down the fence. He is carrying his experiences with him but is no longer afraid to move on.

9 of Cups (March 1–10, 10°–20° Pisces, Mutable Water)

The 9 of Cups presents the opportunity to create your own reality with the gift of creative imagination. You have dipped nine cups into the pool of the unconscious and have successfully faced all terrors to take the path home. Now you know how to come and go from the land of the Moon (the unconscious) with ease. This card represents working with dreams and intuitive techniques. You can visualize what you desire with such clarity that it comes into being.

You have the resources and the knowledge to nurture others along the same path you have traveled.

The problem comes when you begin to think that this is all there is. You become complacent and self-satisfied. Although the tasks are completed, you may not want to move on; you get stuck in sensuality or gluttony, or wrapped up in your fantasies and illusions. This, then, is the vision of Maya (Hindi for "illusion"), that is attributed to the Moon.

9 of Swords (June 1–10, 10°–20° Gemini, Mutable Air)

The 9 of Swords presents the opportunity to grieve, face the demons, or weather the nightmares through the gifts of time and patience. With the 9 of Swords as a Lessons and Opportunities Card, you face the self-cruelty aspects of your idealism and perfectionism. You can find endless faults with yourself, mostly projections of your own fears. Your dreams and memories remind you of the things you should have done or things you once had but now are lost. Also, as a highly empathic 18-9, you might be taking all the sorrows of the world on your shoulders.

And yet, confronting fears and experiencing grief are ways of purging yourself. The 9 of Swords is essential before any process can be complete. You must transform your pain, first by reexperiencing it, then by identifying the source of the emotion in order to know what to change. When you find yourself in the midst of stress or depression, realize that it is part of a larger cycle of events and is usually the last despair of your rational mind before new possibilities break through from the unconscious.

9 of Pentacles (September 2–11, 10°–20° Virgo, Mutable Earth)

The 9 of Pentacles presents the opportunity to complete the "work" of self-development through confidence in your self-discipline and patience. You are in harmony with Nature around you. Just as the grapes will ripen in their own time, you know everything will bear its fruit. Although the woman keeps a hawk to remind her of her instincts and intuitions, she knows to keep such a wild creature hooded when not in use. You are alone here, as you are in each of the other 9s, indicating that you have had to turn to yourself to reap the reward of self-development.

The 9 of Pentacles is called "gain" and indicates everything you can gain from your work and skills, including the luxury of leisure and solitude. Another aspect of this card is the loneliness that can come from cutting yourself off from your emotions and personal contacts. In your struggles to reach the top, you may lose your ability to be wild and free. Do you feel confined in your grape orchard, hooding your desire for free expression (as the bird is hooded), and (as with the gloved hand) keeping your personal contacts at a distance?

CHAPTER 14

Your Year Cards

For each year of your life, you have a card from the Major Arcana called the Year Card. It represents the tests and lessons you experience in any given year. Some Major Arcana cards will appear as your Year Cards over and over, while others you will never get. The events that happen to you in any year offer the opportunity to master new skills and discover more about yourself and your needs. The Year Card points out what that learning will be about. It indicates the kind of archetypal energies that are constelled in that year, suggesting personal qualities you can work with, such as assertion, compassion, and relating. Knowing your Year Card makes you more aware of the overall situation at your disposal and the kinds of learning opportunities it presents during that year.

Your Year Card

Following the example below, add the month and date of your birth to the current year and reduce it to 22 or less.

Month of Birth	8
Day of Birth	26
Current Year	+ 2012
	2048

$2 + 0 + 4 + 8 = 14$ (Temperance)

In determining the Year Card, always keep the highest number under 23 and don't reduce it!

Find your own Year Card by adding:

    The month of your birth: ____

    The day of your birth: ____

    The CURRENT YEAR: + _____

    Equals: _____

    ___ + ___ + ___ + ___   = ____ (Year Number)

For the current year _____, my Year Number is _____, which corresponds to the Major Arcana card: _____.

The Commencement of Tarot Year

You might ask yourself, when does my Year Card begin, on January 1 or on my birthday? The answer is both! There are two different cycles that overlap, to some extent, depending on how late your birthday is in the year. I look at both, but many people prefer to focus on just one of these two cycles, shown in Chart 10 on page 173.

People with birthdays at the beginning through middle of the year will have little trouble using the January-to-January cycle for most purposes. It is easiest to recognize and identify the outer events that happen to you (January to January) rather than your inner motivations and modes of expression (birthday to birthday). Those with birthdays in the last two months might find most of their associations with a card falling in the following calendar year. For instance, at the beginning of a Hermit Year, all your friends seem suddenly unavailable. At parties you can't seem to connect, etc. Thus you are forced into spending more time alone. By your birthday, you've realized how much you can accomplish, as you enjoy the time to complete things and do some reflecting. Then, in January, as you move into a Wheel of Fortune Year (outer events cycle), you are thrown into the whirl of social events and sudden opportunities. You react at first with the prudence and circumspection that you came to trust in your Hermit Year, while wishing that those peaceful moments of solitude would return. By your birthday, you are at home in the whirl.

The Year Card Chart

It is well worth calculating your Year Cards for your entire life: ninety or one hundred years. For this purpose, use Chart 11: The Year Card Chart on page 175, which was designed by Bay Area tarotist Twainhart Hill. It helps you quickly determine your Year Card for any specific year. The chart also makes it easy to find the Birth Cards and Year Cards of your friends. I encourage you to photocopy this chart.

To use the Year Card Chart, add up the month, day, and year of your birth. The sum before you reduce it to your Birth Card number is _____. I call it your four-digit Base Number. Find this number on the chart. Next to it is the number corresponding to your Personality Card; mark this as "zero years old" or "Born." You will not be one year old until the following year. Next, take the four-digit Base Number from your Year Card calculations and find this number on the chart, with your Year Card number next to it. Write your *age on your birthday this year* in the space next to it. From the present year you can easily count backward or forward to see the cards corresponding to those other years.

Chart 10: Year Card Cycles

The January-to-January Cycle—Outer Events
Your year begins on January 1 in terms of *events happening to you.* You then begin to learn the lesson of the year through experiences that require you to face the issues represented. This is an outer, event-oriented cycle.

The Birthday-to-Birthday Cycle—Inner Response and Integration
By your birthday, you have integrated the lessons to the extent that you begin *acting out that energy.* In this way, you have a birthday-to-birthday *inner experience* cycle.

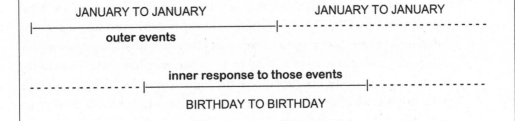

Look at your five previous Year Cards. Lay the cards out on a table or the floor; ask yourself how each of these cards represents lessons you needed to learn in that year. While seemingly simple, this system can tell you a great deal. I am surprised at what I learn about myself just by considering the significance of each card. Each year I dialogue with my Year Card, asking it, "What do I need to learn from you this year?" It may take a while to gain enough perspective to see the real learning. It helps to examine your past cards to see trends that become clear through hindsight. This will also help to refine your foresight in future years.

Make a list of all your Year Cards. Next, write a sentence for each year, telling what happened to you in that year and why it was significant. (Don't worry if there are years in which you remember nothing—that's normal; you'll probably remember something more to add whenever you look at your chart.)

Rather than making predictions for cards in the future, determine where you are in a cycle. For instance, people often make major choices in a Lovers Year (6). In the following year, which is usually a Chariot Year, they act on that choice, focusing on moving ahead along the path set in the previous year. And then in the Strength Year (8), they need to reevaluate whether their heart is still in it. If not, they may lack the fortitude to persevere through the two years until the Wheel of Fortune (10) again brings change.

In the following chapter, I suggest possible meanings for your Year Cards. For more specific information and direct guidance, use the dialogue technique described in chapter 2. Ask the Year Card directly what meaning it has for you and how to obtain the most from your year.

Using the Year Card Chart

If you examine the Year Card Chart, you will notice several interesting things. Because our mathematical system is decimally based, the numbers run in ten-year cycles (although in some cases the single-digit numbers are actually reduced 23s, 24s, and 25s). These ten-year cycles have a line separating them in the chart. So every ten years, you jump to a new cycle of numbers, usually beginning one number higher than the previous cycle. Depending on your age, you may not experience the highest-numbered Major Arcana cards in your lifetime. For instance, after January 1, 1988, there were no more 19-10-1 personalities born, although they had been relatively abundant previous to that. They will begin appearing again after 2069.

Chart 11: Year Card Chart*

Left number = Base number: sum of month, day, and year. Right number = Year Card

1919	20	1960	16	2001	3	2042	8	2083	13
1920	12	1961	17	2002	4	2043	9	2084	14
1921	13	1962	18	2003	5	2044	10	2085	15
1922	14	1963	19	2004	6	2045	11	2086	16
1923	15	1964	20	2005	7	2046	12	2087	17
1924	16	1965	21	2006	8	2047	13	2088	18
1925	17	1966	22	2007	9	2048	14	2089	19
1926	18	1967	5	2008	10	2049	15	2090	11
1927	19	1968	6	2009	11	2050	7	2091	12
1928	20	1969	7	2010	3	2051	8	2092	13
1929	21	1970	17	2011	4	2052	9	2093	14
1930	13	1971	18	2012	5	2053	10	2094	15
1931	14	1972	19	2013	6	2054	11	2095	16
1932	15	1973	20	2014	7	2055	12	2096	17
1933	16	1974	21	2015	8	2056	13	2097	18
1934	17	1975	22	2016	9	2057	14	2098	19
1935	18	1976	5	2017	10	2058	15	2099	20
1936	19	1977	6	2018	11	2059	16	2100	3
1937	20	1978	7	2019	12	2060	8	2101	4
1938	21	1979	8	2020	4	2061	9	2102	5
1939	22	1980	18	2021	5	2062	10	2103	6
1940	14	1981	19	2022	6	2063	11	2104	7
1941	15	1982	20	2023	7	2064	12	2105	8
1942	16	1983	21	2024	8	2065	13	2106	9
1943	17	1984	22	2025	9	2066	14	2107	10
1944	18	1985	5	2026	10	2067	15	2108	11
1945	19	1986	6	2027	11	2068	16	2109	12
1946	20	1987	7	2028	12	2069	17	2110	4
1947	21	1988	8	2029	13	2070	9	2111	5
1948	22	1989	9	2030	5	2071	10	2112	6
1949	5	1990	19	2031	6	2072	11	2113	7
1950	15	1991	20	2032	7	2073	12	2114	8
1951	16	1992	21	2033	8	2074	13	2115	9
1952	17	1993	22	2034	9	2075	14	2116	10
1953	18	1994	5	2035	10	2076	15	2117	11
1954	19	1995	6	2036	11	2077	16	2118	12
1955	20	1996	7	2037	12	2078	17	2119	13
1956	21	1997	8	2038	13	2079	18	2120	5
1957	22	1998	9	2039	14	2080	10		
1958	5	1999	10	2040	6	2081	11		
1959	6	2000	2	2041	7	2082	12		

*Year Card Chart originally designed by Twainhart Hill, based on the work of Angeles Arrien.

Certain numbers or cycles predominate depending on when you were born. Each generation has its own characteristic pattern of Year Card numbers. This represents a stage in the cyclical ebb and flow of what's generally called the Christian or Common Era as defined by the Gregorian calendar. Remember that the Year Cards, like the Personality and Soul Cards, give us a look at ourselves in a mirror colored by the Western Anglo-European-dominated society we live in. Perhaps we need a second spiritual lunar calendar such as the ancient Mayans used, in which to see a clearer reflection of our soul's true potential.

People born in any one year could have any of forty-two possible four-digit Base Numbers, but, depending on the year, these reduce to a far more limited range of cards. For example, people born in 2004 can only have Personality Cards between 3 and 13, or ten of the twenty-two total constellation patterns. Someone born in 1959, or looking at the Year Cards for that year, will have only fifteen possibilites. A person born in 1892 could have any of eighteen possible cards from 5 to 22, but not Single 2s, 3s, or 4s—which did not become possible until January 1, 1957. After 1991 there are no more 19-10-1s or 22-4s until the close of the 21st century. These give us our generational factors.

One example of this generational factor is that many people born between December 31, 1957 and January 1, 1998, had the High Priestess as their Personality Card. Their birthdays added up to 2000! This card has not figured as a Personality or Year Card for the last nine hundred years, since January 1, 1098, CE. She will not appear as a Birth or Year Number again for approximately eight thousand years! She appeared just before a period that was been marked by social myths of our time—for instance, prophecies of native peoples all over the world that this is a time of great transformation and possible destruction. Most of these myths allow for a choice or decision to be made by human beings about how to relate globally in order to save our planet. Some of these prophecies claim that a rise in Goddess consciousness and the conception of the Earth as Gaia was essential for making the right choices during this vulnerable time.

It is interesting the number of contemporary politicians and first ladies who are 20-2s, beginning with Ronald Reagan, Jackie Kennedy Onassis, Tony Blair, Bill Clinton, Al Gore, and Barack and Michelle Obama. Also, Prince Charles is a 20-2, while his son William is of the younger generation of 11-2s. The great danger in 20-2s is that they can foster a "cult of personality" through the media, for which Russian leader Leonid Brezhnev, another 20-2, was noted.

Missing and Most Repeated Year Cards

In a lifetime of eighty or so years, the average person will experience the majority of the Major Arcana as Year Cards. Look through your chart to determine which cards (and therefore lessons) you will *never* experience. These are not necessary for you in this lifetime, representing qualities probably already well developed. Which cards will you receive most often? These are your greatest lessons to learn and probably the most difficult, but you are not alone—your entire generation has a similar focus.

Your Karmic Year

The four-digit Base Number that is the sum of your birth month, day, and year can, itself, be looked at as an important year for you. It represents a year that especially tests and challenges you to develop your potential. I call it your Karmic Year because unfinished issues from the past that express "soul" themes come up in that year, giving you an opportunity to complete them or at least recognize your task and consciously begin the process of completion. Some people have found that their Karmic Year starts them in a new direction or introduces a theme or focus into their lives that takes on a central importance later.

An example of the Karmic Year is pertinent to everyone. According to the Mayan calendar, its Great Cycle of 5,125 years is completed in 2012, which, according to legends, indicates a great shift in world consciousness and communication. It was preceded on August 17, 1987, by what was called the "Harmonic Convergence," described as the moment at which acceleration phased into synchronization in preparation for the galactic climax. If you take this as a birthday and add the digits in 8/17/1987, you get 2012, which is its Karmic Year. Reducing this four-digit number gives us the Hierophant (5). It is, therefore, a year of teaching and learning, of new knowledge revealed. According to this theory, 2012 completes a task that began on the Harmonic Convergence and challenges us to develop a new potential.

Getting in Touch with Your Soul Purpose

Look at your Year Card Chart again. Every ten years, you will have experienced your Personality, Soul, or Hidden Factor Card as a Year Card. Circle these on your chart and note their actual calendar year and your age. During these years, you were probably drawn to and involved in the things that are especially important to your soul purpose in this lifetime. You were probably doing or directly searching for something through which you could express your highest potential. Look at your achievements, actions, travels, relationships, studies—how you spent your time and what you hungered to do. Where did your fantasies and dreams lead you in those years? These are the things that are probably most in line with your soul purpose.

Occasionally, you will find that in one or more of these personally important years, you felt your greatest frustration and pain. This happens when you feel powerless to follow your own needs and instincts or to develop your interests. You might then project your own potentials onto someone else who awes you with their ability, or perhaps you resist their influence and thus reject the qualities and learning that the card represents. This happens when your task seems too powerful for you. When you project your potentials onto a powerful person outside yourself, that person actually indicates the possibilities accessible to you, which you can gradually assimilate and eventually express in your own lifework and personality. Each time your Personality, Soul, or Hidden Factor Card appears as a Year Card—in ten-year cycles—you will have an opportunity to work with the constellated energies of your destiny.

Milestones and Turning Points

To find the significance of any major event in terms of your personal development, look at your Year Card Chart to see when that event took place. Then look at the card for that year to see the nature of its energy. For instance, if you married in a Lovers Year, it would be obvious that you learned about your wants and needs in a relationship and how another person mirrors your own self-image. But people get married under the auspices of all the Year Cards. So, if you were married in an Emperor Year and you are a woman, you might have taken the initiative. You might also have been learning to organize and establish a firm foundation. Or, if you felt uncomfortable asserting yourself, you might have chosen an older father figure as your mate to teach you what the Emperor energy is about. A Wheel of Fortune Year, by comparison, would have emphasized lessons of change and expanding horizons that you experienced as a result of the marriage. The Year Card associated with your marriage or any ongoing commitment will generally characterize your entire involvement in it.

The Age of the High Priestess

On the Year Card Chart, you will find the four-digit Base Number 2000. It marks the beginning of a whole new generational cycle and ushers in a period during which the High Priestess appeared as a Single 2 Birth Card; that is, as both Personality and Soul (instead of in combination with an 11 or a 20). Furthermore, most people who became adults in the second half of the 20th century experienced the High Priestess once in their lives as a Year Card. If you were born after 1998, you will never experience a High Priestess year, but both the 11 Year (Justice or Strength) and the 20 Year (Judgment), which you would get instead, are part of the High Priestess constellation and resonate with her energy.

The premillennium years showed a great reawakening of the Goddess and widespread interest in women's spirituality that ranged from honoring the Goddess in her myriad forms (sometimes called "Isis of a Thousand Faces") to new appearances of the Virgin Mary to renewed interest in Mary Magdalene as the secret consort of Jesus. There was a resounding call to women to enter the priesthood. I found that many women and men experienced significant spiritual awakenings in their High Priestess Year, becoming involved in psychic, intuitive, or healing studies and often first discovering the myths and religion of the Great Goddess during that year.

The Minor Arcana as Year Cards

While the Minor Arcana are not individually described here, they are indicators of the gifts and challenges (lessons and opportunities) you will have in the corresponding year. Lay out cards from the Minor Arcana that correspond to a memorable year in your past. Look at how these cards might

Year _____	Why Memorable _____ _____ _____
Year Card _____	Principle of Its Constellation _____ _____ _____
Minor Arcana Cards	**Specific Situations from that Year that Correspond with the Card**
_____ of Wands	_____ _____
_____ of Cups	_____ _____
_____ of Swords	_____ _____
_____ of Pentacles	_____ _____
Describe the major lessons and the abilities developed:	_____ _____

express the situations that gave you your most powerful learning experiences that year. (For instance, in a Chariot Year (7) all the minor 7s will be significant.)

Follow the format on the facing page to explore each of your Year Cards to see the major lessons and the abilities you have developed.

Continue this exercise with other significant years from your past. Don't try to "predict" how they might function in the current or coming years unless you understand how these cards have already expressed themselves in your life.

Other Periodic Cards

The Generic Year

Every year has its own Year Card that exists for everyone. For instance, the year 2012 adds up to 5. It's the "Year of the Hierophant." Simply add the digits in any year.

Your Personal Month Card

Add the month you were born plus the day you were born to the current year plus the current month.

Cycle Themes

Year cards run in a consecutive sequence of usually ten years and then jump to a new cycle that begins one card higher than the previous cycle. The first Year Card in any cycle will set the tone or theme for that entire period of your life. For instance, each year in the ten year sequence that begins with the Lovers will deepen your lessons regarding what true relationship is all about for you.

CHAPTER 15

Interpreting Your Year Cards

The following interpretations of the Major Arcana as Year Cards suggest lessons to be learned in each year (see chart 11, the Year Card Chart, in chapter 14). They are intended to be suggestive rather than authoritative. Don't use them as a substitute for working with the cards yourself. In other words, try to discover directly what they have to tell you. The various symbols on your current Year Card are psychic (and sometimes literal) tools you can use. Ask the figure(s) on the card what the symbols are for and how to use them. Dialogue with your Year Card, addressing one or more figures on the card in turn. One way to begin a dialogue is with the question, What do I need to learn from you this year? Do this with a feeling of spontaneous nonchalance (a characteristic of the Divine Fool). Begin playfully and say whatever comes to mind without thinking about it, so that your pen is in constant motion.

Date these dialogues and keep them in your tarot notebook, along with written observations about previous years and the correlations of the cards to the events of each year (see page 180). You may also want to use the margins of this book to note (next to the description of each card) your age and the year(s) during which it is your personal Year Card.

Remember that the Year Card will not tell you *what* will happen, but rather it will help you focus on the lesson, for you, in *whatever* happens. You will find, however, that, when a Year Card repeats, certain themes unique to you will also repeat but at new levels of a developmental spiral.

Your Magician Year

No one in our era can experience the Magician as a Personality, Hidden Factor/Teacher, or Year Card. Since January 1, 998, the number 1 has not appeared by itself, and it won't again until we get dates adding up to 10,000, beginning on December 31, 9957 CE. You might, however, want to consider the role of the Magician in Wheel of Fortune and Sun years.

Your High Priestess Year

The High Priestess as a Year Card will appear once in the life of some people born before 1998, There are no more High Priestess Years after January 1,1998, until December 31, 9958—which will add up to 10,001 (which reduces to 2). If you were born with a four-digit Base Number greater than 2000 (the sum of your birth date—see previous chapter), you will not experience the High Priestess at all. This does not mean you cannot develop her qualities. If the work has been done well by those who came before, then you will have more opportunity to access her wisdom than previously.

Look at your High Priestess Year if you had one. It was part of a two-year cycle of feminine energy, as it is followed by an Empress Year. Otherwise, examine your Justice (11) Years (or Strength if you use that card as 11) and Judgment (20) Years to see how you could be using the Priestess energy in your life. Women are very important to your learning. Often there is an increased interest in the psychic, metaphysical, or dream worlds. It is a year of learning to trust in yourself and of being independent and self-sufficient. Many people are drawn to the women's spirituality movement that emerged with this generation of feminists.

As a woman, you may find that people come to you for advice and understanding—as a confidante or lover to many but belonging to none. As a man, you might find yourself inspired by a woman in your work or personal life, a muse to your creativity. As a projection of your anima, she awakens in you the feminine principle.

Take your vacation and holidays at seaside or watery places—for healing and meditation and to bring yourself back into balance with Nature. Be aware of the cycles of the Moon and how they affect you. This is a year in which you must trust your instincts and inner knowledge to guide you to the lessons you need to learn. Sometimes you come face-to-face with your deepest fears and hopes and, especially, dreams. (Chapter 13 has further commentary on the High Priestess.)

Your Empress Year

The Empress first appears following the High Priestess Year, extending the feminine cycle into a second year and projecting the High Priestess self-sufficiency out into the world. She no longer appears after January 1, 2008, except for one reappearance when your Year Card adds up to 2100. Otherwise, the Hanged Man (12) or World (21) takes her place and carry her energy with them. The Empress has the inner knowledge of the High Priestess, but now it is expressed through the Empress' creative imagination. During an Empress Year, people are very productive, and the mind becomes a rich field of ideas. The response to everything is more sensual, intensifying your awareness of color, form, and style.

You're more disposed to relate to others in an Empress Year. Other people will be attracted to you as well, sensing your openness to them and responding to your hospitality. Because of your heightened sense of harmony and beauty, you want to be surrounded by beautiful things, especially in your home and on your body. You may change your clothing style or otherwise modify your appearance. Watch your weight as well as your pocketbook, for the Empress's sense of luxury can extend into overindulgence.

Since your Empress year suggests a connection with Mother Earth, it is a good time to get out into the country or work in a garden as much as possible. Maternal issues are prominent, either through relations with your mother, or your own desire to mother or care for others. You can be very fertile as well as creative, so, if this applies, there is a ripeness for pregnancy either with a child or a project. Men are just as fertile with ideas, the need to nurture something, and they are ripe for a relationship. You can develop the gracious, hospitable, and sensitive-to-emotions side of yourself—if you dare. The capability to nurture and care for the growth, health, and well-being of others is heightened at this time.

Your Emperor Year

The Emperor Year is the first year of a two-year cycle of learning to establish your own authority. It represents fathers and patriarchy—deciding "who gives the orders around here." Father issues therefore stand out: being a father, dealing with your own father, accessing your "father within," or relating to a father-figure. The Emperor tries hard to establish rules of order, creating stability in his environment. In such a year you will either be doing this yourself or reacting to orders coming from outside yourself. In the latter case, you may be rebelling against what you see as an imposition on your freedom by the dictates of others.

When the Emperor follows the Empress Year, which is a year of abundant creativity, you then take your work from the private sphere and seek a way to go public. You focus on getting recognition or approval for your work and finding ways to establish yourself in business and the marketplace. You initiate projects that will hopefully make your name. You pioneer new things. You go forth to conquer the world.

Your lessons focus on establishing authority for making your own rules or on learning how to live with the rules of others. You become assertive, and even forceful in presenting your ideas. There can be confrontations with the "state" or with the law. You need to know your domain so that you can work efficiently within it. You risk becoming so dictatorial that you stifle those around you. Overly dependent on linear reasoning, your thinking can become "square." Leadership and management roles in this year may advance you to positions of responsibility and prestige.

Your Hierophant Year

The Hierophant Year is the second in the power and authority cycle (following the Emperor). People often go back to school, complete a course of study, or receive on-the-job training or perhaps counseling. If you are a teacher, trainer, or counselor yourself, this can be an important year to establish yourself in the field or to develop your professional skills. As the Minor Arcana 5s show, you learn best this year through adversity or when faced with problems to solve (as the 5s all tend to be problematic). So this may be a year of stress, threatening the stability you tried to establish in the Emperor Year. You may respond by rigidly adhering to tradition, also indicated by this card's correspondence to Taurus. You can take advantage of this year by learning to listen to your own inner counsel. Taurus is ruled by Venus (Empress); the Moon (High Priestess) is "exalted"— meaning that it is a good time to rely on inner knowledge.

Educational or corrective institutions, religious organizations, and corporations can assume the role of authority figures in this year, and the rebellion you may feel is more generic than personal, although it may be represented by a single person. Or you could become the spokesperson or rep for such an organization. You are confronted by all your indoctrinated "shoulds" and "oughts," which you will try to either uphold or oppose. Examine your values and beliefs to determine which ones still apply to your life. Ask yourself which ones limit and which ones produce growth. You can often tell when a Hierophant situation is activated because your emotions get involved. Trace those emotional reactions back to the old teachings that generated them; then assess them for their current appropriateness. In a Hierophant Year, there is usually someone you look up to as an authority, perhaps a guru or spiritual leader or maybe just someone you go to for advice. You probably find people turning to you for assistance since you represent access to some kind of knowledge at this time. When passing along traditional teachings, listen carefully to what you say. Are you speaking from your heart in accord with your inner wisdom, or are you routinely transmitting dogma? Recognize your ability to find your own answers.

Your Lovers Year

In a Lovers Year, the focus is on relationships. People initiate them and end them or occasionally will not be in any relationship at all because they are unwilling to accept less than what they want and need. This may also pertain to relationships with family, coworkers, and friends.

As a card related to Gemini and ruled by Mercury, one of your lessons is to learn to communicate openly and honestly, with nothing concealed. You expect this from others, as well as yourself, in a Lovers Year. The greatest lesson: What do you want and need in relationships? The people with whom you seriously relate reflect your own self-image, and so in a Lovers Year, to learn how you feel about yourself, look at how others view and treat you.

This is also a year to begin turning to yourself for much of the support and encouragement you need. You do this by realizing that you can communicate with an inner voice (often perceived as being of the opposite sex) that has a direct line to your highest Self. Learning about yourself through what you project onto others is also a major theme for the year. As you withdraw your expectations and projections from the people around you, you are more able to see others for who they truly are. This year, you begin to blend and balance the masculine and feminine energies within yourself.

An old title for this card is "The Two Paths," reminding us that a Lovers Year is a year of *choices* and often involves a fork in the road or major turning point in your ten-year cycle. Your relationships will have a major influence on your decisions and may lie behind the need to make those decisions now. Remember that forthright communications are the hallmark of the year and essential in making all decisions.

Your Chariot Year

In the Chariot Year, you act and move ahead on the decisions made in the Lovers Year. (For instance, you may decide to end a relationship in a Lovers Year, but won't do so until the Chariot Year.) The Chariot Year focuses on your goals, so you harness your energies to move forward and adventure forth. As 7 is a number of initiation, a 7 Year is one in which to take your abilities to the next level. You have to prove your expertise by handling difficult situations, often with conflicting aspects. True mastery requires that you work on self-control and self-discipline. If you give free rein to your instincts and emotions (represented by the sphinxes), they may tear you apart. This can be experienced as some kind of breakdown (losing your temper or worse) or an accident (sometimes literally acted out in your automobile/chariot).

You may be called upon to act as a warrior in a Chariot Year. The moons on the shoulders of the charioteer signal a need to serve and protect others or to champion a cause. Like the knights of old searching for the Grail, when you are goal oriented and have a definite direction in which to move, your Chariot Year has the most meaning. You are developing assertion and creating an identity in the world. If you drive too hard, you could become belligerent and egotistical, running roughshod over everyone else.

To help you assert yourself in the world, you put on some sort of suitable armor, uniform, or persona and appearance. For instance, an expensive suit promotes you as a successful business person, while a special uniform or set of tools inspires confidence in your mastery. Such devices also cloak your sensitive feelings and insecurities.

People often travel or relocate in a Chariot Year, yet as a card relating to Cancer, a sense of roots is necessary for you to feel secure in a possibly turbulent year. Occasionally, you become so attached to home or protected by armor that you "turn to stone," becoming an immovable object. As the Moon rules Cancer, being near water can help you relax those touchy emotions and soothe your jangled nerves.

Your Strength Year

In your Strength Year, the central questions are, Is my heart in what I am doing? Is it what I truly desire? After a year of suppressing your feelings in order move ahead, you find your essential emotions reemerging. In fact, you will need them if you are to continue in your chosen direction. Without renewed passion, you may not endure the challenges and your fears about them. Thus, you could be forced to redirect your efforts. It's time to look at your instinctual nature and deal with any fears you have around it. A connection with animals can be especially important this year.

As a card relating to Leo, this year you experience a "lust" (as Crowley calls this card) for creativity and self-expression. Like the sap rising in spring, you feel a lust for life and a desire to demonstrate your affections, to take the risk of declaring and acting on what you love. It can be a year of sensual and sexual exploration. Hopefully you will direct this passion into meaningful projects and not waste it or allow it to become a destructive force. In ritual magic, this is called raising a "cone of power," which, when released, must be directed toward a specific purpose, or else its energy can wreak havoc. So look carefully at what you are doing, because you are metaphorically "playing with fire." And, like fire, your emotions can be a great civilizing force or a great destructive one, depending on how you use and direct them. Face your rage. Embrace what you feel to be ugly or beastly in yourself, because through such acceptance you build strength of character.

The other side of the Strength Year can be very difficult. It may challenge you to use all your fortitude in order to persevere through situations of great difficulty, such as career, health, or family problems. You struggle to balance your own needs with the needs of those you love. You may be tested in your ability to handle something heart-rending, to stick with it no matter how hard it gets. By being courageous, you build inner strength as you plumb the depths of your heart. Strength is the beating pulse of the heart that says "One step at a time, I continue in the direction my heart calls." From those things you love, which often conflict with each other, you discover what you really want.

Justice as the Number 8

If you see Justice as 8, then it will follow the Chariot Year instead of Strength. This is a good opportunity to see which card works best for you. What seems like perseverance with Strength can be indecision or waffling with Justice. Both can require balancing the needs of one aspect of your life with those of another. With Justice, you'll probably focus more on the adjustments you have to make as the result of decisions and directions taken in the two prior years. It's time for a calling to account of what you earlier set in motion. This more rational take on the year requires negotiations and contracts that may have been overlooked in the forward momentum you have been building up. Honesty, clarity, and commitment are called for, especially in reaching agreements with others.

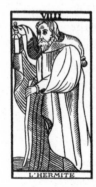

Your Hermit Year

In a Hermit Year, you find yourself more isolated and alone than usual, often right from the beginning of the year. You try to get together with friends, but they are busy, have moved, or are involved in other things. But then you find that you like having more time to yourself. There are things you need to reflect on and things to complete, and you need time alone to do this. In a 9 year, the last of the Root Numbers, you need to finish any projects and tie up loose ends from the past several years so that you will be unencumbered and can begin new things in the following year. Tie them up and send them out of your life, or else they'll become part of the baggage that hangs you up in a Hanged Man Year.

Your Hermit Year is a year of introspection; you look back at where you've been and forward to where you're going. Acknowledge your accomplishments and see what you have learned in this last cycle. You are standing on the peak of some kind of achievement—what is it? It's time to reconnect with your long-term goals. The Hermit has actually captured the star from the Star card and is using that vision to light the way. What is the light that illuminates your path?

You may find a teacher or guide to help you in a Hermit Year. Such a person usually seems older and wiser and represents a role model to emulate. Or you can be such a guide to someone else, remembering that with the Hermit energy, you teach more by example than by what you say. Despite your preference for withdrawal, your knowledgeable perspective and compassionate humanitarianism can benefit many people within your circle. Therefore you might be called upon to be a leader or to motivate others.

After the energy expenditure of the Strength Year, you may feel the need of some well-deserved rest. So let any wounds heal and reconnect with your sense of Self. As this is a card corresponding to Virgo, in a Hermit Year you work hard and selflessly to prepare for the future. Remember that prudence can become overcautiousness, persistence can become obstinacy, and wisdom can become sanctimoniousness.

Your Wheel of Fortune Year

The beginning of a Wheel of Fortune Year is usually unmistakable. After a year of solitude and inner focus, you find yourself out in the limelight. You're in the middle of a social whirl or spinning like a top.

With the Wheel of Fortune Year as your Year Card, you have come to another turning point. From your past experience, you bring seeds for a new direction but also burdens and obligations. The wheel is the equilibrium of contrary forces, irreversibly set in motion. There can be a lot of highs and lows. You probably move or change jobs this year or make some other turnaround in your life. I've seen people lose their job, apartment, and boy- or girlfriend all at the same time. Yet, as there's an aura of prosperity and luck about this card, these people usually end up better off at the end of the year than when they began. From the introspection of the Hermit, you now find yourself being more social again and expanding your horizons. New opportunities and choices present themselves, and you'll see options you never noticed before.

Depending on what projects you completed last year, and how well, you begin to see the results in this year. You receive recognition for your accomplishments and appear in public or are thrust out beyond your usual niche in some way. You may find yourself flying high and wide, literally or figuratively.

It's an excellent time for educational pursuits, communicating, or publishing and for initiating or expanding projects—although these seeding actions might not bear fruit for some time yet. Now's the time, though, to set goals, acknowledge dreams, and make long-range plans, visualizing the whole before becoming embroiled in the details. This is also a year in which things literally turn up, often as the results of processes begun long ago. For example, friends not seen in a decade may pop in. In terms of learning, they serve to make you aware of the effects of your actions over this period, with all the growth and changes time brings.

All in all, this is a fortunate year, in which experience gained as the seasons turn helps you focus on your new direction.

Your Justice Year

The Justice Year heralds a new beginning with decisions to be made. But first, you need to assess the pros and cons of various proposals. It is a year of adjustment, and you will especially need to assimilate the changes that occurred during the Wheel of Fortune Year. You will reap what you've sown so far.

In a Justice Year, you could be involved in legal matters (the scales of justice) or handling financial affairs (the scales of business). You might consider a partnership of some kind, whether in business or your personal life. Contracts and documents are therefore important and should be examined carefully. For instance, getting married in a Justice Year has special significance as a contractual agreement. It's a good idea to clarify what you expect from any partnership or business deal.

In our society, you were trained (especially if you're a woman) to compromise and share—to assess what the other person probably wants, and then figure out how far you go along with that, before you even know clearly what *you* want. Sit down by yourself and make notes about what you would want if you could have *anything* in the world. Don't hold back. Write down your fantasy situation of perfection without compromise. Then, negotiate. If everyone involved did this, it would open the way to mutual trust and eliminate resentments that can hang you up in the year that follows. In any case, the challenge is to be true to yourself, to see clearly what things you can let go of without resentment and what you cannot give up. Justice is a symbol for your inner court that determines personal innocence or guilt. Anything in which you get involved that is not fair to you will become untenable in the following year.

Therefore, this is a year to accept responsibility for yourself, to assess the effects of your actions and judgments, and to make adjustments as necessary. You need to evaluate the changes that have been happening in order to determine what you want to keep in your life and what no longer truly or fairly expresses who you are. You need to judge how you spend your time and energies and whether you are getting fairly recompensed for your efforts. If you are self-employed, adjustments in what you charge or how you do things may be necessary.

Strength as the Number 11

If you see Strength as 11, then it will follow the Wheel of Fortune Year. Here is another good opportunity to see which card works best for you. This is a year of creative and passionate self-expression, but it requires struggles, self-discipline, and stamina. After the social whirl and expanded opportunities that arose with the Wheel, you have to figure out how to handle them all with energy and grace. You have to wrestle things into a shape you can live with—whether it's creative materials or old fears or relationships with others. Your ability to stand strong may be tested at a new level, and weaknesses could have consequences in the following year. Is it the laws of nature or the laws of social interaction with which you are dealing?

Your Hanged Man Year

In a Hanged Man Year, you will have to release things from your past. Sometimes, when this involves the loss of someone you are attached to, it feels like a betrayal. The painful or wounding experiences of such a year, however, serve the purpose of inward spiritual growth. Relax and let go. By releasing old patterns and surrendering fixed ideas, new ones can form in accord with new commitments. Sacrifices are made in Hanged Man Years in which you put someone else's needs first or sacrifice a lesser thing for the sake of a greater.

It can be a year in which you feel confused or thwarted, with life on hold and activities suspended. You may devote yourself selflessly to some task, or you may have to deal with an "impossible situation" requiring you to trust unquestioningly in some force beyond you. The Hanged Man is a symbol of mystical isolation in a ritual of purification. Thus, the sacrifice of your self-interest in dedication to a cause will bring understanding of the deeper meaning of your acts.

If you find yourself in situations in which you feel powerless and unable to act, you may turn to fantasy, alcohol, drugs, or workaholism—anything to escape. A completely different perspective can help; don't expend energy negating a problem; instead put your focus and energy on its opposite. It can mean a reversal of everything you formerly stood for. Humility is essential, as you discover in your Hanged Man Year that there are many things you cannot control. Nevertheless, you can experience the spirit of divinity flowing through you, releasing you from limitations in your imagination, art and devotions.

Your Death Year

It is rare that in your Death Year an actual death will occur, for it signifies transformation and regeneration as well as termination. In general, it's more a time to shed old skin for new growth. Following a Hanged Man Year in which you faced whatever was hanging you up, now you are liberated, often resulting in a fresh surge of energy. You cut through stagnation to get to the things that work for you. By trimming off the deadwood and dying aspects of your life, you allow all the life force to flow into healthy parts so that they can spring forth anew. Whatever is destroyed this year makes way for new life.

While you may experience feelings of being dismembered, you will find yourself getting down to the bare-bones scaffolding of your life or of a creative project. Once you've gotten rid of all that's unnecessary, what's left is something you can really trust and believe in. With nothing to block them any longer, your creative energies are set free to explore new possibilities.

So the Death Year is actually a year of great vigor, liberated from inadequate forms. There can be a tremendous power and drive to assert your life force and face your greatest fears.

Since Scorpio is the corresponding sign, you have the force to plunge deeply into investigating hidden things, to do research, or to be involved in underworld schemes. You might court danger, enjoying the thrill of living close to the edge. Having the ability to merge totally with something else means that your experience will be deeply transformative. Your sexual experiences, likewise, can be ones in which you lose your sense of Self in merging with the other—what in Elizabethan times was known as the "little death." You are aware of life and love, but can also become jealous and possessive; if so, beware—for what you try to possess may be wrenched away even more painfully. The question you need to ask yourself in a Death Year is, What needs to be cleared away so that new growth can surge forth unhampered?

Your Temperance Year

Your Temperance Year is one in which you creatively combine things in new and different ways. You find resources and assistance you didn't know were available before—both from peers and spiritually. Your major lessons may be about compassion, reconciliation, and healing breaches—how to turn problems into blessings. You have the inner endurance to slowly wear away all obstacles with patience and grace. Some people find they can learn to play with time—stretching it out and slowing it down deliberately. Synchronicities and everyday miracles happen in quite extraordinary ways.

As a year associated with Sagittarius, it is time for the rejuvenation of your higher mind—for philosophy, communications, or healing. You are interested in new forms for old things and how to revive stale ideas. You may even work on some kind of restoration or conservation project. You can bridge and make connections, perhaps through networking or by acting as a mediator. You will tackle problem-solving situations and are willing to experiment and look for ways that involve adaptation and moderation. Perhaps you turn to spiritual guidance, but you want practical results.

If the Death Year was painful and disintegrating, then in the Temperance Year, take time to restore yourself, balancing your energies and building your new Self. You may go traveling or redistribute your energy or possessions. Being near water, taking time alone to commune with your inner Self, or seeking out an understanding friend will all be of great help. If you have been through this before, you can now serve as a compassionate friend and healer to another.

Your Devil Year

In your Devil Year, you want to develop the resources you discovered in the Temperance Year. You established lines of communication and networks last year, and now you want to use them to build grander projects. You look for schemes that promise success. Capricornian ambition makes you work hard, and humility and patience won't come easily.

This is a great time for enjoying the material things in life. Have some fun. Be devilish. Stir things up. The danger is that you become possessed by your desires, overindulge in pleasures, and try to control others to get what you want. The key lesson is often about which indulgences and desires produce healthy growth and well-being and which ones enslave and bind you. Where does guilt and fear keep you from doing something? If you were unwilling to let go of something in a Death Year or reconcile your loss in the Temperance Year, it can come back to haunt you in the Devil year.

You may feel blocked and angered by the "big boys" like government, the military, big business, organized religion, or anyone who tries to control or manipulate you. If so, you may want to break taboos, cheat on your taxes, or become involved in disruptive action. Pessimism and distrust can weigh heavily. Sometimes you just need to walk away.

In the Devil Year, you'll want to look at your shadow issues, uncover anger and resentment, and discover where power, creativity and love without fear really lie. It's time to defeat the adversary of unwarranted guilt. Fight back with a sense of humor. Use mirth and imagination to free yourself from bondage to negativity. If you learned to play with time in a Temperance Year, you can learn to play with the "weightiness" of things in a Devil Year.

Your Tower Year

Your Tower Year is one of revolution, with the shattering of unnecessary forms and structures. It presents an opportunity to dissolve barriers between yourself and others and discover what is really important to you.

The extent of change this year depends on what happened last year. If you built a tower of achievement by using your power over others, this will be a year of violent testing. Even if your achievement was modest, expect tremors in your life. Organizations fall, belief structures crumble, and repressed forces are likely to release suddenly, as indicated by the correspondence of this card to the planet Mars. Falsehoods will be revealed. You either consciously break through old forms with new insights, or Nature may do it for you through accidents, natural disasters, or other people's actions. You may lose or change jobs, relationships, or living arrangements. Your physical appearance is affected: you have surgery, an accident, burn up with fever, or lose weight. There's often a need for purging and burning away obstructions.

Look at where you want to regroup and reform and take action to bring it about consciously. Release energy blockages by becoming aware of them and acknowledging the feelings they engender. When you lose your temper, get stressed, or behave badly or inappropriately, you have located blocked and repressed energy. When released consciously, this energy can power you through previously insurmountable problems.

Wherever you have become rigid and are no longer able to grow; now is the time to liberate yourself. The question of the year is is, How do I break open my blockages without causing massive destruction? First, accept that action is necessary. Draw upon intuitive hunches, enlightened ideas, or "improbable" solutions; act on them as new possibilities for future development.

This is an excellent year to make breaks with the past. Literally and figuratively, clean up your house and your act. Break some old habits and start some new ones. Let go of preconceptions about how things are going in your life and make room for a fresh, new future.

Your Star Year

Your Star Year is usually a time of reflection and hope. You are completely exposed, as all falsehoods and false ambitions were stripped away last year. You can rejoice in your freedom and effortlessly grow toward new aspirations, using abilities previously untapped. You may feel overwhelmed by potentialities and unknown frontiers yet aware that all answers lie within you. The challenge is to be totally honest about all your hopes, dreams, and desires. How comfortable you are being vulnerable depends on the work you did over the preceding years regarding letting go of fears and blocks.

Another possibility for a Star Year is that you awaken from your previous year's shake-up to emerge as some sort of luminary: You are in a state of grace, admired by others, a fixture in the firmament. To truly shine, you need to use your talents and abilities.

The Star Year offers you the opportunity to begin to see the pattern of your destiny, to recognize the images that most influence your life, and to acknowledge the light that guides you. By unrestrainedly giving yourself up to your destiny and protective stars, you will be guided on your journey.

In a Star Year, corresponding to Aquarius, you have aspirations for humankind: You perceive the grand patterns and connecting links among particular groups and the needs of the people. You may identify with altruistic causes in which you channel your energies through good works and humanitarian projects, claiming nothing for yourself. You are then noticed for your grace and inner illumination. Ask yourself: What are my hopes and what am I willing to do to achieve them?

Your Moon Year

Your Moon Year can be one of disillusionment with the ideals you worked for last year. This is actually a test to see if such ideals can last through the hounding of others and your fears that your dreams aren't substantial enough. Your sensitivity to the mass consciousness of the public is very strong, deeply affecting your individual identity. You are confused about which are your own values and feelings and which are from the collective unconscious—things being worked out on a world level that you are experiencing instinctively. Events this year involve unforeseeable factors and consequences.

The Moon is a card of karmic relationships, so you are engaged in issues that affect other lifetimes, past and future. You may draw people to you that you have known in another life or who have passed over in this one. Confusion, unnecessary drama, and misunderstandings can arise when you respond to situations from either childhood or karmically triggered emotions.

This can be a year of psychic and intuitive awakening as indicated by the corresponding sign Pisces. You may be drawn to the occult, mysticism, or spiritualism. Working with dreams, symbols, therapy, and the imagination can be very rewarding. In fact, this part of your life might seem more real and vivid than ordinary, waking life. It can appear as if other people are speaking a different language as your interests and theirs diverge. Make sure you understand what is illusion and what is real as your ordinary reasoning powers are eclipsed and the mytho-poetic-shamanic consciousness takes over. However, you can use your imagination to great effect by visualizing and affirming whatever you want to create. It is important to continue functioning in the mundane world. Metaphorical and symbolic interpretations of life situations might help give meaning to anything confusing or disturbing that you are experiencing. Try looking at life events as if they were dreams.

Open your senses and follow your gut instincts. During a Moon Year, you may feel there is more to this world than you ordinarily perceive.

Your Sun Year

The Sun Year represents success. It augurs the birth of a new project conceived in the dreams and imagination of the previous year. You radiate good will, and people love to bask in the light of your enthusiasm and happiness. You arrive at new realizations. Situations that were cloudy last year become clear, and secrets may be revealed. You will be relieved of the fears you have been carrying. Reconciliations with others are possible now. If you have kept faith with your dreams, now you will reap the rewards. The lesson involves recognizing where the center of your universe lies. What makes you happy? What is your gravity center?

It's a good year to be around children, for it is a more playful time than usual. Get out in the sun, go on vacation, get fit, relax a little. Spend time in Nature and with animals. Your ideas and projects bear fruit as you discover how much can be achieved through affirmative thinking. Ride your instincts with confidence, and you'll find they won't let you down. Be warmhearted and generous; you can afford it and will be rewarded in turn. Occasionally, issues around burnout and exhaustion can arise from focusing all your energies on a single, central source.

The Sun is the source of riches both temporal and spiritual but also of radiation and sunburn. Cultivate prosperity consciousness and let each day bring more wisdom and understanding. Generally speaking, it's a lucky year; many opportunities will present themselves, so be ready respond.

Your Judgment Year

In a Judgment Year, corresponding to Pluto, you come face-to-face with your own mortality, whether through a personal experience, the death of someone you know, or the ending of something. It's the end of one era and the beginning of a new one. An evaluation of your life and accomplishments

may take place. The results of this eventually will be liberating, although the process is slow and it may take a long time to realize the full implications of the events of this year. A full-scale restructuring of some aspect of your life is likely to occur. You are unexpectedly freed from a limitation or obstacle. This can open you to a whole new calling or profession.

You are also concerned with transformations within your family structure or community. If you've awakened to a new level of awareness or experienced a spiritual rebirth, you'll want to persuade others of your new perspective. Persuasion can be good in some contexts, like sounding the alarm around issues that require global action. However, your personal power is as strong as it will ever be, and the effect on others can have significant consequences, especially if you are criticizing or judging them. Avoid using your power for personal aggrandizement, and instead apply it unselfishly for the good of others or society. As the cross on the banner shows, you are at a crossroads, and it's your choice how you respond when destiny calls.

Your World Year

Your World Year indicates the completion of major projects, being at the end of a cycle, and giving birth to a holistic and independent sense of Self. It can be a very successful year, witnessing the culmination of some larger process. You may find yourself working within a narrow or even confined sphere, although possibly on tasks of wide applicability. As with the preceding Judgment Year, your issues and those of the masses are actually inseparable.

The urge to mother and nurture have implications of global or universal import that can affect Mother Earth. You need to establish firm contact with your own nature, as it serves as a foundation to your outer world projects. Take care of your health and physical body.

You want to be free from any dependence on others and would like to make your unique mark on the world. Orienting yourself to your surroundings is important. Know where you are in the scheme of things. As they say in real estate: location, location, location. Your success in getting your bearings will have a major impact on the following year—usually that of the Fool, when chaos steps back in.

The World card symbolizes the concept of creative cosmic synthesis. You will need to integrate your physical Self with your spirit Self. Dancing, as pictured on this card, is symbolic of the creation of the universe and suggests a way to align yourself with whatever is being brought into form. The hermaphroditic qualities of the dancer indicate that you do things that draw on a full range of human characteristics and will not be constrained by gender.

Your Fool Year

The last possible Fool Year (22) for an individual would have been January 1, 1991, and there won't be another one for about 250 years, but reverberations of it may be felt in Death and Emperor Years. In your Fool Year, a year of *loco*motion, you are very likely to make a major move, travel in a carefree manner, or at least take unusual or unexpected trips. You take risks and do things that seem quite out of character. Travel gives you the opportunity to experiment with new personas and to forget your responsibilities for a while. You live in the present, following every momentary whim. In caring only for the moment, you may do some foolish things from a long-term perspective, but you can't think about that now. The future seems far away, and the past is forgotten.

You are heedless of order, admit you know nothing, wear mismatched clothes, and upset standards of conduct and society in general. You may annoy people because you mimic their folly, refuse to act falsely, and parody their values. This makes you the Fool, and it's clear you don't fit in with the norm.

Yet in a Fool Year, you are divinely inspired. You follow your instincts and frequently turn up in the right place at the right time. Your naiveté and innocence (a kind of temporary insanity) enable you to see things from a fresh perspective and to discover exciting possibilities where others with jaded senses perceive nothing. You will succeed in doing things that others, far too prudent, won't even attempt.

Your haphazard attitudes can create problems for you in the years that follow. When you overturn traditions and espouse anarchy, you stir up trouble. On the other hand, your belief in the basic joy and spontaneity of life is exalting. You are an original being, representing a wonderful truth: The world is full of possibilities if you will only step off the beaten track.

THE TOWER.

THE MAGICIAN.

THE SUN.

WHEEL of FORTUNE.

THE EMPEROR.

THE CHARIOT.

DEATH.

THE STAR.

TEMPERANCE.

THE HIGH PRIESTESS.

JUDGEMENT.

JUSTICE.

THE HIEROPHANT.

STRENGTH.

THE FOOL.

THE MOON.

THE DEVIL.

THE EMPRESS.

THE WORLD.

THE HANGED MAN.

THE LOVERS.

THE HERMIT.

CHAPTER 16

Soul Groups and Relationship Dynamics

Just as the tarot can be laid out in three rows of seven cards or in groups based on Root Numbers, there is another pattern for laying out the Major Arcana that specifically elucidates the Lifetime and Year Cards. I first learned it from Vicki Noble and Jonathan Tenney, who wrote about it in *The Motherpeace Tarot Playbook*, but then I discovered that other tarotists such as Papus and Lois Ellis had worked with this pattern, too. I encourage you to lay out your own Major Arcana as described and see what you discover in the process.

Begin with your Major Arcana in order. For the time being, put the Fool aside. You'll need a large table or floor space. You are going to create three groups of seven cards, such that the three groups form the points of an upward-pointing triangle.

We'll begin laying out the last three Major Arcana cards (19, 20, 21) but, after that, follow the numerical order beginning with the Magician. Place the Sun as the first card of group 1, almost as far away from you as the space allows. To your far left and near the front put Judgment (group 2). To your far right and level with Judgment put the World (group 3). The Magician goes directly above the Sun, touching it. The High Priestess is directly above Judgment, and the Empress is above the World. The Emperor goes with group 1 immediately to the right of both the Magician and the Sun (halfway up the Magician and halfway down the Sun). The Hierophant goes similarly with group 2 and the Lovers with group 3. The Chariot returns you to group 1 and goes under the Emperor, and so on. Continue distributing the cards into these three groups so that they surround the first card in each group in a clockwise manner. See the illustration on the opposite page.

Because of the ways they relate to each other, we'll call these groups *Dynamics*.

- **Dynamic 1**: card 19 is in the center, with cards 1, 4, 7, 10, 13, and 16 clockwise around it.

- **Dynamic 2**: card 20 is in the center, with cards 2, 5, 8, 11, 14 and 17 clockwise around it.

- **Dynamic 3**: card 21 is in the center, with cards 3, 6, 9, 12, 15, and 18 clockwise around it.

If you use round cards, you'll discover that six cards form a hexagram and fit perfectly around the center seventh card with their edges just touching adjacent cards.

Prepare to be further astonished: The three cards that form the central vertical axis in each group are the cards found in the first three constellations:

- Magician, Wheel, and Sun

- High Priestess, Justice, and Judgment

- Empress, Hanged Man, and World

Cards diagonally across from each other in a Dynamic are the constellation pairs. If you wish, place the Fool at the center of all three groups of cards. In which Dynamic do your own Birth Cards fall? You are not only identified by a constellation, but also by your Dynamic Group, which also lends characteristics to Year Cards. The identifying characteristics are presented in chart 12 on page 205.

Year Cards cycle through the three Dynamics, creating a rhythm in the way each year responds to the energies of the preceding year and yields to the following year. What was integrated in one year gives way to new intentions, only to be followed by evaluation in the next, etc. The exact qualities depend on the specific cards involved.

The Dynamic in which your Birth Cards appear points to the kinds of energy dynamics you'll encounter with people of other Birth Cards. Chart 13 on pages 206–207 marks a few of the ways people relate to each other according to their Dynamic. By examining people you know, you'll discover other interesting characteristics. There are obviously good and bad relationships in each category. Here, I've used examples of famous love, creative, and business partnerships.

Recognizing differences and exploring relationship dynamics is one of the most interesting and beneficial aspects of working with Birth Cards. It can lead to an acceptance of diversity and compassionate understanding of others.

Chart 12: The Three Dynamic Groups

Dynamic 1	Dynamic 2	Dynamic 3
Conscious	Intuitive	Imaginative
Rational	Emotional	Synthesizing
Aggressive	Receptive	Integrative
Focused	Absorbing	Formative
Intentional	Reactive	Motivating
Thinking	Knowing	Being
Outer	Inner	Interactive
Willing	Reflecting	Transforming
Initiating	Channeling	Adapting
Asserting	Judging/Evaluating	Mediating
Desiring	Accepting	Expressing

Chart 13: The Six Relationship Dynamics Patterns

D1 + D1	Because aggression and competition can be strong, relationships between people in this Dynamic do best when a great challenge is present, there are clear boundaries or rules, and the individuals are working toward a common goal. The presence of a conscious focus seems to stimulate both people to achieve their highest, although egos can certainly get in the way. Risk taking can provide big payoffs or escalate out of control. *Examples:* Bonnie (Parker) and Clyde (Barrow) (outlaws) Marie and Pierre Curie (husband-wife team of chemists) Steve Jobs and Steve Wozniak (Apple Inc. cofounders) Bill Gates and Paul Allen (Microsoft cofounders) Larry Page and Sergey Brin (Google cofounders)
D1 + D2	This combination tends to fall into the traditional trap of dominance and submission, or actor and receiver, in which one person is needed to fill in what the other lacks. This can work well when both respect the role the other plays. Problems arise, for example, if one person grabs the limelight such that the other feels used, betrayed, or slighted. When they work together, they can be brilliant. *Examples:* Karl Marx and Friedrich Engels (cofounders of Marxism) Humphrey Bogart and Lauren Bacall (actors, costars, spouses) Margot Fonteyn and Rudolf Nureyev (ballet duo) John F. Kennedy and Jackie Kennedy Onassis (U.S. president and first lady) Princess Diana and Prince Charles (Princess and Prince of Wales)
D1 + D3	This is, generally speaking, a very imaginatively creative Dynamic. At its best, there's an almost uncanny ability to perceive and nurture the creative spark in each other. But that doesn't say that these relationships will be easy. The individuals' visions, styles, and needs can be quite different and require connections and understanding outside the partnership. Flexibility is called for, or the relationship becomes brittle and will break. *Examples:* Sigmund Freud and Carl Jung (psychoanalysts) Frida Kahlo and Diego Rivera (Mexican artists, spouses) John Lennon and Paul McCartney (songwriting partners, members of the Beatles) Ozzy and Sharon Osbourne (singer-songwriter and wife-manager) Ben Cohen and Jerry Greenfield (cofounders of Ben & Jerry's ice cream)

D2 + D2	While we might think this combination would be too passive, in fact, Dynamic 2s seem to work well in combined personal and business relationships, forming strong intuitive links. Judging just what the other needs, they can provide each other with support and security. However, when emotional stress, addictions, and psychodrama take hold, the individuals in this sensitive partnership can become overly reactive, taking out the stress on their partner and others around them. *Examples:* 　Richard Burton and Liz Taylor (actors, costars, spouses) 　Jackie Kennedy and Aristotle Onassis (former U.S. first lady and second 　　spouse, Greek shipping magnate) 　Lucille Ball and Desi Arnaz (comedians, actors, costars, spouses) 　Barack and Michelle Obama (U.S. president and first lady) 　Beyoncé Knowles and Jay-Z (recording artists, collaborators, spouses)
D2 + D3	At their best, this pair learns to accept the other person as they are and to work in harmony. This seems to be a great combination for deep, long-lasting friendships with gentle competition. There's just enough difference to stimulate, an ease with compromise that doesn't require total merging, and not a great need for dominance. They often establish individual identities and may even go their own ways, but their interaction seems to benefit both themselves and others. *Examples:* 　Franklin Delano and Eleanor Roosevelt (U.S. president and first lady) 　Paul Newman and Joanne Woodward (actors, costars, spouses) 　Bill and Hillary Clinton (U.S. president and first lady, politician). 　David and Victoria Beckham (British footballer and singer-songwriter) 　Prince William and Princess Kate (Duke and Duchess of Cambridge) 　W. S. Gilbert and Arthur Sullivan (operatic collaborators) 　Bill Hewlett and Dave Packard (cofounders of Hewlett-Packard)
D3 + D3	This combination seems to work best when the couple shares, nurtures, and expresses dreams and romantic ideals together. While great sacrifices can be made, the relationship is served when each makes the sacrifices for a larger cause and they work together toward transformation. While occasionally a strength, the tendency to merge identities or accept the fantasy of such a merger can become a problem if the separate individuality of either is suppressed. *Examples:* 　John Lennon and Yoko Ono (artist, collaborators, spouses). 　Elizabeth Barrett and Robert Browning (poets, spouses) 　Elvis and Priscilla Presley (singer and spouse) 　Sonny and Cher Bono (husband-and-wife music duo)

THE MAGICIAN.

+

THE DEVIL .

=

THE TOWER.

TAROT

+

JUDGEMENT.

+

THE MOON.

+

JUDGEMENT.

=

DEATH.

=

JUSTICE .

CHAPTER 17

Your Name Cards

The Significance of Your Name

From earliest antiquity, in most cultures, the name of a person was synonymous with their soul. This is a reflection of a long-ago golden age when magic and reality were all one. Name-giving was an important rite. In some cultures, newborns had to be named before they could be suckled. In others, the child was named by a shaman or tribal elder who used divination to discover the name already known to Spirit that expressed that child's purpose and character. To name a thing or to know its name is often seen as a way to gain power over it. One's real name, that is, one's soul name, was often a secret known only within the immediate family.

Names have always been profound psychological expressions of one's true Self, and even in written form, one's name is a hieroglyph of spiritual power. Consider the secret Hebrew name of God, known as the Tetragrammaton since it is symbolized by the four consonants YHVH. The vowels were not marked and it was forbidden to be pronounced. Even among Christians, the concept of name has been equated with character and destiny, and so children are often named after saints whose qualities the parents wish them to reflect. Today, people are more likely to name a child after a movie star, sports hero, or character from a book but, again, with the hope that a little of their personal magic will rub off on the child. Therefore, historically and symbolically, your name is a vehicle of your power and your personal magic. As it says in Ecclesiastes (7:1), "A good name is better than precious ointment" and, although it refers to reputation, it also suggests the power of naming.

The Name Cards

In addition to Birth Cards determined by your birth date, you have a set of cards from the Major Arcana called Name Cards that are determined by your birth name. There are cards for each letter of your name, literally spelling it out in images, and other cards derived by the numerological addition and reduction of those letters. By means of the tarot, you can discover the hidden significance of why you were given your particular name and what it tells you about your character and your soul's destiny. Again, as with the Birth Cards, you will find this information most valuable once you have used it on yourself and friends. Then you will begin to recognize the trends and patterns. All these Lifetime Cards are tools for understanding and should be used as intuitive indicators, not as absolutes.

Your Lifetime Cards, which consist primarily of Birth Cards and Name Cards, are like personal readings that apply to you your whole life long. Should you ever change your name, you are choosing to modify or redefine your personal direction, as discussed later in this chapter. You can consider anniversary dates (or spiritual rebirth dates, etc.) as the beginning of a new phase of your life or a dedication to a chosen purpose, but you can never get rid of your actual birth date and your official birth name. Granted, there will always be people with unusual birth circumstances: I have met people with two birth dates, not knowing which is correct, and I've known children who were not named until more than a year after they were born—their birth certificates simply say "Baby Girl Jones" or "Baby Boy Williams." In such cases you must work with whatever feels right to you or accept all the possibilities as aspects of yourself.

Numerical Equivalents

There are two major methods of determining numerical equivalents for the letters of your name.

The first is the standard English system (see below), not used in this book, in which the twenty-six letters are numbered consecutively from 1 to 9 and then begin with 1 again. *A* equals 1, as does the 10th letter, *J*, and the 19th letter, *S*.

A=1, B=2, C=3, D=4, E=5. F=6. G=7. H=8. I=9, J=1. K=2, L=3, M=4, N=5, O=6, P=7, Q=8, R=9, S=1, T=2, U=3, V=4, W=5, X=6, Y=7, Z=8

The second system is a Qabalistic one which attempts to match the English alphabet with the Hebrew alphabet of only twenty-two letters. Since each Hebrew letter *is also a number*, once you are sure of the corresponding letter from English to Hebrew, you know the number. However, none of the various systems for transliterating the English alphabet into Hebrew is precise, as they should be based on sound and not spelling. This is shown by the wide disagreement found among authorities. The Hebrew letter *Heh*, for instance, stands for our *h* and sometimes our *e*, while *Cheth* is *ch* in some systems and *h* in others. *Teth* is usually *t*, and *Tav* is *th*, but in some lists they are switched, and *Tav* is occasionally *x*. *Tzaddi* is especially difficult, as it is usually designated as a *tz* sound such as that found in *czar* (spelled with a *cz* to make it even more difficult). You can see the problems!

I have chosen to use the numbers of the twenty-two Major Arcana as the numeric base. To create a symbolic representation of my essential Self through the medium of the tarot cards, I matched them with the English alphabet in the order that every child learns, imprinted as deeply in my unconscious as in my conscious mind, just as I teach it to my child in the traditional alphabet song.

Linguists have determined that babies, before they are a year old, recognize and have learned to form all the basic sounds of the language or languages spoken to them daily. After the age of ten, it is difficult if not impossible for a person to learn another language without an accent. As with the Gregorian calendar, we have all been imprinted with particular cultural conventions that frame our perceptions of reality.[14] It makes little sense to spell an English name with Hebrew letters unless you are committed to working with Kabbalistic magic.

In chart 14 on page 212, each letter directly corresponds to the number below it and to a card from the Major Arcana corresponding to that number. Thus, *A* = 1 = the Magician, *L* = 12 = the Hanged Man, etc. The numbers in this chart are called "Key Numbers" and are the numbers used in all calculations. Any two-digit Key Number can be reduced down to its "Root Number," which is always a single-digit number between 1 and 9. The Root Number is the number used in standard numerology calculations, whereas *in this book you always work with the numbers 1 through 22*.

You'll notice that in English there are four more letters than there are Major Arcana tarot cards. Thus, the letters *W, X, Y,* and *Z* correspond to

A	B	C	D	E	F	G	H	I
1	2	3	4	5	6	7	8	9
J	K	L	M	N	O	P	Q	R
10	11	12	13	14	15	16	17	18
S	T	U	V	W	X	Y	Z	
19	20	21	22	5 Fire	6 Earth	7 Water	8 Air	

the numbers 23, 24, 25, and 26, *but for our purposes here are automatically reduced to their Root Number and card,* that is, W = 23 = 2 + 3 = 5, X = 24 = 2 + 4 = 6, Y = 25 = 2 + 5 = 7, and Z = 26 = 2 + 6 = 8. The reduced numbers are the ones you should use in all calculations involving the final four letters. They also represent the four elements that correspond to the four tarot suits: *W* = Fire, *X* = Earth, *Y* = Water, and *Z* = Air.

Your Basic Name Cards

Now let's use the preceding chart to find some of your personal Name Cards. Place all the vowels above your name and all the consonants below. Add them separately as shown and reduce the sums to a number that is twenty-two or less. (Do this in the space provided in chart 15: Your Personal Cards Chart, on page 214.)

For example:

	1		7		1			5		9		5			5	5		= 38	= 3 + 8	= 11
M	A	R	Y	K	A	T	H	E	R	I	N	E	G	R	E	E	R			
13		18		11		20	8		18		14		7	18			18	= 145	= 1 + 4 + 5	= 10
Sum of vowels plus consonants																		= 183	= 1 + 8 + 3	= 12

(*Note: Always add whole numbers together before reducing!*)

Adding the vowels together and reducing to a Major Arcana number of 22 or below gives you your Desires and Inner Motivation Card. (In my case, above, this is the 11th trump: Justice, which is in the constellation of the High Priestess.)

Adding the consonants together and then reducing that sum gives you your Outer Persona Card. (In my case, this is the 10th Trump Card: the Wheel of Fortune in the constellation of the Magician.)

Your Destiny Card comes from adding together all the numbers in your name and then reducing them to 22 or below. (In my example, I have the 12th Trump Card: the Hanged Man in the constellation of the Empress.)

Your Personal Blueprint

Let's look at this entire concept more closely. According to Hermetic and metaphysical philosophy, the individual soul chooses a life to be born into for the particular lessons and challenges it will find there. Usually it is a life that will offer the greatest opportunity for soul development through a framework of experience offered by a particular historical time; the national, ethnic, and cultural belief structures; and the genetic contributions of the physical parents. As Jane Roberts's spiritual mentor, Seth, says in *The Nature of Personal Reality*, "Unconsciously, then, you have within you what you might think of as a set of blueprints for the particular kind of physical reality you want to materialize. You are the architect."[15] Your Name Cards can therefore help you realize the particular qualities and individual characteristics that are innately yours.

Your job is to use the talents you have to the best of your ability—knowing, as Seth puts it, "that in [your talents] lies your own individual fulfillment."[16] This, then, is your destiny! Your Birth Cards and Name Cards are indicators of talents, abilities, and characteristics that you can develop by creatively facing the challenges that are your lessons in daily life. Your job is to actualize your *name* to the best of your ability. Free will means that you can choose to do this or not. If you don't, then your name becomes all those things you are "fated" with. This reminds me of a study I read about in which it was found that people with really unusual names tend to stand out, either as unusually individualistic, creative, and successful, or as lonely, disturbed, and maladjusted.

Chart 15: Your Personal Cards Chart

Using your name as it appears on your birth certificate (that is, your full, original name), change each letter into its corresponding number as given in chart 14, the Alphabet Key Numbers Chart. Later you can determine the numbers of any other name(s) you currently use.

- Write your name in the space provided below.
- Above your name, write the numbers corresponding to the vowels: A, E, I, O, U, and Y (if it is used as a vowel, as in the name Mary).
- Below your name, write the numbers corresponding to the consonants (including Y if it is used as a consonant, as in the name Beyoncé).
- Total the individual vowel and consonant numbers before reducing.

Vowels:	= ____
Full name:	
Consonants:	= ____
Sum of vowels plus consonants (not reduced)	= ____

My Desires and Inner Motivation Card (Vowels)

Total (reduced) = ____

Major Arcana card = _____

Root Number = ____

Constellation of _____

Principle of _____

The Desires and Inner Motivation Card indicates what inspires your actions and what drives your urges. It represents the spiritual and karmic forces at work, wanting to be expressed. It shows how you feel, and your inner strength

My Outer Persona Card (Consonants)

Total (reduced) = ____

Major Arcana card = _____

Root Number = ____

Constellation of _____

Principle of _____

The Outer Persona Card indicates your surface qualities and public identity, how you present yourself, and how you are experienced by others. It suggests your physical expression and how you manifest your inner drives in the outer world.

My Destiny Card (Vowels plus Consonants)

Total (reduced) = ____

Major Arcana card = _____

Root Number = ____

Constellation of _____

Principle of _____

The Destiny Card shows why you were born, what you were named to do, and the kinds of experiences necessary to accomplish that task.

Charles Garfield's work on "peak performers" in business and industry indicates that people, operating at their peak, value achievement in their work and in the full development of their human faculties. Garfield says, "they have what used to be called character: an inner strength that comes from an existential decision to excel,"[17] and they have a need for challenges through which to develop that excellence. Any of us can become peak performers if we accept the challenge of using our talents to their fullest extent.

In this regard, the individual letters of your name represent basic beliefs or assumptions that are natural to you and which form your character. (For instance, in my name, the letter $M = 13 =$ Death and indicates that I experience life deeply by transcending the barriers between things. My pattern is to continuously regenerate by eliminating or cutting off forms that no longer serve their purpose. Since M is the initial letter of one of my names, this becomes a leading or primary characteristic.

Even more important than the totals of your name are the patterns made by all the individual cards in your name. Also, since each card is in a Tarot Constellation, those constellations that appear most often, as well as those not represented at all, are indicators of major personality characteristics.

A = Magician (1)

B = High Priestess (2)

C = Empress (3)

D = Emperor (4)

E = Hierophant (5)

F = Lovers (6)

G = Chariot (7)

H = Strength (8)

I = Hermit (9)

J = Fortune (10)

K = Justice (11)

L = Hanged Man (12)

M = Death (13)

N = Temperance (14)

O = Devil (15)

P = Tower (16)

Q = Star (17)

R = Moon (18)

S = Sun (19)

T = Judgment (20)

U = World (21)

V = Fool (22)

W = Hierophant (5)

X = Lovers (6)

Y = Chariot (7)

Z = Strength (8)

"Spelling" Your Name

(1) Laying Out Your Cards

Lay out the cards from the Major Arcana that "spell" your entire name, using the list of letters and cards above. Because there will probably be repetitions of several letters, hence repeated cards, you will need one of the following: the Major Arcana from several decks, photocopies of the repeated cards, or pieces of paper (cut to size) on which you write the names of the repeated cards. Counting how many times the most frequent letter comes up will tell you how many different decks are necessary.

Place the vowel cards slightly higher than the consonant cards so that you can clearly see which is which. If using multiple decks, arrange the cards from your decks in any combination that appeals to you. Try several variations. Refer to the earlier illustration as an example of how to layout your cards.

(2) The Vowel Cards

Examine the vowels in your name. Try to get a sense of their energies. Remember that the vowels are your basic desires and inner motivations. They tend to propel you and give you the drive to accomplish things. They show what is likely to bring out your inner strengths. The first vowel in your name is especially important—your most characteristic energy expression.

Short interpretations of the vowels are provided below, including their source in the Hebrew alphabet. These descriptions are provided primarily to give impetus to your own interpretations.

At the end of each entry are various names from mythology that begin with that letter. Because these mythic names are seldom used for individuals and immediately evoke certain characteristics to anyone familiar with their stories, they often demonstrate the archetypal energies of the letter. Look up some of these figures in the mythology section of your library, on the Internet, or in the *New Larousse Encyclopedia of Mythology*. For instance, notice how many of the *I* names make long journeys or searches, especially into the underworld. You will discover other such "coincidences" that will help you understand these letters.

Vowels are either long or short in sound. A long vowel sounds like the letter itself. The short vowel can have a variety of other sounds. Check the pronunciation section of any dictionary for examples of long and short vowel sounds. The long vowels tend to be more active, assertive, and projective in their qualities, while the short vowels are more inner, receptive, and self-possessed.

THE MAGICIAN.

A (Derived from *Aleph.*) The Magician is communicative, skillful, and full of new ideas. He is multitalented but can become scattered. His task is to remain focused. This card gives you a focused will, high aspirations, and a pioneering spirit. It is impulsive, begins things, and creates activity but requires others to follow through. It can be selfish and egotistical. The Magician knows what he wants. (*Adam, Agni, Amaterasu, Amon, Anahita, Anubis, Aphrodite, Apollo, Athena, Astarte, Ashera, Avalokitesvara.*)

THE HIEROPHANT

E (Derived from *Heh.*) The Hierophant is confident, authoritative, and silent when he wants to be. Especially if you have several E's you tend to be active, adventurous, and curious, changeable but opinionated. Learning is a great motivator for you. Perception is a strong quality as you seek significance and meaning. Sensuality and spirituality are major forces in your life. This letter's individual power is lost when it is silent at the end of a word, but it then helps to make the preceding vowel more active. In this context, the Hierophant either helps to support all that has gone before it, or it can become dogmatic and rigid. (*Ea, El, Elijah, Enlil, Epona, Erinyes, Eros, Europa, Eurynome, Eurydice, Eve.*)

THE HERMIT.

I (Derived from *Yod.*) The Hermit is careful, prudent, and patient, with a desire to complete things. You are stimulated by the intellect and seek wisdom but approach things critically. You search for perfection. You need peace and time to reflect. People with many I's can have natural healing qualities. You find value in the inner worth of things, with love as your prime motivator. You can be overly sensitive and tend to pessimism, irritability, and quarrelsomeness. (*Icarus, Ida, Imams, Imhotep, Inanna, Indra, Io, Iris, Ishtar, Isis, Israel, Isvara, Izanagi, Izanami.*)

THE DEVIL.

O(Derived from *Ayin*.) The Devil is earthly, powerful, and ambitious, and it experiences things holistically. It concentrates, absorbs, and draws things to itself, with a natural drive to organize and an ability to understand and visualize whole systems. You will finish what you start, rarely acknowledging defeat. You can be stubborn and tenacious, melancholy and brooding, and sensitive to criticism, in which case you withdraw into yourself. Many "O"s will slow a person down through trying to take in everything. You are then cautious and obstinate. Eliminating the superfluous will help free up an O person. (*Obatala, Oceanus, Odin, Odysseus, Oedipus, O-Kuni-Nushi, Olympia, Omphale, Orion, Orpheus, Oshun, Osiris.*)

THE WORLD.

U(Derived from *Vav*.) The World is sensitive and nurturing, and it desires to protect and contain. It resists outer influences, fears ridicule, and is basically conservative; it maintains personal dignity and exclusiveness and can appear aloof and clannish. It feels free to express itself creatively only under conditions with sharply defined boundaries and limitations yet likes to travel. You U's are very responsive to those who need your protection or assistance or who fear being scattered. You are intuitive and likely to be a good judge of character. (*Uazit, Uma, Uni, Unkulunkulu, Uraeus, Urania, Uranus, Ur-Nammu, Uzza, Uzume.*)

THE CHARIOT.

Y(Derived from *Yod*.) The Chariot is intuitive and introspective with a talent for penetrating mysteries. It is emotional, irresponsible, yet assertive and challenging. It can harness the imagination to work toward goals but hates any bondage, desiring, above all else, freedom of movement. "Y's require mental, spiritual, and physical fulfillment and the freedom to pursue it. They develop the patience to work toward long-term goals. They need to be careful of losing their temper or getting "carried away" with things. (*Yahweh, Yama, Yarilo, Yemaya, Yggdrasil, Yseult, Yuki-Onne.*)

(3) Your Personal Rhythm

Can you feel the rhythms that the vowels create in your name—the energy pulses or beats? Notice when and where they repeat and what it does to the structure of your name.

Each of your names has its own beat and rhythm. According to numerologist Martita Tracy, "You are an instrument. Your physical experience and conditions of your life are the results of the harmonies or discords played by you—or upon you—by your personal name."[18] Initially, let's take just your first name and learn how to beat its rhythm out with your hands. Let your left hand beat the consonants and use your right hand for the vowels, clapping your hands against your knee. Emphasize the first letter of your name as the downbeat. You can use marks similar to those used for scanning poetry to mark the beat like this:

```
  ´   ^   ´   ´   ^   ^   ´
  W   I   L   L   I   A   M
```

Write out your full name here with the vowels and consonants marked as beats:

_____

Beat out the rhythm for one name at a time. Finally, when you can do all the beats easily, put them together so that you can beat out your whole name as one long personal rhythm, repeating it in cyclic pulses of energy. Do this until it becomes automatic and you don't have to think about it. Sway to the rhythm. Feel it deep within you as a pattern you were given at birth. Feel yourself moving through the years with this pattern. Stay with it for awhile. Once you can feel this rhythm within yourself, try any other names you have used, such as nicknames. Get a feel for how the rhythm is different. What has changed?

(4) Musical Correspondences

There are several systems of correlating the Major Arcana with musical notes. The Musical Correspondence Chart below uses the system developed by Paul Foster Case, based on the Order of the Golden Dawn correspondences.[19] Use any of these systems or one of your own devising and play your name on a musical instrument. Using the name spaces provided below, mark the corresponding musical notes below the letters of your name. If you play the tune, it will probably not be melodious, but allow yourself to experiment and play around until you find something that sounds like you. Don't be afraid to create your own system. One way would be to choose a tune that fits your name and then develop the correspondences from that.

Chart 16: Musical Correspondence Chart

A (Magician)	E	N (Temperance)	G#
B (High Priestess)	G#	O (Devil)	A
C (Empress)	F#	P (Tower)	C
D (Emperor)	C	Q (Star)	A#
E (Hierophant)	C#	R (Moon)	B
F (Lovers)	D	S (Sun)	D
G (Chariot)	D#	T (Judgment)	C
H (Strength)	E	U (World)	A
I (Hermit)	F	V (Fool)	E
J (Wheel of Fortune)	A#	W (Hierophant)	C#
K (Justice)	F#	X (Lovers)	D
L (Hanged Man)	G#	Y (Chariot)	D#
M (Death)	G	Z (Strength)	E

(5) Leading Letters

Look at the first letter of your first name. This is what you lead with. If it begins with a vowel, you've already examined it while looking at your drives and motivations. Leading with a vowel means you lead with your energy and emotions. It might give you the ability to act quickly, but usually without thinking first. For instance, the name *Elizabeth* starts with an *E*. With The Hierophant as the associated trump, it means something like this: "You confidently and authoritatively express your opinions, yet your curiosity motivates you to seek experience with new things." With a consonant first, you will "characteristically" react first with the qualities of that letter.

(6) The Consonants

Notice how consonants in general give a certain quality or "air" to the name. There are many more consonants than vowels. They are more personal and lend nuance to your basic drives. They define you more clearly. Their function linguistically is to differentiate between sounds. They create rhymes. Note especially the first consonant in each of your names. By changing it you radically alter the name; for instance: Ted, Ned, Fred, Jed, Red.

Keep in mind that the meanings given here for each letter are merely my own personal suggestions. Let the cards themselves, particularly in combination with each other, suggest their meanings to you in your own name. By looking at the cards laid out in your name, you will begin to see how they integrate and flow together.

B (Derived from *Beth*.) The High Priestess is receptive to the subtle currents of emotion around her. She is an intuitive, sensitive dreamer yet ordered and wise. She is self-sufficient, independent, and secretive. Good at diplomacy and mediation, she builds and constructs forms and combines what already exists in novel ways. (*Baal, Baba Yaga, Bacchus, Balder, Baphomet, Bast, Bel, Bellerophon, Blodeuwedd, Bona Dea, Brahma, Bran the Blessed, Brigit, Buddha.*)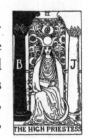

C (Derived from *Gimel*.) The Empress is concerned with the creative, imaginative, and aesthetic aspects of anything. This card/letter is sociable, cooperative, loving, gracious, and noble of bearing. (*Cain, Cassandra, Castor, Cerberus, Ceres, Cernunnos, Cerridwen, Chango, Chalchiuhtlicue, Chiron, Circe, Coyote, Cybele.*)

D (Derived from *Daleth*.) The Emperor is efficient, orderly, practical, and conservative, with a keen, discerning mind. This card/letter is purposeful—jumping at opportunities and tenacious with possessions. Self-expression is difficult, so it needs encouragement. (*Daedalus, Daevas, Dagda, Dainichi, Dakini, Danu, Demeter, Devi, Diana, Dionysus, Domovoi, Dumuzi, Durga.*)

F (Derived from either *Peh* or *Vav*.) The Lovers card is very aware of life's choices and is sometimes weighed down by the responsibility, struggling with dilemmas. It suggests a need for companionship. When inspired and in harmonious surroundings, it works to actualize dreams, while disharmony and strife bring anxiety. (*Fates, Faunus, Firanak, Flora, Fortuna, Frey, Freyja, Frigg, Fudo-Myoo, Fujiyama, the Furies.*)

G (Derived from *Gimel*.) The Chariot knows the value of leadership and goals. This card/letter is assertive, determined, and active. It is concerned with controlling the emotions, requiring meditation or exercise for focus. You will find it hard to work with others, as you struggle and see opposition in other people's points of view. Thus, you prefer to control or nurture and care for them. (*Gaea, Gandharvas, Ganesha, Ganga, Garuda, Gawain, Geb, Genii, Gilgamesh, Gorgons, Graces, Guinevere, Gwydion*.)

H (Derived from *Heh*.) Strength uses its talents to aid others, the community, the nation. It is broadminded and tolerant, courageous and fearless, with innate spiritual power. At its best, it means you work from the heart. (*Hades, Hanuman, Hapi, Harmonia, Hathor, Hecate, Hel, Hephaestus, Hera, Hercules, Hermes, Hestia, Horus, Hoshang, Huitzilopochtli, Hygieia*.)

J (Derived from *Yod*.) The Wheel of Fortune is a leader who moves easily with change. It suggests that you have good friends but can be overly influenced. It is enthusiastic, benevolent, and loves new ideas and things, being naturally inventive and original itself. You strive to improve and expand on things. (*Jadapati, Jade, Janus, Jason, Jehovah, Jesus, Jemshid, Jocasta, Jove, Joy, Juno, Jupiter*.)

K (Derived from *Kaph*.) Justice is concerned with truth and honesty. This card/letter indicates a decisiveness, is analytical, and depends on reason. It makes adjustments easily and seeks to maintain a balance. It means you can be articulate or literary, using words to good advantage. It is firm and unyielding when justice is offended. (*Ka, Kadi, Kali, Kami, Kannon, Kashiwano-kami, Keres, Kherpera, Khepri, Kore, Krishna, Kuan-yin*.)

L (Derived from *Lamed*.) The Hanged Man sacrifices himself for his dreams. This card/letter has a love of justice but leans toward irony, pessimism, and worry. It indicates that you find happiness in service to others. It needs a stimulus or push to get going. (*Lada, Lagash, Lakshmi, Laomedon, Lancelot, Lao-tzu, Leda, Leto, Libera, Lilith, Llew, Loa, Loki, Loo-Wit, Lucifer, Lug, Luna*.)

M (Derived from *Mem.*) Death efficiently brings about physical change and effectively eliminates past issues and concerns. Bitterness and sorrow are associated with this card/letter, but it is also concerned with regeneration and reconstruction. It makes you a capable and intuitive leader or executive. This letter goes with great depth of feeling but has difficulty taking things lightly. It is sensual. (*Ma, Maat, Macha, Maia, Maitreya, Mama Quilla, Marduk, Mars, Medea, Medusa, Mercury, Metis, Midas, Minerva, Minotaur, Mithra, Mohammed, the Muses.*)

DEATH.

N (Derived from *Nun.*) Temperance is outgoing, adaptable, and versatile. It can be nervous and restless and overly conscious of details. It likes travel and exercise. You react to others with compassion but have strong personal values. (*Nammu, Narcissus, Neith, Nemesis, Nephthys, Neptune, Nereus, Nergal, Ningirsu, Ninigi, Ninlil, Niobe, Norns, Nuada, Nun, Nut.*)

TEMPERANCE.

P (Derived from *Peh.*) The Tower is power oriented and potentially explosive. This card/letter suggests tremendous willpower and moral courage but quickness to anger. It is concerned with reform combined with great power of expression and can make you either a philosopher or a revolutionary. It focuses only on its own sense of power and place. (*Pachamama, Pallas, Pan, Pandora, Parsival, Parvati, Pegasus, Persephone, Perseus, Phaedra, Pluto, Poseidon, Prometheus, Prajapati, Psyche, Ptah, Pygmalion.*)

THE TOWER.

Q (Derived from *Qoph.*) The Star is inspiring, hopeful, and cheerful. It is proud spirited and calmly powerful and is therefore often followed by others. It is also insatiably curious. You use your intellect well and can work on a vision that will not manifest until a distant future. At its worst, the letter suggests unscrupulousness and dogmatism. (*Qadesh, Qamaits, Qebhsnuf, Quetzalcoatl.*)

THE STAR.

R (Derived from *Resh*.) The Moon inspires confidence through its intuitive understanding. This card/letter has a keen sense of discrimination and deep stores of knowledge. It bears hardship well and quietly but has some problem or sorrow not revealed to others. It follows its own sense of timing. It makes you magnetic and generous and perhaps draws you to the occult. (*Ra, Radha, Rama, Ravana, Rhadamanthys, Rhea, Rhiannon, Romulus and Remus, Rudra*.)

S (Derived from *Samekh*.) The Sun has a powerful will yet is benevolent, outgoing, and optimistic. It is self-regenerating, inspiring, and independent while loving social contact. This card/letter may manifest in your desire to appear wise and all-knowing and to be known as a peacemaker. You are an original and independent thinker but sometimes lack sincerity and frankness. (*Samson, Satan, Saturn, Savitri, Sekhmet, Selene, Seth, Shakti, Shamash, Shango, Shekinah, Sin, Shiva, Siddhartha, Skalds, Solomon, Soma, Sphinx, Sybil*.)

T (Derived from *Teth* or *Tav*.) Judgment has a "call" or purpose, often with some spiritual dimension. It is domestic and a peacemaker but concerned first with self-mastery. People with this card/letter are concerned with raising mass consciousness. They can be critical and love to investigate anything they question. They love a challenge. (*Tammuz, Tanet, Tara, Tartarus, Tefnut, Tethys, Tezcatlipoca, Themis, Theseus, Thetis, Thor, Thoth, Tiamat, Tirawa, Tlaloc*.)

V (Derived from *Vav*.) The Fool has the mark of the master. People with this card/letter are very individualistic, take risks, and are inveterate vagabonds (even if only in their minds). They can become scattered when pulled to the new and unusual or become depressed from attempting to cut themselves off from sensation. They need to be appreciated. (*Valkyries, Vanir, Varuna, Venus, Vesta, Victoria, Vidar, Vishnu, Volcanal, Vulcan*.)

W (Derived from *Vav.*) The Hierophant in his fiery, consonantal phase is proud spirited, versatile, and clever. People with this card/letter are good diagnosticians and determined and tenacious in their loves and desires. They like to give advice or counsel and are good learners. They feel comfortable with things that are "ordered" and follow laws or rules. (*Wakan-Tanka, Walpurga, Wen Ch'ang, Woden.*)

THE HIEROPHANT

X (Derived from *Tav* as cross.) This letter represents the Lovers in its earthly form. The card is concerned with success in business and worldly matters, crafts and artistic endeavors. It is quite aware of the burdens of responsibility but, at the crossroads of life, is willing to take the hard and difficult path if sure of a reward. You choose friends who will profit you. (*Xerxes, Xipe Totec, Xiuhtecuhtli, Xochiquetzal.*)

THE LOVERS.

Y (Derived from *Yod.*) This letter represents the Chariot in its watery and consonantal form. It is psychic and prophetic, with a talent for penetrating mysteries, assertive and determined when its idealism is aroused. It can be mediumistic and channel energies. (*See the vowel listing for Y for mythic names.*)

THE CHARIOT.

Z (Derived from *Zayin.*) This is Strength in its airy form. These people are extremists. They have self-confidence, push, and the energy to go for what they want. They magnify and exaggerate situations and seek to organize and control others, or else they become very restless. They can be very successful through promoting and developing the creative ideas of others. (*Zagreus, Zarathusthra, Zend-Avesta, Zenobia, Zephyrus, Zeus.*)

STRENGTH.

(7) The Name Patterns

Divide each of your names into syllables. Look at any diphthongs or blended sounds; overlap these cards to indicate that they don't stand alone. (A good dictionary will provide the pronunciation and syllable division of most names.) Combine the meanings of the cards in these groups.

As an example, my middle name is Katherine, which I pronounce *Kath'-er-in*. The first syllable is *Kath*, containing a *th* blend; it is emphasized. In the second syllable, the *e* is barely heard, sliding into the *r*. And the final *e* in the last syllable is silent. The *th* blend of Judgment (*T*) and Strength (*H*) is suggestive of my call to be useful to others. The leading letter/card of Justice (*K*) emphasizes *honesty and articulateness*, while the connective vowel card, the Magician (*A*), stresses my drive to be focused in order to communicate. Thus the first syllable clearly harmonizes with my work as teacher and author. In the second syllable, the almost silent Hierophant (*E*) points to my need to learn intuitively—Moon (*R*). The remaining Hermit (*I*) and Temperance (*N*), with a silent Hierophant (*E*), point to a restless energy that insists on perfection and attention to detail in learning, as well as compassionate concern for the well-being of others.

Your Name Mandala

Take the cards for each one of your names and arrange them in any pattern that feels balanced or right to you. Don't worry about correct order—just create a picture with the cards that seem to express your name. Study each name. Your destiny is to fulfill your overall personality characteristics—to actualize your name. Although this gives you your basic Name Mandala, there is much more you can discover about yourself from your name.

Adding It All Up

Most of us are given three names at birth: a first or personal name, a middle name, and a last or family name. The following processes will give you some idea of how each of these names affects you individually. But many of you will not have the "usual" English and American name structure. For instance, I have a cousin who was given only a first and last name. Finally, in college, she legally added a middle initial (but no name) in order to end the hassle of having application forms returned or rejected for leaving an item blank. Adapt the following ideas in any way that seems appropriate for your situation, especially if your name follows some other naming tradition or is unique.

Your Personal Name

Your first name is also called your "given name." It is usually very personal. Until this century, only one's family and friends used it. It was a sign of intimacy and trust to permit someone to address you by your first name. Today we are more casual and openly friendly, so this is probably how you usually identify yourself. (A little later I'll discuss nicknames and other names you assume for yourself.) Your first name is the "I," or thinking Self, and deals with what you are most conscious of in yourself. It is also most closely aligned with your peers in your generation. The popularity of certain first names comes and goes in the form of fads, societal mores, styles, and even events. You may have an uncommon first name for your generation that was quite ordinary in another, or vice versa. For instance, I've never known anyone my age named Jason, yet now I know more than a dozen, all born since 1972. Many children born during the 1960s and '70s were given names that reflected their generation's preoccupation with Nature, cultural heritage, or mythology. Thus, first names are generally indicative of historical eras.

Your Middle Name

Your middle name may represent a variety of things. It is usually your hidden Self, in that most people don't know you by that name, so it can indicate an undeveloped potential. If it is your mother's maiden name, it has a genetic and hereditary function, referring to ethnic roots that may not otherwise be apparent. If it is also a "given" name, it may be from the family roots, like being named after Great-aunt Arabella, or perhaps it reflects some of your parent's further-out fantasies. Ask yourself (or your parents) why you were given this name. You must judge for yourself the significance of this position in your name but, in general, it indicates subtle inheritances, things you don't know about yourself or personal aspects with which you may not outwardly identify (unless you use your middle name as your personal name). It also acts as a connecting link between your personal Self and your social/cultural Self.

Your Family Name

Your last name (on your birth certificate) is likely to be your father's last name, although that is not necessarily the case. It could be your mother's last name, a combination of your mother's and father's last names, or a completely original name given just to you (the rarest of all). I call it your family name, because even if you took it for yourself it tends to categorize you in some social or cultural framework. Your last name represents your most formal Self and usually comes from your cultural and hereditary background. It is the "we"-thinking Self, with which you identify with some group of which you are a part, from nuclear family to national or ethnic kinship. When family names are changed during immigration, it generally marks a commitment to the new nationality and a reforming of family values.

PERSONAL/ FIRST NAME CARD	MIDDLE NAME CARD	FAMILY/ LAST NAME CARD
Conscious sense of Self	Hidden Self	Formal Self
Personal and generational	Genetic and hereditary	Social and cultural
"I"-thinking Self	Undeveloped potential	"We"-thinking Self

Your Individual Name Cards

The cards that spell your name and the cards that represent the numerical total of each name should be examined with the following keywords in mind:

Use Chart 17 (pages 230–231), Name Cards and Life Potential Card Chart, which comes after these instructions to add up each of your names individually and thus determine the tarot card that sums up each.

First Name Card

Add all the vowels in your first name and write the total on the chart where indicated. Do the same for the consonants, writing the total in the space provided. Add these two together (from your first name only) to find Sum 1 and reduce to a number that is 22 or below. This indicates the tarot card that represents your Conscious Self, called your First Name Card. Write this on the chart.

Middle Name Card

Do the same with your middle name to find the card that expresses your Hidden Self, called your Middle Name Card.

Last Name Card

Then do the same with your family name to determine the card that expresses your Social Self, called your Last Name Card.

Theme Chord

The three cards you have just identified are like individual musical notes that express the essence of each of your three names. Together they strike a chord, a combination that is your three names in unison. I call this three-card combination your Theme Chord. It "sounds" the dominant chord in the "theme song" of your life. (These three cards may or may not have a constellation in common.) The way to reflect upon your Theme Chord is as a three-card tarot spread, using the keywords on the previous page as the three position meanings.

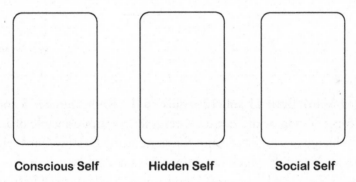

Conscious Self   Hidden Self   Social Self

Your Destiny Cards

When you add up the numbers in your name, you may notice that there are a variety of ways to do it, and each way will give you slightly different sums. For instance, if you sum up your first, middle, and last names separately, reduce the numbers to tarot cards between 1 and 22, and then add these totals, you might arrive at an answer of 21 (The World); yet by adding up all the letters in your entire name before reducing them, you would get a 12

Chart 17: Name Cards and Life Potential Card Chart (Part One)

INDIVIDUAL NAME CARDS	Unreduced totals	Reduced to 22 or below
First Name:		
Vowels:	= _____	
Letters: _____		
Consonants:	= _____	
Sum 1 = _____	= _____ : _____	
		First Name Card
Middle Name:		
Vowels:	= _____	
Letters: _____		
Consonants:	= _____	
Sum 2 = _____	= _____ : _____	
		Middle Name Card
Last Name:		
Vowels:	= _____	
Letters: _____		
Consonants:	= _____	
Sum 3 = _____	= _____ : _____	
		Last Name Card

(Hanged Man). Both 21 and 12 reduce to the Root Number 3 and so are in the constellation of the Empress, representing the principle of Love and Creative Imagination. (This is not the same as the Destiny Card referred to in *Tarot for Your Self*, which is a Minor Arcana card, which in this book is called your Zodiacal Lesson and Opportunity Card) As used here, the Destiny Cards are cards from the Major Arcana with standard numerological correspondences.

There are three different ways of adding the numbers in your name to reach a grand total, resulting in your Destiny Card(s), individually known as your Theme Note Card, your Rhythm Card, and your Melody Card. These cards are always from the same constellation and add up to the same Root Number. They are variations on your basic destiny theme (as noted by your name).

Chart 17: Name Cards and Life Potential Card Chart (Part Two)

DESTINY CARDS

Theme Note Card *(use reduced sums)*:

Sum 1 + Sum 2 + Sum 3   = _____:_____

Theme Note Card

Melody Card *(use unreduced sums)*:

Sum 1 + Sum 2 + Sum 3 = _____   = _____:_____

Melody Card

YOUR PERSONAL CARDS *(from Chart 15)*

Desires and Motivation Card:

Reduced sum of all Vowels   = _____:_____

Desired and Inner
Motivation Card

Outer Persona Card:

Reduced sum of all Consonents   = _____:_____

Outer Persona Card

Rhythm Card:

Desires and Inner Motivation Card + Outer Persona Card   = _____:_____

Rhytjm Card

My Theme Note Card, Melody Card, and Rhythm Card (my Destiny Cards) are all in the

Constellation of _____

Principle of _____

The following card(s) of this constellation did not appear as Destiny Cards and therefore are

Hidden Factor Name Card(s): _____

LIFE POTENTIAL CARD:

Birth day + month + year   = _____ (Base Number)

Sum 1 + Sum 2 + Sum 3 (not reduced)   = _____

· Reduce total to 22 or below   = _____

_____
My Lifetime Potential Card

Theme Note Card

Add together the reduced sums of your first, middle, and last names as indicated on the chart. Reduce them in turn to a tarot card number (22 or less). This is your Theme Note Card, the single "note" that expresses the sum of your Theme Chord (the three cards derived from your first, middle, and last names). By referring to chart 16, Musical Correspondence Chart, earlier in this chapter, you can actually sound out your Theme Note as well as your Theme Chord.

Rhythm Card

Earlier in this chapter you added up all the vowels in your entire name to give you your Desires and Inner Motivation Card, and you added all the consonants in your name to find your Outer Persona Card (refer to chart 15, Your Personal Cards Chart). Simply add the number of these two cards together (reduce the sum to 22 or below, if necessary). Since your vowels and consonants represent the inner beat of your name, I call this card your Rhythm Card. It sums up your personal beat and shows the way in which you manifest the tempo of energy flow in your life.

Melody Card

Add all the individual numbers in your entire name together before you reduce (in the chart, take the total of Sum 1 + Sum 2 + Sum 3, then reduce). This process requires you to listen to each card's unique tone, played one after another as your personal melody. I call this your Melody Card. The sum is its essence.

Hidden Factor Name Card

Since your Theme Note Card, Rhythm Card, and Melody Card are derived from the various ways in which you can sum up your name (you are adding the same numbers, only reducing the totals at different places), they will all add up to the same Root Number and are therefore in the same Tarot Constellation. This constellation is the final expression or summing up of your personal destiny as described by your name. Any card in your constellation that does not appear as Theme Note, Rhythm, or Melody Card acts like the Hidden Factor Card did in your birth date calculations. This is your Hidden Factor Name Card(s).

Chart 18: Name Cards Checklist

Desires and Inner Motivation Card	= Reduced sum of full name vowel numbers
Outer Persona Card	= Reduced sum of full name consonant numbers
First Name Card	= Reduced sum of all first name numbers
Middle Name Card	= Reduced sum of all middle name numbers
Last Name Card	= Reduced sum of all last name numbers
Theme Note Card	= Reduced sum of the previous three cards
Rhythm Card	= Reduced sum of the first two cards above
Melody Card	= Reduced sum of all full name numbers (Sum 1 + Sum 2 + Sum 3)
Destiny Card Number)	= Any of the three previous cards (same Root
Hidden Factor Name Card	= Any remaining card(s) of same Root Number as the above card
Life Potential Card	= Reduced sum of full name numbers plus birth date Base Number

Note: "Reduced sum" means any number from 22 to 1, which is then equated with the Major Arcana card of that number.

Life Potential Card

This is the card that sums up both your name and birth date. It shows your greatest potential and the highest that you may achieve. It is always read in its most spiritual and idealistic manner to represent the ultimate goal that you may achieve by marshalling all your forces to fulfill your destiny according to your soul purpose. Take the four-digit total of the month, day, and year of your birth (don't reduce), and add to it the total of all the unreduced letters of your name (Sum 1 + Sum 2 + Sum 3). Finally, reduce this number to between 1 and 22. This is your Life Potential Card.

Counting Constellations

The numbers in the chart below correspond to the nine tarot constellations. We will use the square to determine which constellations are emphasized in your name.

Chart 19: Constellation Count Chart

1	2	3
4	5	6
7	8	9

First, you need to find the Root Number of each letter in your full name: Write the letter of your name in the spaces below, with the corresponding Key Numbers (1 to 22, corresponding to the tarot cards, see chart 14, Alphabet Key Numbers Chart), then reduce each of the numbers to its Root Number (1 to 9).

For example:

Letters:	M	A	R	Y	K	A	T	H	E	R	I	N	E	G	R	E	E	R
Key Numbers:	13	1	18	7	11	1	20	8	5	18	9	14	5	7	18	5	5	18
Root Numbers	4	1	9	7	2	1	2	8	5	9	9	5	5	7	9	5	5	9

My Name:

Letters: _____

Key Numbers: _____

Root Numbers: _____

Now, for each letter of your name, place a mark in the above square (dot, check, line, etc.) somewhere within the box of its Root Number. Then do the same for each of the cards found in charts 15 (Your Personal Cards

Chart) and 17 (Name Cards and Life Potential Card Chart) (there are at least nine of these).

Which constellations are the most strongly represented (probably with five or more marks for the average name)?

What are their core principles?

Tarot Constellations	Principles

Which constellations and principles are not represented in your name at all?

Tarot Constellations	Principles

Any constellations that are missing indicate characteristics or qualities that you lack. Unless these are compensated for by your Birth Cards, you will probably find yourself strongly drawn to people in this constellation (or constellations). These are qualities that you have to consciously work at developing, because they are not part of your natural expression. Nevertheless, they are strong motivators because you see them outside of yourself and are probably fascinated by them. This may give you some insight to as to why you are irresistibly attracted to certain people.

Changing Your Name

At long last, we get around to looking at any other names you may have: nicknames, married names, spiritual names, professional names or aliases, or other name changes. You can never totally change the basic underlying rhythm of your birth name, which is why you've spent so much time getting to know it here. Other names, though, represent the ways in which you have chosen to modify or change or add to your destiny. They are very important. When you take a new name, there is a corresponding change in your outer life. Often when you take on the name of a husband or partner or create a new one for the two of you, the new name will indicate what you are taking on in that relationship.

The nicknames that other people call you indicate your particular characteristics to which they respond. These represent the part of you that they align with and probably suggest what they need from you. You represent to them what they call you. They will also bring out those traits in you.

Although you might want to check out a name change with numerology or the tarot cards before you finalize it, I do not believe that there are any "bad" or "wrong" names or that, because your Birth Card is one number, your Destiny Card *should* add up to a certain number in order to be in harmony with it. Many people have made growth-producing challenges out of difficult and inharmonious number patterns, developing great strength, compassion, and personal abilities out of so-called adversity. Every name has its own potential; the harmony comes from maximizing the lessons contained therein.

When you take on a new name, you can inaugurate it with a ritual. This ritual should be your own, but basically you might want to include some of the following:

Acknowledge and thank the name you are putting aside for all you have learned from it. Perhaps begin with your old name laid out in cards and then change it card for card, noting the cards you need to add and those you must take away. Rearrange them to form the new name.

Go over the new name with all the ideas from this chapter, getting to know it and its beat, rhythms, and melody. Acknowledge aloud the qualities and personal characteristics that you have chosen to bring into your life through this name. Call them to you as you call out your name.

If you are hesitant or ambivalent about taking this name, such as a married name or alias, include affirmative statements that will help you get the most from your experience with this name. Your intuitive feelings of ambivalence might show up in comparing your birth name with the new one, especially if you now have to take on many qualities that were lacking or weak in your original name. Look to see the kinds of lessons you are most likely to face so that you will recognize them when they occur.

Your Magic Mirror and Life Mandala

Take all the cards that make up your name and lay them on the floor in any pattern that feels right to you, so that it forms a mandala or complete picture. (This is your basic Name Mandala, but now you can work with it magically.) If you wish, place power objects or personal symbols for the elements around your cards. Put a small mirror in the center and look at yourself so that you can see only your eyes in the mirror, while the cards around it become your "face." Breathe deeply, evenly, and rhythmically. Become aware of your strengths and weaknesses, what you possess and what you lack. Remember that your name carries a magical rhythm and melody that can be heard on other planes of existence. Realize that if you fight against that rhythm and song, it will limp along, stifled and crippled. Reclaim your personal energy! Feel it within yourself. Beat out the sound of your name. Move with it, creating a dance of vitality and joy. Rise and spontaneously improvise your own individual movements. Dance your name; dance your destiny. Realize that the dance doesn't stop; it is only that you are not always aware of it. Learn to dance your dance consciously. This is a beginning.

If you are taking a new name, make a magic mirror for it and look at yourself in your mirror. In your imagination, step bravely through this magic mirror and into your personally chosen destiny. You may wish to photocopy, photograph, draw, or collage the image you have created with your cards. Add pictures from magazines and postcards. Use an actual mirror or some other symbolic image as the center. Hang this image on your wall.

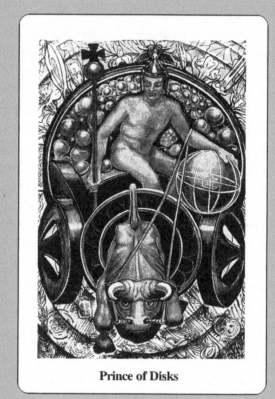

Prince of Disks

CHAPTER **18**

The People or Court Cards

In *Tarot for Your Self*, I presented a chapter on the People Cards and thought I had said everything about them, but of course I had only scratched the surface. In *Understanding the Tarot Court* (cowritten with Tom Little), we explored these cards in much more depth. In this chapter the focus is on who you are in the tarot court.

The number of new tarot decks being designed and published each year seems to be increasing steadily. Many of these decks are taking the people out of the medieval court environment and exploring new contexts for how we experience them. In the process they are also changing what they call the Court Cards, renaming them as Family Cards, People Cards, Tribal Figures, Royalty Cards, and even the Three Faces of the Goddess.

In this book, you are asked to consider who you are not only as a King, Queen, Knight, or Page, but also as Prince, Princess, Son, Daughter, Warrior, Servant, Patriarch, Matriarch, Guardian, Guide, Seeker, Novice, Child, Crone, Sage, Angel, Muse, Shaman, Priestess, Knower, Gift, Apprentice, Speaker, Companion, and more.

Who Are You in the Tarot Court?

One of the most familiar uses of the Court Cards is as the Significator in a spread. A Significator is a card that represents the person or issue for which the reading is being done. Most often it serves as a sign or token of that person's identity and presence, a proxy in cardboard, existing at the same level of symbolic reality as the cards providing the response. It can also represent the intent or purpose of the reading or the subject of concern, rather than the person being read for (in which case, any of the seventy-eight cards can be used).

Most of the time it's okay to not use a Significator, even when a spread calls for one. (Occasionally a Significator, left in the deck, makes the cards surrounding it more important or indicates the direction of movement in one's affairs). If you strongly identify with a particular Court Card you might want to leave it in the deck and pay special attention if it turns up in the reading. Cards that you connect with specific people in your life often *signify* that person's influence on the situation being depicted.

When a court card appears in a reading, it can represent yourself or someone else. More specifically, it represents an aspect of your personality or a style, attitude, or a role that you or someone else is assuming. More abstractly, it can be an energy or influence at work in your life. Traditionally, Knights also represent travel and action, and Pages can signify news, thoughts, or messages.

The traditional method for choosing your Significator is by sex, age, hair color, and/or sun sign. However, physical descriptions based on European ranges of eye and hair color are not relevant to the majority of people on this planet. I suggest using the following standards loosely, if at all.

Traditional Associations for the Suits

Wands	Cups	Swords	Pentacles
Fire signs	Water signs	Air signs	Earth signs
Blond to red hair	Light brown hair	Brown hair	Brunette or black hair
Blue or hazel eyes	Blue, brown, or hazel eyes	Brown eyes	Blue or black eyes

Traditional Associations for the Ranks

Kings	Queens	Knights	Pages
Mature or married man	Mature or married woman	Young or unmarried man (under thirty)	Young, unmarried woman or child

As you will discover, it's not always this easy. There's always a part of you that's a child to your mother, and you may be a King or Queen when you are in charge but a Knight or Page when taking orders from someone else.

Another way to choose your Significator is to lay out all sixteen people cards and choose the one you most identify with at the moment. When reading for someone else you can have them spontaneously choose their own card from among the sixteen.

Alternatively, the querent can randomly select a card from either the whole deck or just the people cards, which can then be interpreted as showing the aspect of the querent that is asking the question or involved in the situation.

Which Card Are You?

Before you go any further, you might want to look through the court or people cards in your deck and intuitively select the one that seems most like you. Card picked: _____

How are you like this card?

The Roles You Play

Whatever these cards are called, they primarily represent the roles, masks, or subpersonalities we wear and with which we identify ourselves.

There are many ways to determine the roles you play and the different aspects of Self. One technique that may hold some surprises for you is to go through your closet and look at the clothes you have. Who are the different characters within yourself who wear these costumes? There is perhaps your business-suited downtown self, your casual weekend traveler persona, and your Saturday night special. Then there's the hiker, backpacker, skier, swimmer, boater, cyclist, or biker. And what about those sensual nightclothes, or that outfit stuck in the back that your mother bought you, or your equally buried hippy togs waiting for a revival; and are the paint-spattered jeans those of an artist or a housepainter? Obviously there are a lot of "yous" around.

Another place to look for your roles is on your bookshelf, with its old and new interests, its hobby and activity guides that reflect your fantasies of what you'd like to do and be. Look around the other rooms of your house for additional clues as to the myriad aspects of Self that can found there.

Let's take a look at all these facets of you, which are like the mirrored faces on a disco ball reflecting different things under different lights.

In the space below make a list of six or seven of the roles you play or masks you wear in your life right now. (If you did the similar exercise in *Tarot for Your Self*, you'll find it useful to do it again, as your responses may differ, based on changing perceptions of yourself.)

1.

2.

3.

4.

5.

6.

7.

Now separate all the People Cards from your deck and look through them, keeping their elemental qualities in mind.

Developmental Stages

These cards represent stages in your psychological development and in the development of your skills, as well as personality types. I will use traditional names from this point on. Compare these cards from the Waite-Smith tarot with the images from your favorite deck. How does your deck express similar concepts and how is it different?

The Pages

The Pages (also Child, Princess, Daughter, Servant, Novice, etc.) are the least developed and most immature but open and willing to take risks. As a Page, you are an eager learner trying things out, an apprentice using and carrying knowledge whose significance you don't yet fully understand. You are curious and hopeful, wondering and amused. Pages have some of the qualities of the maiden on the Strength card. They are also similar to the Fool in that both can represent innocence, trust and new beginnings. They are related to the element Earth.

The Knights

The Knights (also Seeker, Prince, Son, Warrior, Amazon, Dancer, etc.) have reached the stage of thinking they now know something. As a Knight you are exploring what you can do with your skills; you are actively using and further honing them. You are discovering things for yourself and learning from experience but may be rebelling against conventions. You seek challenges and adventure and can be aggressive or even reckless. Knights are similar to the Chariot card. They are usually related to the element Fire.

The Queens

While the Queens and Kings are equally skilled, the Queens have fully developed talents that are personal and interpersonal. (They are also known as Woman, Mother, Matriarch, Mistress, Guide, Sibyl, Gift, Priestess, etc.)

Queens focus on understanding the deeper underlying meanings of things and, at their best, are benevolent and inspiring. As a Queen of Cups or Pentacles you are sensitive, caring, nurturing, and comforting. As a Queen of Wands or Swords you are directing, teaching, observing, motivating, and implementing. Queens accomplish things. They give advice. Queens are most like the Empress. They are related to the element Water.

The Kings

The Kings (also Man, Father, Chief, Patriarch, Guardian, Sage, Shaman, Speaker, etc.) demonstrate their talents, which are outer and public. They seem confident of their expertise and secure in their positions, but they can easily become rigid and outmoded; their energy is on the wane. As a King, you administer, judge, take charge, and handle your outer affairs competently. You establish procedures and build empires. Kings show where you have developed mastery, but also where you can be inflexible, and where you think you have nothing more to learn. Kings are much like the Emperor. They are usually related to the element Air.

Developmental Role Exercises

Quickly and without thinking too carefully about it, look through these cards and pick one card for each role that you play as noted in your list above. Be spontaneous rather than analytical. If possible, do not use a card more than once. Write their names in your list next to the roles they represent for you.

After you have chosen your cards, answer the following questions: Have you used all the suits? If any suits are missing, which are they and what qualities do they represent? Where in your life are you able to manifest these missing qualities?

Which suit predominates? What does this say to you about conditions in which you are most comfortable? Do that suit and its related element also appear in other symbol systems (your astrological chart, dominant Jungian functions, etc.)?

Is there any figure (King, Queen, Knight, Page) that you did not choose or don't feel comfortable with? At which developmental level is it? Is it masculine or feminine? Older or younger than you feel yourself to be? What qualities does this missing figure(s) represent that you haven't listed among your roles?

Which figure did you use most often? At which developmental level is it? What does this indicate about your own perception of self-mastery?

With all sixteen People Cards spread before you, look at the Kings. Acknowledge some area of your life in which you have developed outer mastery and can demonstrate it to others. In this you are kingly. Pick one of the Kings to represent this in yourself. Also, state your expertise:

Look at the Queens. Acknowledge some area of your life in which you have developed inner mastery and can nurture that in yourself or another. In this you are queenly. Pick one of the Queens to represent this in yourself. Also state your expertise:

Look at the Knights. Acknowledge an area of your life in which you actively using a skill, or putting energy into an area of interest or inquiry (a quest). In this you are knightly. Pick one of the Knights to represent this in yourself. Also, state your skill or interest:

Look at the Pages (Princesses). Acknowledge an area of your life in which you are taking a risk, learning something new, or acquiring some information through your senses. In this you are like a youthful Page. Pick one of the Pages to represent this in yourself. Also, state your information or learning:

For instance, as a mother I feel I am the Queen of Cups to my daughter. When writing books and presentations, I become the Queen of Swords. I am the King of Wands when expounding passionately on my favorite topic—the tarot. To my mother I will always be her Page of Cups, learning to grow up, and in my determination to create a stable financial base I am the Knight of Pentacles, and so on.

Now, just to take this a bit further: List three or four of the major people in your life. Do it right now.

1.

2.

3.

4.

Next to each person's name, write the Court Card that you most associate with that person *as he or she relates to you.*

Take a moment to look at what you've written and realize that each of these people have their own masks and roles just as you do. Try to imagine which Court Card each of these people *would have picked for themselves.* How are your impressions of them different from how they would probably see themselves? When you get the opportunity, ask these people to pick the card they feel most describes them and find out why.

From the Courts to the People

The People Cards are difficult yet intriguing. Most tarot students and even longtime tarot readers have more trouble with these than with any of the other cards. The traditional Court Cards depicting figures from a medieval court are about as foreign to my personal experience as one can get. Of course I can envision my father and mother in the roles of king and queen, and I've known a few knights in shining armor in my time. And my daughter occasionally looks as sweet and winsome as the Page of Wands.

But for the most part, I've wondered when the Knight of Pentacles appears if he's someone at work, an old boyfriend, someone I haven't met yet, or any of a half dozen Earth-sign people I know.

In creating their decks, many tarot artists simply follow traditional royalty designations. Yet the court environment is irrelevant in our society. It lacks the richness of personal symbology, as revealed by the awkwardness of Court Cards in readings. Luckily many of the contemporary tarot designers have been intrigued by this family of figures and are reconceptualizing them according to our contemporary settings, mythological symbologies, and current psychological understandings of human nature. They are revolutionizing our fixed conceptions of the Court Card roles and creating different models for us to reflect on.

Even if you use a deck with the traditional Court Cards, your appreciation of them can be deepened by the work these tarot artists have done.

One of the first decks to radically reconceptualize the Court Cards (and to make the deck round) was the Motherpeace tarot created by Vicki Noble and Karen Vogel. Their People Cards are named Shaman, Priestess, Son, and Daughter. Shamans represent power and experience and control the qualities of their suit. Priestesses work from the heart. They receive and channel the forces of the suit and are concerned with the sacredness of life. Sons represent the ego. While they have a light, playful quality, they are also focused and goal oriented. Daughters are more sensory and represent the child within us all.

Angel of Music   *Child of Painting*   *Man of Science*   *Woman of Poetry*

Ed Buryn, in *The William Blake Tarot of the Creative Imagination*, calls the court Person Cards and named them Angel, Woman, Man, and Child. He notes that the word *person* comes from *personare*, a face mask used by actors, signifying "to sound through." A person is a character and a role as well as a body and a personality. In keeping with the theme of the deck, these cards represent the artists and the heroes in us all. An Angel is a sacred persona, a Child represents the face of innocence, and the Woman and Man are the archetypal feminine and masculine qualities and roles within each of us.

The Gaian tarot by Joanna Powell Colbert features Elders, Guardians, Explorers and Children. Elders pass on the wisdom and teaching of the suit,

Child of Earth

Elder of Air

Explorer of Fire

Guardian of Water

keeping the long view in mind. They represent dissemination and release. Guardians nurture and preserve the qualities of the suit. They represent midlife and fruition. Explorers are actively engaged with discovering the qualities of the suit. Representing young adulthood, they investigate paths and options and are driven by their quests and goals. Children remind us of our sense of wonder. They represent birth, beginnings and learning, as well as acting as messengers.

There are many other decks that express, through crosscultural symbolism, our developmental processes and inner psychic states. You might wonder how to resolve the differences between a Queen, Priestess, Guardian, and Woman, for instance, yet they can all broaden our understanding of the essence of the feminine.

Each deck contains its individual symbolism that can guide you through your inner landscapes. Therefore it is important to find a deck that expresses the values with which you feel most in accord. To some extent, each deck (because the pictures themselves are so evocative) must be interpreted within its own symbology.

The Golden Dawn Decks: Thoth and Waite-Smith

Major confusion arises when people try to reconcile Aleister Crowley's Thoth deck with traditional court designations like those found in the Waite-Smith deck. However, both decks arose out of a magical organization known as the Hermetic Order of the Golden Dawn, founded in London in 1888.

The Golden Dawn associated the court cards with the Tetragrammaton, or four-lettered, unspoken name of god, Yod-He-Vau-He, which letters are related to the elements in a developmental process such that:

Yod/Fire	=	instigating energy	
He/Water	=	response to and support of that energy	
Vau/Air	=	working out of that energy	
Final He/Earth	=	the energy materialized	

This scenario required that the most dynamic, active, and forceful court

Chart 20: Comparison of Golden Dawn–Based Court Cards

Characteristics	Yod/Fire	He/Water	Vau/Air	final He/Earth
Golden Dawn	King	Queen	Prince/Emperor	Princess/Empress
Thoth	Knight	Queen	Prince	Princess
Traditional and Waite-Smith	Knight	Queen	King	Page

card come first and be supported by the following card—hence the active Knight was elevated to the Yod or King position as consort to the Queen (He). To create a balance of male and female, the other two Court Cards became the son and daughter or Prince and Princess of the Knight (King) and Queen. The Princes were Kings in training (and were also called the Emperors). Golden Dawn members were told to write these new titles on their continental decks, changing the Knights to Kings and the Kings to Princes. The intentions of these three groups can best be determined as follows:

Knight of Cups   Prince of Disks   Princess of Swords   Queen of Wands

As Chart 20 shows, the primary couple in the Thoth deck are the Knight and the Queen. They are accompanied by their children, the Prince and Princess. The reason for this switch changes the meanings of these cards and needs to be told, as it has from time immemorial, in the form of a fairy tale.

Once upon a time, communities were so isolated they became genetically inbred, lessening vigor and fertility. Because the rulers were often seen as gods, their health and well-being symbolized that of the land and the entire community. As a king became old and infertile, or was injured (like the Fisher King in the Grail legends), the land would dry up and become a wasteland, or the king would be unable to vanquish a ravaging monster. And so it came to pass that new blood (and genes) were needed to revivify the royal lineage passed through the queens. When a strange knight rode into town, he faced a test to determine his strength and wisdom. He was required to vanquish a dragon or a sphinx, solve a riddle, or kill the old king. If he succeeded, he was given the hand of the queen in marriage. The son of their union was the prince, who was in training to be king. He was required to be a diplomat and a leader but not to possess the fieriness of spirit required of the knight. The princess was their daughter but also represented the young fertile state of woman, whereas the queen mother represented the royal lineage itself.

Thus, we have to read the characters in the two decks differently—Crowley's Knight is more powerful and masterful than Waite's Knight, taking on many of the qualities of Waite's King yet retaining the vitality and adventurousness of Waite's Knight. Crowley's Prince is a King in training, demonstrating the diplomacy, art, and artifice of its suit. And Crowley's Princess emphasizes feminine potential rather than the childlike aspects of Waite's Page card.

Our Inner Family

The People Cards can be seen as steps or stages in our growth and development. They illustrate the different kinds of mastery that we must bring into balance within ourselves to be full, rounded individuals. They are our inner family, as well as the people we know. And as we are always sliding up and down the scale of so-called maturity, we can appear in any of these forms.

For example, when you offer your advice to someone, based on your wide experience, you speak with kingly authority. But at fifty-five years of age, when you take up the guitar for the first time, you approach it like a Page, with the innocence of a child. You risk appearing naive or even silly. Luckily, we are usually able to switch roles when appropriate. And in a tarot reading, we have the opportunity to see just which persona we are displaying to determine how appropriate it is to the particular situation in which we are involved.

A Numerical Analysis of the People Cards

The tarot cards can be seen as a model of coming to "know ourselves"—an admonition written on the gate of the Oracle at Delphi. Since numbers so often form the inner structure of the Tarot, we can turn to them in our attempt to better understand the Court Cards. There are no individual numbers associated with the Court Cards, but there are sixteen of them. Perhaps there is a significance to this.

The 16th Major Arcana card is the Tower, which is also known as the House of God, Tower of Destruction, and the Great Liberator.

This is the card that liberates us from the structures and forms that keep us from perceiving our true Self. In it, the lightning bolt of Truth destroys all false boundaries and beliefs. And the structures, boundaries, and beliefs that are destroyed in this card are, of course, the roles that each of us play in our daily lives. These roles are the masks behind which we hide. They are the walls we build to keep us from the realization of who we really are. These roles and personality structures become fences behind which we isolate ourselves from one another. They form our "identity," or that which makes us different from others. These enclosing walls protect us from the unknown; thus we nest down in a structure of false security, false because these personality structures—ones like those you've listed earlier in this book—are not who you really are. You are not the walls around you, but rather the multiform spirit that resides within.

Thus, the Tower expresses the fact the Court Cards are the roles we play, the masks behind which we hide, and the towering forms into which we've crystallized, which must ultimately be destroyed if we are to awaken to who we really are. The Tower stresses the impermanence of worldly position and rank and the false sense of importance and pride of achievement in which we cloak ourselves. We are truly liberated when we have no more roles to play; when our infinite possibilities are no longer limited.

Now, if we numerically add 1 + 6, we get 7, and perhaps the 7th Trump Card can tell us something more about the essential nature of these sixteen Court Cards.

Seven is the number of the Chariot, also known as Victory or Mastery. The vehicle pictured on the card represents our own personal temple from

which our power flows into our daily experience. The Holy Order of Mans, in their work on tarot called *Jewels of the Wise*, explain how we have built vehicles or enclosures to imprison our inner subconscious Self. These are enclosures within which we cultivate who we are and develop our various masteries in our daily life.[20]

The lunar masks on the charioteer's shoulders and the duality and mixed characteristics of the sphinxes show that we wear the masks to pose our own riddle to the sphinx's question, Who am I? The zodiacal belt suggests that we wear these masks of personality as long as time and space bind us.

Our individual vehicle is the enclosure in which we cultivate ourselves. The court cards are therefore the ways in which we gain mastery and perfect ourselves. They are the developmental steps we take to discover our own identity. Like the Chariot, the court cards show us how to develop control over our physical environment, how to harness our personal resources toward our purpose, and how to use our skills and abilities to move us instinctively through the challenges presented in the Minor Arcana Number Cards. The Court Cards depict us on a journey of self-development. As the Bhagavad-Gita says, "The Self is the rider in the chariot of the body, of which the senses are horses and the mind the reins." We are the Self within an ever-changing vehicle consisting of social and developmental roles.

And, thus, we see how we develop and perfect our personality structure, and then, as in the Tower, go through a process of breaking down all that is false in that structure, only to slowly build it up again. We then discover that that too is not who we really are. And so we continue until we have

burned away all the forms that keep us from mirroring Truth and Perfection. Then, we too can see our reflection in the Holy Grail as pictured in the Thoth Chariot card.

Finally, let's look at the sixteen Court Cards again, and at the number 16. It is made up of two other numbers: the 1 and the 6. Translated into the Major Arcana, these are the Magician and the

Lovers. This seems appropriate because, in interpretation, the court cards work in two core ways:

First, as the Magician indicates, these cards always represent some aspect of the person the reading is about: old Numero Uno; "Number One"; me, myself, and I.

Secondly, as the Lovers shows, the court cards also refer to someone you are in relationship with. In the Lovers card, a mirroring is taking place between the inner and outer Self. As Paul Foster Case points out, the conscious mind looks to the subconscious mind, which is focused on the Higher Self for guidance. We can look at the people we draw into our lives as mirrors of our own inner processes—sometimes our shadowy negative self-images, and other times those highest qualities we are blind to in ourselves.

So when the Court Cards appear in a spread, it is important to read them from both points of view: as an aspect of yourself, and in the role of others teaching you about yourself.

And, of course, $1 + 6 = 7$, and so we are back to the Chariot: We develop self-mastery through our interactions with others, by seeing the different aspects of ourselves reflected in some way by everyone we come in contact with.

The People Card Reading

This is a simple two-card reading, yet I've found it helpful in understanding the changing dynamics of an ongoing relationship, or to gain a quick insight into why certain people come briefly into your life. You can also discover things about yourself of which you were never consciously aware before. Use it for all kinds of relationships: family, friends, coworkers, teachers, lovers, and between different parts of yourself. It can be expanded for more information, as I'll describe later.

Using only the sixteen People Cards, you will choose one card to tell you what qualities you are learning from a particular person at this time. And a second card to tell you what qualities they are learning from you at this time. These images will probably correspond to how these people currently appear to you and how you appear to them. If there is a disparity between the qualities the cards describe and your perception of yourself, you can ask why you are unaware of these qualities.

Although you can do this reading by yourself, you will have more insight as to how it works if you first try it with a friend. Each of you randomly picks a card representing what you are learning from the other. Then tell your partner what you are learning from them, based on the card you drew. You may be very surprised by what they see in you. They might perceive you as having qualities you've never seen in yourself. Once you have experienced this with a friend, you will be better prepared to understand what such a reading can mean when you do it alone.

Selecting the Cards

Shuffle your sixteen People Cards, then spread them in a fan, face down.

1. With your left hand, pick a card to represent the qualities you are learning from the other person. Place this card to the left.

2. With your right hand, pick a card to represent the qualities they are learning from you. Place this card to the right of the first card.

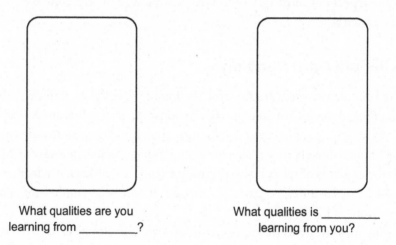

What qualities are you
learning from _____?

What qualities is _____
learning from you?

Expanding the Reading

If you want more information, then by drawing three additional cards for each of the above cards, you can determine the kind of situation in which you will find your learning opportunity.

Shuffle the remainder of the deck together (leaving out all the People Cards). Cut the deck into two stacks, cutting from the right to the left. Turn over the top three cards from the left stack and place them under your People Card to represent what you are learning. Turn over the top three cards from the right stack and place them under the other People Card to represent what your friend is learning. Blend the meanings of the three cards until they seem to describe a recognizable situation or interplay in your relationship. You might find that they will show the developmental stages of your interaction and learning. For instance: (1) how it was, (2) the current situation, and (3) its potential.

Doing this exercise together with a friend is even more enlightening than doing it by yourself, as you can discuss what you feel you have to give and receive from each other and just how you go about doing that.

The 8–11 Controversy

In writing this book, one of my greatest dilemmas has been deciding what to do with the Strength and Justice cards. Since my first (and only) deck for many years was the Waite-Smith deck, and my early studies all supported that order, I hold a personal allegiance to Strength as card number 8 in the sequence and Justice as number 11. This is different from most Continental European decks, epitomized by the Tarot of Marseilles, in which Justice is number 8 and Strength is number 11. This numbering sequence first appeared in 1557 on the pack developed by Catelin Geofroy of Lyon, France. But it was not until the 17th century that the numbering stabilized and the images known as the Marseilles type appeared.[21]

Historically, several variations in the tarot sequence exist, and tarot scholars and deck creators continue to suggest alternative orders.

The oldest numerical listing of the tarot cards is found in the *Sermones de Ludo Cum Aliis*, a late 15th-century discourse against gambling. There the cards are listed in the following order:

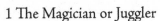

1 The Magician or Juggler	12 The Hanged Man
2 The Empress	13 Death
3 The Emperor	14 The Devil
4 The Popess	15 The Arrow or Tower
5 The Pope	16 The Star
6 Temperance	17 The Moon
7 Love	18 The Sun
8 The Triumphal Car	19 The Angel or Judgment
9 Strength or Fortitude	20 Justice
10 The Wheel	21 The World
11 The Hunchback or Hermit	0 The Fool[22]

There is a 16th-century uncut sheet of cards from the Rosenwald Collection of the National Gallery of Art in Washington, D.C., in which both Strength and Justice are numbered 8 (VIII).[23] Florentine Minchiate decks often place the four cardinal virtues (Temperance, Fortitude, Justice, and Prudence [the Hermit]) together between the Chariot and the Wheel.

Since I have chosen to use numerological systems in many of my books, the numbers of the cards become vital. Some new tarot deck designers have returned to the Marseilles numbering because they feel it is more "traditional," although the Marseilles system is hardly the oldest one. *In this book, I chose to follow the Waite-Smith numbering, which makes Strength 8 and Justice 11.*

A. E. Waite, a member of the Hermetic Order of the Golden Dawn, was the first person in modern times to use these numbers on a published deck. Waite, himself, makes only the following statement about this change:

> For reasons which satisfy myself, this card [Strength] has been interchanged with that of Justice, which is usually numbered eight.
> As the variation carries nothing with it which will signify to the reader, there is no cause for explanation.[24]

He revealed as much as he dared about a tarot secret he had been sworn to conceal.

There is a popular tarot myth that says Waite's deck was deliberately misnumbered as a subterfuge to conceal the true path from the uninitiated. Another myth claims that only Waite's numbering reveals the true wisdom of the tarot. In reality, all the orders of the cards have served a purpose in their own time and place that we can't always discern.

The departure from the Marseilles order was originally made by Kenneth Mackenzie, an inveterate designer of rituals for esoteric orders and a cryptographer. Professionally, he was a translator of books on Egyptology, mythology, and folklore and author of a Masonic encyclopedia. In 1861, Mackenzie visited the great French magus Eliphas Lévi to test his own tarot theories. He thought to publish a book on the cards but, when asked about it later, wrote to W. Wynn Westcott, one of the founders of the Golden Dawn,

> With reference to the Real Tarot ... I am not disposed to communicate the Tarot system indiscriminately although I am acquainted

with it. To do so would put a most dangerous weapon into the hands of persons less scrupulous than I am.[25]

Upon Mackenzie's death, Westcott purchased a box of his papers from Mackenzie's wife and, soon after, hired S. L. MacGregor Mathers to translate a cipher manuscript containing initiation rituals for a magical order in which the tarot served as the basis of the levels of initiation. This cipher manuscript became the core document for the Hermetic Order of the Golden Dawn, founded in 1888, for it contained a brilliant set of correspondences connecting the tarot with astrology and the Hebrew Qabalah, based on the change in numerical sequence. The majority of 20th-century innovations in tarot have arisen from these Golden Dawn teachings.

Paul Foster Case, also an initiate of the Golden Dawn and founder of the Builders of the Adytum (BOTA), which still publishes his tarot correspondence course, follows Waite on the numbering of the cards. Aleister Crowley remained undecided about the numbering system until his artist, Frieda Harris, demanded he choose so she could paint the numbers on the cards. Although he uses the Marseille numbers, he simultaneously uses the Golden Dawn astrological and Qabalistic attributions in which Strength follows the Chariot and Justice follows the Wheel of Fortune.

In the Golden Dawn system the Fool (0) equals the Hebrew letter *aleph* (which letter, in Hebrew, also serves as the sign for 1). The Magician, which is numbered 1, is associated with *beth* (which *is* the number 2) and, thus, this system seems out of alignment. But, there is a method to this madness. The oldest Qabalistic text, the *Sepher Yetzirah*, speaks of the creation of the world through the Word of God. The Hebrew letters and sounds are described as the building blocks of creation and each one corresponds to a sign of the zodiac, element, or planet. When the Fool is first, it is the element of Air, and all the other cards line up with the Hebrew letters and their zodiac signs in a way that made sense to the Golden Dawn—except for Justice, which was paired with *teth*/Leo, and Strength, which was paired with *lamed*/Libra. Once these two cards were switched, pairing Strength with *teth*/Leo (the lion) and Justice with *lamed*/Libra (the scales), everything was felt to be in place.

Angeles Arrien has said that the two cards were actually once one card with two sides, back to back. They may have represented two aspects of the operation of a single power. It is interesting that the Rosenwald Collection of tarot cards from the 16th century has both Strength and Justice numbered VIII, even though it was an obvious mistake in which one was probably numbered nine (VIIII) before a slip of the carving knife. The close relationship between these two cards is also explained in the Golden Dawn cipher manuscript:

> VIII Justice = *Lamed* and Libra, and XI Strength = *Teth* and Leo, which causeth a transposition, for these are cognate symbols. But at one time the sword of Justice was the Egyptian knife symbol of the sickle of Leo while the scales meant the Sun having quitted the balance point of highest declination [summer solstice]. So the female and the lion gave the idea of Venus, Lady of Libra repressing the fire of Vulcan (Saturn in Libra) exalted. But earliest was the Lion Goddess to Leo and Ma'at to Libra with her scales, and this is better.[26]

The single power found in both these cards is *Law*. Strength represents "natural law," in which a being is required to live and act in accord with its nature. A lion should not be punished for killing a lamb in order to eat, for its nature is to do so. But, were it to wander through village streets, it would be out of harmony with the laws of its nature and probably diseased. Justice, then, represents the attempts of a culture to codify the natural laws, creating a standard against which our actions can be weighed objectively. It is when society's laws are not in accord with natural law that we have injustice—when we force a being to do something that is not in its nature, or not to do something that is. In a manuscript originally circulated only among members of the GD, Mathers says that Strength is "power not arrested," while Justice is "Strength and Force, but arrested, as in the act of Judgment."[27]

The reordering of the cards marked an initiation into a new esoteric order requiring a new interpretation of the cards and, perhaps, a rectification of a teaching that had lost its balance. When Strength follows the Chariot, we see in these two cards a comparison of two forms of power and victory. The Chariot requires physical force that is used to dominate Nature through exerting power *over* the elements. Strength demonstrates the value of the soul and the body working in unison and perfect trust to achieve its natural power *within*. In this way, the Strength figure becomes the female Magician, which is demonstrated when the cards are placed in three rows of seven cards each, so that Strength, as the 8th card or octave, appears directly below the Magician. The Hermit, which then follows Strength, represents

Chart 21: Alpha-Astro-Numeric Correspondences

Letter	Shape	No. Equiv.	Meaning of Shape	English Equiv.	Eliphas Lévi (French School) (1856)		Golden Dawn (English School) (1888)	
Aleph	א	1	Ox, Cow, Bull	A	Juggler	♎	Fool	♎
Beth	ב	2	House, Courtyard	B	High Priestess	☽	Magician	☿
Gimel	ג	3	Camel (transport)	G	Empress	♀	High Priestess	☽
Daleth	ד	4	Doorway (to open)	D	Emperor	♃	Empress	♀
Heh	ה	5	Window (to see)	H, E	Pope	♈	Emperor	♈
Vav	ו	6	Nail (to build)	U, V, W	Lovers	♉	Hierophant	♉
Zayin	ז	7	Sword (to cut)	Z	Chariot	♊	Lovers	♊
Cheth	ח	8	Fence (to enclose)	Ch	Justice	♋	Chariot	♋
Teth	ט	9	Serpent (to twist)	T	Hermit	♌	Strength	♌
Yod	י	10	Hand (to jot)	I, J, Y	Wheel of Fortune	♍	Hermit	♍
Kaph	כ	20	Palm (to grasp)	C, K, Kh	Strength	♂	Wheel of Fortune	♃
Lamed	ל	30	Goad (to chastise)	L	Hanged Man	♎	Justice	♎
Mem	מ	40	Sea, Womb	M	Death	▽	Hanged Man	▽
Nun	נ	50	Fish (to move)	N	Temperance	♏	Death	♏
Samekh	ס	60	Peg (to support)	S, X	Devil	♐	Temperance	♐
Ayin	ע	70	Eye (to part)	O	Tower	♑	Devil	♑
Peh	פ	80	Mouth (to feed)	P, Ph, F	Star	☿	Tower	♂
Tzaddi	צ	90	Scythe (to harvest)	Tz	Moon	♒	Star	♒
Qoph	ק	100	Back of Head, knot	Q	Sun	♓	Moon	♓
Resh	ר	200	Face (to reason)	R	Judgment	♄	Sun	☉
Shin	ש	300	Teeth (to harp)	Sh	Fool	△	Judgment	△
Tav	ת	400	Sign (to mark)	T, Th, X	World	☉	World	♄

the hermaphrodite (like the seer, Tiresius, in the Greek dramas), composed of both masculine and feminine energies unified in one being. When Justice follows the turn of the karmic Wheel of Fortune and precedes the Hanged Man and Death, it indicates that force must be "arrested" and a judgment made before the punishment or sacrifice is determined and carried out. When Justice appears in the middle position in the three rows of seven, it becomes the pivot or mediating point for all the cards that come before and after it. It is worth mentioning that the third cardinal virtue in the tarot,

Temperance, is the last card in the row, so that the entire middle row is bracketed by and centered on the virtues.

Variations in tarot order reflect variations in worldview, at first among the different city-states in Italy and then between the French and English orders of magicians. As people experiment with changing the sequence of cards, it becomes clear that some are extremely personal while others serve a larger proportion of humankind. The latter will stand the test of time until a radical revisioning of who we are requires even more radical changes.

The Qabalah of the Nine Chambers

In his introduction to the *Kabbalah Unveiled*, S. L. MacGregor Mathers presents three forms of word analysis by permutation through which to find hidden meanings and correspondences among Hebrew words. One of these is known as *Aiq Beker* or "The Qabalah of Nine Chambers," which was also used by the Masons as a cipher for the secret word lost at the death of the architect, Hiram Abif—a story that's at the center of Masonic initiation.

The Nine Chambers form a chart by which one can convert Hebrew letters to their numerical roots (1 = 10 = 100) and is a major technique for creating sigils and talismans. Similar to the term *QWERTY* for a typewriter keyboard, the name *Aiq Beker* (*AiQ BKR*) is derived from the Hebrew letters in the first two chambers: *aleph/yod/qoph* and *beth/kaph/resh* (read right to left in the chart below). This grid is used as the template from which to permutate the letters in words in order to discern hidden truths. This Pythagorean "rule of 9," in which numbers could be reduced to their *pythmenes* (roots or thrones) was used by Hippolytus with the Greek alphabet and, according to him, by the Egyptians. It was said to bring qualities of peace and harmony to the universe.

The chart should be read from right to left. The numbers 500 and above correspond to a "final" form that some Hebrew letters assume and have no corresponding Trump Cards.

The following text was written by Aleister Crowley (Frater

Chart 22: The Nine Chambers Chart

3 Sh L G 300 30 3	2 R K B 200 20 2	1 Q Y A 100 10 1
6 M S V 600 60 6	5 K N H 500 50 5	4 Th M D 400 40 4
9 Tz Tz T 900 90 9	8 P P Ch 800 80 8	7 N O Z 700 70 7

Perdurabo) between 1907 and 1911 and makes the correspondence between the Qabalah of Nine Chambers and the tarot Trumps clear.

Except for the position of the Fool, note that the Trump Cards are disposed in groupings corresponding to a person's Lifetime Cards—that is, the tarot constellations. In this case, however, each constellation or "chamber" is determined by the Root Number of the Hebrew letter, not the number on the card. It is for this reason that the Hermit and Moon are placed in the first chamber with the Fool. No one in the Golden Dawn seems to have developed this concept further in relation to the Trumps.

NOTE BY H. FRA. P[erdurabo] 4° = 7□ ON THE R.O.T.A.

BY THE QABALAH OF NINE CHAMBERS

from LIBER CCXXXI
(This book is true up to the grade of *Adeptus Exemptus*.)

Units are divine — △ The upright Triangle.

Tens reflected — ▽ The averse Triangle.

Hundreds equilibrated — ✡ The Hexagram their combination.

(The Thoth card names and astrological correspondences (in bold face) below were added by me to the original text to make the tarot associations clearer.)

1. "Light." — [Here can be no evil.]

   1: *Aleph* / **Fool** / **Air.** The hidden light—the wisdom of God foolishness with men.

   10: *Yod* / **Hermit** / **Virgo.** The Adept bearing Light.

   100: *Qof* / **Moon** / **Pisces.** The Light in darkness and illusion. (Khephra about to rise.)

2. "Action." —

   2: *Bet[h]* / **Magus** / **Mercury.** Active and Passive—dual current, etc.— the Alternating Forces in Harmony.

20: *Koph* / **Fortune** / **Jupiter.** The Contending Forces—fluctuation of earth-life.

200: *Resh* / **Sun** / **Sun.** The Twins embracing—eventual glory of harmonised life under Sun.

3. "The Way." — [Here also no evil.]

3: *Gemel* / **Priestess** / **Moon.** The Higher Self.

30: *Lamed* / **Adjustment** / **Libra.** The severe discipline of the Path.

300: *Shin* / **Aeon** / **Fire.** The judgment and resurrection. (0 = 10 and 5 = 6 rituals.)

4. "Life." —

4: *Dalet* / **Empress** / **Venus.** The Mother of god. Aima.

40: *Mem* / **Hanged Man** / **Water.** The Son Slain.

400: *Taw* / **World** / **Saturn.** The Bride.

5. "Force" (Purification). —

5: *Heh* / **Emperor** / **Aries.** The Supernal Sulphur purifying by fire.

50: *Nun* / **Death** / **Scorpio.** The Infernal Water Scorpio purifying by putrefaction.

This work is not complete; therefore is there no equilibration.

6. "Harmony." —

6: *Vau* / **Hierophant** / **Taurus.** The Reconciler (Vau of Yod-Heh-Vau-Heh) above.

60: *Samekh* / **Art** / **Sagittarius.** The Reconciler below (lion and eagle, etc.).

This work also unfinished.

7. "Birth." —

7: *Zain* / **Lovers** /**Gemini.** The Powers of Spiritual Regeneration. (The

Z.A.M. as Osiris risen between Isis and Nephthys. The path of *Gemel*, Diana, above his head.)

70: *Ayin* / **Devil** / **Capricorn.** The gross powers of generation.

8. "Rule." —

8: *Chet* / **Chariot** / **Cancer.** The Orderly Ruling of diverse forces.

80: *Peh* / **Tower** / **Mars.** The Ruin of the Unbalanced Forces.

9. "Stability." —

9: *Tet* / **Strength** / **Leo.** The Force that represses evil.

90: *Tzaddi* / **Star** / **Aquarius.** The Force that restores the world ruined by evil.

Note that, in this paper, Crowley puts Justice/Adjustment with the Priestess and Judgment/Aeon. Likewise, Strength is with the Star.

Summary of Card Names

The Lifetime Cards

Chart 23: The Lifetime Card Chart

	BIRTH CARDS	NAME CARDS	

Major Arcana or Trump Cards	**Personality-Soul Pattern:**
	• Personality Card
	• Soul Card
	• Hidden Factor Card
	          = Shadow Card
	          = Teacher Card
		•Desires & Inner Motivation Card
		•Outer Personal Card
		
		Destiny Cards (same Root Number):
		          • Theme Note Card
		          • Rhythm Card
		          • Melody Card
		          • Hidden Factor Name Card
		
		Theme Chord:
		          • First Name Card
		          • Middle Name Card
		          • Last Name Card
			• Life Potential Card
			=
			(Birth Card
			+
			Name Card)

Minor Arcana cards	**Number (Pip) Cards**	• Lessons and Opportunities Cards • Zodiacal Lesson and Opportunity Card	
	Court or People Cards	• Significator Card	

The Year Cards

A Major Arcana card for each year of life.
   ✦ Karmic Year Card

Endnotes

1   See Stuart R. Kaplan, *The Encyclopedia of Tarot*, vols. 1 and 2 (New York: U.S. Games Systems, 1978 and 1986), or Michael Dummett, *The Game of Tarot: From Ferrara to Salt Lake City* (London: Gerald Duckworth and Co., 1980).

2   Joseph Chilton Pearce, *Exploring the Crack in the Cosmic Egg* (New York: Pocket Books, 1975), p. 19.

3   M. Esther Harding, *Psychic Energy: Its Source and Its Transformation*, Bollingen Series X, (Princeton, NJ: Princeton University Press, 1973), p. 307.

4   Ibid., p. 308.

5   Marie-Louise von Franz, *On Divination and Synchronicity: The Psychology of Meaningful Chance* (Toronto: Inner City Books, 1980), p. 57.

6   Ibid., p. 58.

7   Ibid., p. 72.

8   Ibid., p. 94.

9   Gertrude Moakley, *The Tarot Cards Painted by Bonifacio Bembo* (New York: The New York Public Library, 1966), pp. 43–53.

10 I originally learned this concept from Angeles Arrien.

11 Muriel Bruce Hasbrouk, *Tarot and Astrology: The Pursuit of Destiny* (Rochester, VT: Destiny Books, 1989; reprint of *The Pursuit of Destiny*, 1941.) p. 28.

12 Ibid., p. 224.

13 M. Esther Harding, *Woman's Mysteries: Ancient and Modern* (New York: Harper Colophon, 1971), p. 125.

14 For information about how language and cultural conventions of time structure our world view, see *Language, Thought, and Reality* by linguist Benjamin Lee Whorf.

15 Jane Roberts, *The Nature of Personal Reality: Practical Techniques for Solving Everyday Problems and Enriching the Life You Know; A Seth Book* (New York: Bantam, 1978), p. 413.

16 Ibid., p. 444.

17 Garfield quoted in Norman Boucher's "In Search of Peak Performance," *New Age Journal*, February 1986.

18 Martita Tracy, *Stellar Numerology* (Mokelumne Hill, CA: Health Research, n.d.), p. 1.

19 Paul Foster Case, *Highlights of Tarot* (Los Angeles: Builders of the Adytum, 1970), pp. 46–47.

20 The Holy Order of Mans, *Jewels of the Wise* (San Francisco: Holy Order of Mans, 1974), pp. 73–79.

21 See Stuart Kaplan, *The Encyclopedia of Tarot*, Vols. 1 and 2, and Michael Dummett, *The Game of Tarot*, for specific references and a scholarly discussion on this topic.

22 See Stuart Kaplan, *The Encyclopedia of Tarot*, Vol. 2 (New York: U.S. Games, 1986), pp. 182–196, for a full discussion of sequence and titles of the Major Arcana with charts comparing the variations among twenty-six decks from the late 1500s to 1909.

23 Ibid., p. 186.

24 A. E. Waite, *The Pictorial Key to the Tarot* (New York: Causeway Books, n.d. [originally 1910]), p. 100.

25 Quoted in Ellic Howe, *Magicians of the Golden Dawn* (York Beach, ME: Samuel Weiser, 1972), p. 29.

26 Darcy Küntz, ed., *The Complete Golden Dawn Cipher Manuscript* (Edmonds, WA: Holmes Publishing, 1996), Folios 36–41, and Carroll "Poke" Runyon, *Secrets of the Golden Dawn Cypher Manuscript* (Pasadena: C.H.S., 1997), Facsimile pages 34–38.

27 From Book "T"—The Tarot, signed "S.M.R.D." (MacGregor Mathers's identifying motto in the Golden Dawn). This manuscript is now available in Robert Wang's *An Introduction to the Golden Dawn Tarot*, and also as volume 9 of *The Complete Golden Dawn System of Magic*, by Israel Regardie.

Selected Bibliography

Since there are now so many noteworthy tarot books, I have limited this bibliography to books most directly related to the concepts presented here.

Amberstone, Wald and Ruth Ann Amberstone. *The Tarot School's Birth Card Notebook. www.tarotschool.com/BirthCards.html.*

Arrien, Angeles. *The Tarot Handbook: Practical Applications of Ancient Visual Symbols.* Tarcher/Putnam, republished 1997.

Bunker, Dusty and Faith Javane. *Numerology and the Divine Triangle.* Whitford Press 1979.

Buryn, Ed. *The William Blake Tarot of the Creative Imagination. Tools and Rites of Transformation,* revised, 2010.

Cehovet, Bonnie. *Tarot, Birth Cards, and You: Keys to Empowering Yourself.* Schiffer Books.

Colbert, Joanna Powell. *Gaian Tarot.* Llewellyn Publications, 2010.

Crowley, Aleister, *The Book of Thoth: An Interpretation of the Tarot.* Samuel Weiser, 1974.

Greer, Mary K. *21 Ways to Read A Tarot Card.* Llewellyn Publications, 2006.

———. *The Complete Book of Tarot Reversals.* Llewellyn Publications, 2002.

———. *Tarot for Your Self: A Workbook for Personal Transformation.* New Page Books, revised 2002

———. *Tarot Mirrors: Reflections of Personal Meaning.* Newcastle Publishing, 1988.

——— and Tom Little. *Understanding the Tarot Court.* Llewellyn Publications, 2004.

Hasbrouck, Muriel, *Tarot and Astrology.* Originally *Pursuit of Destiny,* 1941; republished Inner Traditions/Destiny, 1987.

Michelsen, Teresa C. *The Complete Tarot Reader.* Llewellyn, 2005.

Nichols, Sallie, *Jung and Tarot: An Archetypal Journey*. New York: Samuel Weiser, 1980.

Noble, Vicki and Jonathan Tenney. *The Motherpeace Tarot Playbook*. Wingbow Press, 1986.

Pollack, Rachel. *The Forest of Souls: A Walk through the Tarot*. Llewellyn, 2002.

———. *Tarot Wisdom: Spiritual Teachings and Deeper Meanings*. Llewellyn, 2008.

Von Franz, Marie-Louise. *Divination and Synchronicity: The Psychology of Meaningful Chance*. Inner City Books, 1980.

Waite, Arthur Edward. *The Pictorial Key to the Tarot*. Rider, 1910.

About the Author

MARY K. GREER is an independent scholar, writer, teacher, and professional tarot consultant. She has an MA in English Literature from the University of Central Florida where she also first taught tarot in 1974. For eleven years, she was a teacher and administrator at New College of California in San Francisco, where she taught tarot as an interdisciplinary subject integrating art, literature, history, and psychology. She is the author of eleven books on tarot and on magic.

Mary's books have pioneered entirely new techniques for learning about and working with the cards, including being the first to present in-depth techniques for reading for oneself. In 2007, Mary received the International Tarot Lifetime Achievement Award from the Association for Tarot Studies. She also received the 2006 Mercury Award from the Mary Redman Foundation for "excellence in communication in the metaphysical field," and the 2006 Coalition of Visionary Resources (COVR) award for best divination book. She is also an ordained priestess in the Fellowship and Church of Isis. Visit her at *marykgreer.com*.

To Our Readers

Weiser Books, an imprint of Red Wheel/Weiser, publishes books across the entire spectrum of occult, esoteric, speculative, and New Age subjects. Our mission is to publish quality books that will make a difference in people's lives without advocating any one particular path or field of study. We value the integrity, originality, and depth of knowledge of our authors.

Our readers are our most important resource, and we appreciate your input, suggestions, and ideas about what you would like to see published.

Visit our website at *www.redwheelweiser.com* to learn about our upcoming books and free downloads, and be sure to sign up for newsletters and exclusive offers at *www.redwheelweiser.com/newsletter*.

You can also contact us at *info@rwwbooks.com* or at

Red Wheel/Weiser, LLC
65 Parker Street, Suite 7
Newburyport, MA 01950